PRAISE FOR *PHANTOM PARADISE*

"This is a riveting tale of survival and transcendence. I could not put it down."

KEN BURNS
Filmmaker

"Long since I encountered such a moving, thrilling and readable book. Finished in a few hours non-stop. Such a touching and candid memoir of a repatriate family from Manchuria as well as of a girl of that family starting from scratch to become a top hotelier in DC. You are lucky if you have not read it yet. You still have the joy of reading this fascinating book."

ICHIRO FUJISAKI
Former Ambassador of Japan to the United States

"Not since the wildly popular bestseller *Pachinko* have we had a multi-generational story as revelatory and hair-raising as the one we read in *Phantom Paradise*. Here, all too vividly, we experience the fear, displacement, hunger, and human ravages of an epic war novel. Except that Kay Enokido's story is all too true. Her memoir turns a sharp lens on the little understood occupation of Manchuria and the heart-stopping experiences of a Japanese family as the Empire collapses and they flee through the embers of a savage war."

MARIE ARANA
Author of the prize-winning memoir *American Chica* and inaugural Literary Director of the Library of Congress

"From the very first sentence, Kay Enokido's memoir draws you into the remarkable, untold story of a country that no longer exists and a family that endures through war and exile. Her crisp prose weaves her mother's writing with her own voice to deliver an intimate chronicle of flight, memory, and resilience. I could not put down."

KIM GHATTAS
Author of New York Times Notable Book *Black Wave*

"*Phantom Paradise* is a powerful narrative of survival and transformation and a valuable contribution to our understanding of East Asia's twentieth-century history. Enokido's account of her family's perilous flight from Manchuria in 1945 and her own extraordinary journey from refugee child to successful businesswoman in America offers an unusually personal and engaging perspective on displacement and survival."

GERALD L. CURTIS
Burgess Professor Emeritus of
Political Science, Columbia Universi

"A fascinating account of a period and people often overlooked in Western histories of the 20th century. Kay Enokido draws on her mother's vivid recollections of raising a young family in Japan's Manchurian colony as war's shadow descends. She paints a poignant portrait of a lost empire's broken promises and the consequences for one family. The perspective Enokido brings, after a lifetime of business and personal successes anchored in that turbulent time, is all the more striking."

MARCUS BRAUCHLI
Former Executive Editor of *The Washington Post*
and Managing Editor of *The Wall Street Journal*

PHANTOM
PARADISE

PHANTOM PARADISE

Escape from Manchuria

KAY ENOKIDO

BOLD STORY PRESS

CHEVY CHASE, MARYLAND

Bold Story Press, Chevy Chase, MD 20815
www.boldstorypress.com

Copyright © 2025 by Kay Enokido

All rights reserved. No part of this book may be reproduced or used in any manner without written permission of the copyright owner except for the use of quotations in a book review. Requests for permission or further information should be submitted through info@boldstorypress.com.

First edition: 2026
Library of Congress Control Number: 2025916925
ISBN: 978-1-954805-94-1 (hardcover)
ISBN: 978-1-954805-92-7 (paperback)
ISBN: 978-1-954805-93-4 (e-book)

While this story is based in fact, some names and identifying details have been changed to protect the privacy of individuals.

The calligraphy on the front cover means "Phantom."
Cover and interior design by KP Books

Printed in the United States of America
10 9 8 7 6 5 4 3 2 1

To the memory of my father and mother
who made me who I am;
with my utmost gratitude

CONTENTS

Preface — xi

PART ONE

CHAPTER 1 An Adventurous Young Couple — 3
CHAPTER 2 On the Cutting Edge — 9
CHAPTER 3 The Saddest Day — 17
CHAPTER 4 Take Care of Our Heirloom Sword — 25
CHAPTER 5 Dark Days — 31
CHAPTER 6 The Soviet Union Enters the War — 35
CHAPTER 7 The Doll — 45
CHAPTER 8 Inferno in Manchuria — 53
CHAPTER 9 Mother's Painful Choice — 65
CHAPTER 10 Winter Approaches in Andong — 77
CHAPTER 11 The Train Leaves Tonight — 85
CHAPTER 12 Mother Confronts "Mama" — 97
CHAPTER 13 Furniture Makes the Best Firewood — 107
CHAPTER 14 The Menace of Russian Soldiers — 125
CHAPTER 15 "We Are Equal Human Beings" — 131
CHAPTER 16 Escape from Slaughter — 139
CHAPTER 17 Journey of Repatriation — 149
CHAPTER 18 Unwelcome — 155
CHAPTER 19 Days of Sleep — 175
CHAPTER 20 Failure in Filial Duties — 183
CHAPTER 21 An Arrogant Girl — 193
CHAPTER 22 Three Cups of Coffee — 203
CHAPTER 23 Irresistible Eggs — 209
CHAPTER 24 Dying on Your Own Futon — 213
CHAPTER 25 The Longest Forty-Eight Hours — 223

PART TWO

CHAPTER 26	Miso Soup Together	233
CHAPTER 27	Going to America	243
CHAPTER 28	The Problem with Americans	251
CHAPTER 29	Shinto Ceremony	261
CHAPTER 30	A Hapless Honeymoon	265
CHAPTER 31	Life in New York, California, and Washington, DC	269
CHAPTER 32	Cornell	283
CHAPTER 33	New Beginning	287
CHAPTER 34	Graciousness	289
CHAPTER 35	Crisis with Our Children	293
CHAPTER 36	September 11, 2001	299
CHAPTER 37	Renovation	303
CHAPTER 38	Beyond My Wildest Dreams	307

PART THREE

CHAPTER 39	Apology to My Father	313
CHAPTER 40	Suicide Mission	319
CHAPTER 41	Return to Phantom Paradise	323
CHAPTER 42	Mother's Regret	331
CHAPTER 43	Unable to Say "Arigato"	335
CHAPTER 44	The Search for Missing Pieces	341
CHAPTER 45	Not a Helpless Leaf	353

Acknowledgments	365
Endnotes	369
About the Author	373
About Bold Story Press	375

PREFACE

I was born in Manchukuo, a country that no longer exists. Manchukuo was established in Manchuria (now northeast China) by Japan's military conquest in 1932, and settled by colonizers like our family. It was supposed to be an independent nation, but was considered a puppet state by the international community, and lasted only thirteen years.

Despite the terrible experiences we encountered in our desperate escape from Manchuria after the collapse of the Japanese Empire, a surprisingly large number of Japanese people who lived there still fondly remember it as a "phantom paradise." These were bright, idealistic, and well-intentioned people in pursuit of creating a "new heaven on earth" on the 250 million acres of northeast China that bordered Russia, North Korea, and Mongolia. However, the process of that creation was far from idyllic; it was blighted by conspiracy, aggression, violence, and power struggles. The abrupt end of this "paradise" brought tragedy and misery to the more than one million Japanese citizens who had tasted its ephemeral splendors.

My family was formed, separated, and abandoned in Manchukuo. It was where my future was shaped, though I barely remember my time there; or perhaps I have spent a lifetime trying to suppress my memories. I distanced myself from Manchuria almost all my youthful life. I always told others that I was born in Japan; I did not want to be associated with "invaders" or "poor repatriates." After I married, I attended New York University to major in journalism and East Asian studies. There I discovered histories of Japan and Asia that I had not been taught in Japan.

In 1976, my husband and I were staying at my parents' home in Yokohama, Japan, on our yearly visit. After dinner, as my mother finished up the dishes in her kitchen, I asked if she would write the story of our life in Manchuria. I asked out of both a sense of obligation to have some degree of knowledge about my family's time there, as well as journalistic curiosity about Manchuria. My mother had always enjoyed reading literature and composing poetry in the Japanese haiku tradition. She was sixty-five years old during that visit, and she seemed old, as I was only in my thirties.

She wiped her hands on the white apron covering her casual kimono and said, "*Soo-ne*" (Yeah, hmmm). It was not an enthusiastic yes, but not a definite no either.

My mother tended to be reluctant to show instant enthusiasm. Grabbing any opportunity right away was considered ungraceful, and I had been taught I should not accept any offer quickly; first you decline in order to give the impression that you are someone with a refined manner. I had always followed my mother's credo until one day I realized that the Japanese manner might not work in different cultures. I was visiting an American friend's home in Yokohama, and she asked if I wanted something to drink. I declined because I expected to be asked again, when I would reply, "Yes, please." But that first offer was the end of it. I interpreted

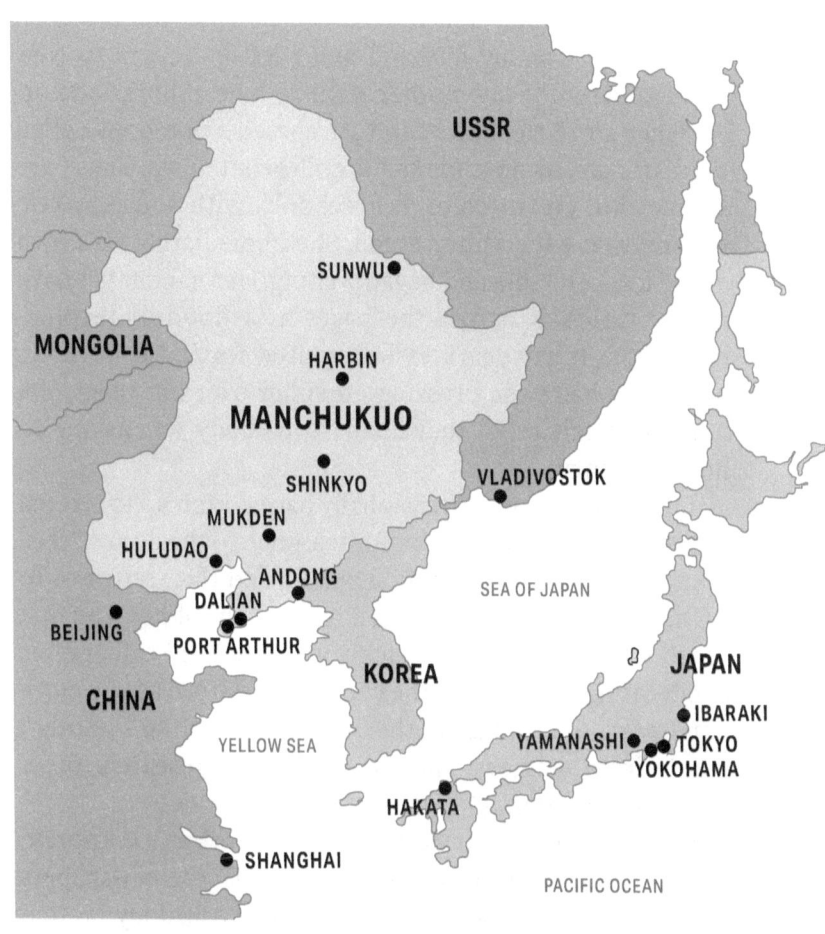

Map during the time when the Japanese Empire ruled Manchukuo (1932–1945).

MAP CREATED FOR *PHANTOM PARADISE* BY DUMONT DESIGN

my mother's response to being asked to write her story not as a rejection, but a "soft yes."

The next day, my husband and I left to return to New York. Apparently, my mother went to a neighborhood convenience store right away and purchased a notebook called *daigaku note*, or notebooks for college students. These are simple thin cream-colored notebooks with soft gray covers and tied with white thread. She immediately sat down at her kitchen table and began writing. Her hand must have moved furiously across the pages as a flood of recollections from thirty years earlier poured forth. I believe her memories had been pressing upon her over the years. She must have felt relief that finally somebody was asking to hear her story.

I imagine she must occasionally have gotten up to stretch. She would have boiled water for tea, gone to the door to feed the stray cat she'd grown attached to, and then returned to her table, placing a pot of green tea in front of her. The first notebook probably filled quickly with her fluid calligraphic handwriting. She went to the convenience store to buy more notebooks. She filled another notebook and still another, purely from memory. She did not do any research; there were no computers.

I had returned to my busy life in New York as a corporate wife, student, and freelance writer for Japanese newspapers and magazines. I almost forgot that I had asked my mother to write about her memories. The following year when I visited her, she handed me three notebooks. I could not hide my surprise.

"Three notebooks?" I said with astonishment and a sense of guilt. When I had asked her to jot down her memories, my request had been somewhat casual. I hadn't expected to receive such serious writing, in such great volume.

"Yes, I could not stop," my mother answered with a shy smile.

I went to my room on the second floor, wondering what might be in these notebooks. I sat down at my old study desk next to a wooden bed and opened the notebook inscribed with the number one on the cover. Her account started the day my father left our home in Shinkyo in May 1945 for the draft, only three months before Japan's declaration of surrender. Shinkyo was the capital of Manchukuo and the place I was born. My mother questioned why a father with three small children had to be drafted. She described how she tried to be brave in sending her husband to the war, and how precious we three children were. My older brother was six, I was three, and my younger brother was one year old. I choked up and put the three notebooks into my suitcase and returned to New York. I did not want to go through her notebooks in haste. I wanted to read them when I was fully mindful in a quiet environment.

When I returned to our apartment in the Upper East Side, and after my husband had gone to work, I opened her notebooks. Morning sun flooded my study through the window facing the UN Plaza. The first page of the first notebook started with a lovely depiction of spring in Manchuria, although she soon described what turned out to be a sad day. I was drawn in again, reading as if for the first time, even though I had read the first few pages in Yokohama. It took me several days to finish. The narrative descriptions of us three small children were adorable throughout her writing; we were so docile and well-behaved. According to her accounts, she did not explain anything to her children, but we sensed we were in an extraordinary situation, and there was no room to complain. What good children we were!

Earlier I had accepted as an unfortunate fate that we happened to be in Manchuria when Japan acknowledged military defeat on August 15, 1945. But my mother's writing of our time in Manchuria opened my eyes and gave me the incentive to learn more about our history, and I found that my family's unfortunate situation had been the result of the deliberate abandonment by Japan's leaders. What else didn't I know?

This account takes place in a time of war. Wars are started, and won or lost, by political and military leaders, but frequently the ordinary people are the ones victimized. In this book, my ordinary family endured the strife and tragedies of wartime just as many other families did during that terrible time. Behind war casualties are countless personal stories. We are not just part of statistical numbers—we are living and breathing human beings.

Our family was fortunate to have persisted, survived, and eventually succeeded to attain peaceful and productive lives. Our miraculous escape from Manchuria in 1946, and what came after it, has carried me ultimately to Walpole, a bucolic village in New Hampshire. There's a manicured town green with a gazebo where bands perform on summer evenings. This is not the life I could have imagined following our escape. Memories of World War II are steadily fading. I wanted to record my family's story as a tribute to my mother, and to pass along the story of her courage to the next generation and many people whom I have not known.

In this book, the reader will hear different voices. First is my mother's voice from her notebooks, translated by me. I have also included translations of published articles from thinkers, artists, and public people who endured the rise and fall of Manchukuo along with us. Further, I added translations of my father's letters that were discovered at a much later stage of writing this book. Finally, my voice is woven throughout in various places.

PART ONE

PREVIOUS PAGE
*Isao 4, and Kashiyo 2, September 26, 1943.
At the Nanrei Zoo in Manchuria
(now Changchun Zoological and Botanical Garden).*

CHAPTER 1

•

AN ADVENTUROUS YOUNG COUPLE

I heard more than once from my mother that she had been nicknamed "The Princess in White Gloves" when she was young. Although I never thought of her as a "princess," the name still gives me a great sense of pride. I never heard my mother brag about her beauty. She was a woman of average height and weight; her facial features did not have anything special to mention. She had silky black hair, but that was not unique among young Japanese women. She did have a delicate bone structure. Her hands were particularly beautiful, with long, nicely shaped fingers. The Japanese say such hands are "like white fish" as a compliment. She was vivacious, active, curious, resourceful, and loved music and literature.

My maternal grandfather instilled in her a sense of pride, a trait he might have had in excess. He instructed his children never to initiate bows to village people but to let them bow first. My grandfather, whom I never met, had little formal education, but was respected by the people in his village in Yamanashi prefecture. He was born and raised when the country was controlled by samurai in a strict feudal order, when most women existed to serve their men. Nevertheless, he was progressive minded. It sounds contradictory, but his public posture as a village chief was not the same as the opinions he held in private.

My mother grew up in an isolated village at the foot of Mt. Yatsugatake, famous for its bitterly cold winter winds. Many families in her village were poor. After completing elementary school, even girls from well-to-do families were expected to go work in factories that made silk yarn and thread. When each school year ended in spring, recruiters from the factories would go to the village to offer jobs to the girls. Girls from poor families saw this as an opportunity to improve their circumstances and enjoy greater freedom; girls from more affluent families went to work as part of their training to become good wives.

My mother's two older sisters followed these village customs and went to work in silk factories after elementary school, although they later went to training schools and passed official examinations to become supervisors. When my mother graduated from elementary school, my grandfather seemed to have had a change of heart. Recruiters came to the village as usual, but he said, "From now on, children should receive an education." Unable to sway her father, the recruiters still offered my mother incentive to work in the factories. But her mother told them quite emphatically, "You cannot take her because her father has decided to send her to upper school."

My grandparents lived approximately 110 miles west of Tokyo with a clear view of Mt. Fuji. My grandfather was not rich, but he enjoyed purchasing beautiful kimonos in distant Tokyo and bringing them back to his daughters. For the people who lived in the remote countryside surrounded by towering mountains, Tokyo was a distant and glorious world in the early 1900s. I imagine my grandfather of modest means enjoyed buying luxurious items, not to spoil his daughters but to show off his "good taste."

One day, he proudly brought my mother a Western dress from Tokyo. She opened the package wrapped in the traditional *furoshiki* (cloth for wrapping parcels) and held up the dress. It was a simple white short-sleeved blouse with a purple pleated skirt at below-knee length, exposing her arms and legs! Her father smiled in anticipation of seeing my mother's delighted face, but she could not smile. All her classmates wore kimonos, covering their whole bodies. She did not want to be different. But she knew she could not disappoint her father, and it never occurred to her to say no to him. She dutifully became the first girl at school to wear Western clothes. Several days later, her classmate from the wealthiest family in the village came to school wearing a Western dress.

My mother was the first girl to leave her village to go to school in Tokyo for further education. For a young girl from the countryside, the opportunity for life in the big city was both enchanting and frightening. My mother told me that the house she stayed in had a tennis court, a grand piano, and several housekeepers, but I never asked more about her life in Tokyo. Who were those people who had accepted a young girl from the countryside for four years? My grandfather, who was just a local politician in a remote village, must have had great connections with money and power in Tokyo.

After the equivalent of high school, my mother went to a medical school to become a nurse. What she really wanted was to study vocal music at a conservatory, but her father flatly denied that request. She had experienced an elegant lifestyle during her stay in Tokyo, and kept that acquired taste her entire life; she gave an impression of being snobbish at times. I must have inherited a bit of this trait, as I have been criticized by my grown (American) children as being reserved.

When my mother was twenty-eight (an old maid in those times), her older sister introduced her to a young man, Masayoshi Enokido. He had been accepted by a university in Yokohama but had chosen not to go. Instead, he had taken a job with Nippon Yusen, the largest shipping company in Japan, so he could travel the world. Unlike typical Japanese, he had big round eyes under thick black eyebrows, a sharp nose, and square jaw. He looked exotic, but contrary to his appearance, he had a strong provincial dialect from the Ibaraki prefecture. People in Ibaraki pronounced the I as "aye" instead of "ee." He pronounced our family name "Aye-no-keedo," instead of "Ee-no-kido," which I hated. Nevertheless, in my mother's eyes, he had an air of sophistication, probably due to his overseas experience. His uniquely stylish clothes charmed her. He was mild-mannered, loved classic music, and was a great swimmer and tennis player. He also wrote poetry, and his handwriting looked like beautiful calligraphy.

My father, Masayoshi, was from a wealthy family with a pedigree dating back to 1172, according to official family records. Our ancestors were samurai, albeit of significantly lower status, thus they were loyal to a regional ruler. As their master expanded his territories by winning battles, our ancestors were given land as a reward. When that style of feudal rule—known as Tokugawa Shogunate—ended, a newly modernized society started in 1868 at the Meiji Restoration; most ordinary samurai became farmers, and the prominent ones became political leaders. The Enokido family were farmers, but they did not farm the land themselves. They had tenant farmers to do that work.

Reflecting his samurai family background, my paternal grandfather was said to be high-handed. He got involved in the civil rights movement of the time, not because of his sense of social responsibility, but rather in pursuit of political power and fame. The Japanese are famous for their maxims, and my paternal grandfather used to say, "Tigers leave skins after they are gone," meaning great people's names are remembered after their deaths. He had a keen sense of honor, but he spent enormous amounts of money on political campaigns to the detriment of the family fortune. Nonetheless, the family continued to convey their proud history from generation to generation. The Enokidos were special, and to be an Enokido, one must do special things.

When my father proposed to my mother, neither set of parents were pleased, in part because a love marriage was rare. Most marriages were arranged to unite two families—not individuals—for their mutual benefit. The young couple's own happiness was not of the utmost importance, but harmonious and socially proper unions were. In prewar Japan, the conventional wisdom for women was "When young, obey your parents; when married, obey your husband; and when old, obey your children, specifically your sons." My mother's sense of independence and self-sufficient lifestyle as a full-fledged nurse appeared to be an ill fit for the traditional role of an obedient bride; she had her own career, as well as being considered old by standards of the day. Mother's father did not respect the Enokidos, who were wealthy but did not have a passion for education. Despite protests from their families, my parents were married in Yokohama, and soon my older brother, Isao, was born in 1938, and my adventurous father announced that they were moving to the new world in Manchuria.

My mother's life as a married woman coincided more or less with the beginning of the Japanese creation of Manchukuo. Manchukuo, established in Manchuria, was at the cutting edge of a quest for passionate idealists and those who hoped to have a better life. Lofty ideas such as *Odo Rakudo* (a utopian state under benevolent rule) and *Gozoku Kyowa* (five races under one union) were symbolized in Manchukuo's national flag.

Those who settled in Manchukuo had an innate desire for bigger things, perhaps rebelling against the island mentality that reflected Japanese conformist thinking. That the adventurous young couple moved there is no surprise. That I was born there was just an accident of fate.

CHAPTER 2

ON THE CUTTING EDGE

There are many different ways to tell the story of Manchukuo, the country established in Manchuria, depending on how far back into history one reaches.

Japan experienced continuous civil wars and social upheavals until the Battle of *Sekigahara* in 1600 when Tokugawa Ieyasu established the shogunate and united the nation. Under the shoguns, Japan maintained peace and a flourishing culture by imposing an isolation policy, called *Sakoku* (chained country), for 265 years. During this period, no Japanese could leave the country on penalty of death, and very few foreign nationals were permitted to enter and trade with Japan. The *Sakoku* ended when Commodore Matthew Perry of the United States arrived in Tokyo in 1853 and demanded that Japan open itself to the world. This eventually resulted in the Meiji Restoration in 1868, when Japan transformed from a feudal society to a modern nation. Once opened up, Japanese leaders, most of whom were ex-samurai or descendants of samurai, recognized the threat from the Western powers that had colonized neighboring Asian countries. In order to defend Japan against outside powers, leaders then set the policy of *Fukoku Kyohei* (Rich Nation, Strong Army).

The first Sino-Japanese war (1894-1895) was between China's Qing dynasty and Japan primarily over influence in Korea. Japan's victory over China in this conflict brought about a complete reversal of the power balance between the two countries. China had acted as the teacher to a smaller and less developed Japan. Empress Suiko, the thirty-third monarch of Japan and the first and longest-reigning empress, started sending official missions to the Sui Chinese dynasty in 607 AD, and by the ninth century, Japan had sponsored nineteen of these missions to learn about the Chinese culture and civilization. The inversion of this relationship had serious consequences later.

In the early twentieth century, Russia was already a significant world power. The autocratic Russian Czar Nicholas II set his sights on Korea and Manchuria's Liaodong peninsula. In an effort to avoid conflict, Japan indicated that if they could maintain influence over Korea, they would not pursue their ambition for Manchuria. Russia refused Japan's offer. As negotiations broke down, the Japanese staged a surprise attack on the Russian navy in 1904. With heavy casualties and losses on both sides, the war ended with Japan's victory in 1905. Japanese victory over these two strong Eurasian nations—China and Russia—greatly enhanced national pride. Overconfidence and arrogance made the Japanese think they were invincible. At the same time, the stunning loss lingered in the minds of Russians, who would later choose to take their harsh revenge when the Japanese "Empire of Manchuria" began to falter toward the end of World War II. Domestically, Japan began to lean toward militarism with a much-strengthened military influence over politics.

Then, when the Great Depression in the US spread worldwide, it hit Japan hard, causing severe food shortages. During this period of domestic and international political instability, a small number of radical Japanese officers of the Imperial Japanese Army conceived a plan to invade northeast China. The region was rich in natural resources, and it was many times larger than Japan, with only a third the population. An added incentive for this takeover was Japan's fear of Russia, which shared over 2,500 miles of border with China. Japan knew Russia was anxious to invade Manchuria, and from there, to invade Korea and eventually Japan.

On September 18, 1931, without approval from the Japanese government, radical officers secretly planted and detonated explosives in the Manchurian city of Mukden near the South Manchuria Railway. The Japanese army proceeded to occupy the major cities with minimal difficulty. Japanese Prime Minister Reijiro Wakatsuki, despite his official non-expansionist policy, was forced to provide the justification of the military action. Within six months of the illicit aggression, Japan established a new nation of nearly half a million square miles, larger than California and Texas put together. The Empire of Japan called the new nation an independent country, but it was under the de facto control of the Japanese military.

Japan's hostile takeover of Manchuria shocked the international community, which expressed outrage. Internally, many Japanese leaders were likewise appalled by the unauthorized invasion, including the foreign minister, the civilian government in Tokyo, and even the commander-in-chief of the army. The Chinese government appealed to the League of Nations. It was not until February 1933 when the Lytton Commission's report was announced before the General Assembly. It concluded that Japan's invasion was aggressive and recommended that Manchuria be returned to China. By then, Japan had firmly secured its control over Manchuria. In response to the report, the Japanese delegation simply declared that they would withdraw from the League of Nations.

The UPI reported, "The stunned international conclave, representing almost every nation on earth, sat in silence while the delegation, led by the dapper Yosuke Matsuoka, clad in black, walked from the hall . . . 'We are not coming back,' Matsuoka said simply as he left the hall."[1] It was reported that even the Japanese emperor was surprised and disappointed by Ambassador Matsuoka's decision to leave the League. It had not been planned; Matsuoka even questioned his own actions after he stormed out from the League's assembly hall. He hesitated to go back to Tokyo directly to face the criticism, so he took detours to Italy and Britain. When he returned to Japan, he was pleasantly surprised that the Japanese people welcomed him as a hero—as someone who had courageously stood up to the formidable Western powers.

The Japanese mass media successfully spread pro-nationalist justification for its act of outright conquest. The government in Tokyo was initially upset by the military actions, but eventually acquiesced to the occupation of Manchuria. Academic institutions started recruiting engineers to plan building heavy industry in the new empire, and government agencies began organizing the resettlement of hundreds of thousands of Japanese farmers to the Manchurian wilderness.

The empire began creating ultramodern cities in Manchuria, enticing the best and brightest scientists, architects, and bureaucrats to create a modern utopia. Poor Japanese farmers were incentivized to establish "Manchurian branch villages," and quickly rose from being tenant farmers in Japan to becoming landlords in Manchuria.

Soon, ambitious middle-class citizens and well-educated young idealists, intellectuals, and civil servants flooded Manchuria with dreams of helping build a utopia. Manchuria became like the expansionist American view of its Western frontier—a territory where it was possible to create a new and better life. For a crowded nation hungry for more land, this vast, sparsely populated land of Manchuria became many different things to many different people. The Japanese government planned to relocate five million people to Manchuria within twenty years. There would be risks, but a passionate spirit of adventure moved many across the Sea of Japan to participate in the effort of constructing a new world. This excitement was global; as the Japanese empire began building a new world, the art movement of Futurism was taking root in Italy and Russia with its emphasis on youth, power, and technology. The word of the day, embodied in the very name of the Works Progress Administration of the United States—perhaps the most ambitious employment and infrastructure program of the era—was "progress." That progress was hard to debate in Manchuria. These immense, barren lands where warlords fought each other fiercely from the end of the Qing Dynasty in 1911 to the establishment of the Republic of China in 1928 were quickly converted to highly industrialized regions, due to Japan's enormous investment of time, money, and human capital.

My parents must have known that the Japanese military invaded Manchuria, but they might not have known that the action was initially against the wishes of their own government. Did they question why the Japanese in Manchukuo enjoyed a better standard of living than they would have back home, with a lifestyle equivalent to the upper middle class? Did they wonder at whose expense it had come? How did they convince themselves there would be no friction between the Japanese newcomers and the Chinese and Korean communities who had previously inhabited the region? It is one thing to be dreamers and believers; it is another thing to treat other groups as second-class citizens.

Perhaps the Japanese of the day, including my parents, were simply unaccustomed to questioning the authorities who promoted a grand concept of the New World.

There were likely many reasons why my parents were drawn to relocate from Yokohama to Manchuria in 1939. I am quite certain that my father was strongly influenced by his older brother, Kunimitsu, whom he idolized. Uncle Kunimitsu, a telecommunications expert, had been sent to the northeast of China as an engineer before Manchukuo was established by the government. His job was to lay the groundwork for future facilities, possibly in preparation for the invasion. Kunimitsu had first traveled to Manchuria in 1928, leaving his wife and their young son in Japan, and returned a couple of years later. During that time, my father met up with Kunimitsu and soaked in his tales of a utopian land.

Was Manchukuo utopian? History Professor Louise Young describes it in her book, *Japan's Total Empire: Manchuria and the Culture of Wartime Imperialism*:

> The builders of Manchukuo were a motley crew. Visions of empire fired the imaginations of a mixed collection of right-wing officers, reform bureaucrats, and revolutionaries of left and right, making bedfellows of erst-while opponents ... This did not mean that they held the same vision of Manchukuo's future. Far from it; their ideas were frequently at odds with one another. Where intellectuals saw in Manchukuo's new colonial cities an urban utopia, rural reformers dreamt of agrarian paradise; where businessmen looked upon Manchukuo as the remedy to a faltering capitalist economy, radical army officers saw it as the means to overturn capitalism itself ... Persuaded that the new empire had something to offer them, groups that had been indifferent or even hostile to expanding

Japan's position in northeast China in the 1920s joined together to build Manchukuo in the 1930s.²

Which category did my father belong to among those motley crews? He was impressed by his brother's personal experience in this new world. In 1932, Kunimitsu was sent back to Manchuria with his family. My father felt he had an opportunity to have the best of both worlds; if he relocated to join his older brother, he could indulge his thirst for adventure while having a reliable family member in the region. This safety net so emboldened my father that when he moved to Manchuria with his wife and one-year-old son, Isao, he did not even have a job.

Once settled in Manchuria, my father started working for a meteorological observatory as a staff member, not an educated scientist or engineer. While we may not have belonged to the privileged class like our uncle Kunimitsu, the benefits given to us as Japanese in an occupied country were so good it hardly made any difference. The Japanese government was eager to shape this frontier as a well-established new nation, and encouraged young people to move in by providing an enticing environment. My parents had left everything behind—the old world, their parents, siblings, and friends—but they were able to slip into a society of privilege.

Salaries were higher (probably 50 percent higher than in Japan), and anything needed for a comfortable life was readily available—nice brick houses with double-pane windows, flush toilets, Japanese food, clothes, medicine, entertainment, and all the conveniences. The Japanese government lavished enormous financial and personnel resources on Manchukuo.

Later, in 2019 when I began my research into the Manchukuo experience, I spoke with Hiroko Kurachi, a woman whose father had been a member of the fearsome Manchukuo *Tokumu-kikan* (equivalent to Russia's KGB). She told me that she had been driven to kindergarten every day by a chauffeur.

"Our life was extravagant," Hiroko said. She was eighty-five years old in 2019 and living in Kyushu, the southwestern-most of Japan's main islands. When we met in a fashionable hotel lobby in Hakata, she shared with me that as time went on, she had a growing realization that, contrary to what we'd been taught in school, Japan had been both an aggressor and a victim in World War II. We both had focused on our miserable evacuation experience from Manchuria and the atomic bombs dropped in Hiroshima and Nagasaki.

"We inflicted so much pain on other Asian people," she lamented.

Many Japanese in the 1930s and '40s were convinced that they were helping Manchuria by converting it into an enlightened, modern, and well-organized state at a time when China had no central government. What evidence did the Japanese have to ignore in order to continue to believe those convictions?

CHAPTER 3

THE SADDEST DAY

Virtually everything I knew about Manchuria came from my mother's recounting. I spent much of my middle childhood in Yokohama sitting next to her while she was sewing. Japan had been totally devastated in the war and was under the control of the American Occupation from September 1945 until the end of April 1952. Mother spoke proudly about her parents, whom I never met. She told me stories about her past and her life with my father. We had no television, no toys, not even enough food. But I never felt we were poor. My mother's stories took me to an imaginary world of splendor. Between translated European children's books and mother's stories, I could indulge myself in a sweet dream world. Unfortunately, she often disrupted that imaginary world by saying, "When we were trying to evacuate from Manchuria..." I kept quiet while she recounted those memories, but I wanted to close my ears. She would mention these miserable stories on various occasions; I wanted to erase that dark portion of my early life.

It took nearly thirty years until I could accept our experience in Manchuria as honest fact. My mother's notebooks connected the dots from the earliest years of my life, and they helped construct a meaningful narrative of our tormented life. Her first notebook started with a beautiful spring day in Manchuria.

> In the spring of 1945, truth was hard to come by in Manchuria. On the radio, the announcers were shouting, "Victory after victory!" Behind their positive words, their tone conveyed a different message that made us uneasy. Nonetheless, we chose to believe in the "Divine Power" of our proud country. And besides, our everyday life was still rather peaceful. The days went by quietly without anything obvious to fear. That is, until my husband was drafted into the Japanese army.
>
> The season was a study in contrasts. Finally, a long frigid winter was over. Flowers were bursting into bloom. Yellow marigolds, white dogwoods, and purple flowers I did not know the name of popped out of their winter doldrums. The cold wind from the vast, open fields no longer pierced our bones. The sky was high and cheerfully blue. An exhilarating season had arrived, but my heart was heavy because it was the day when my husband had to leave us.
>
> His military service classification was not the highest. Under normal circumstances, he belonged to the older age group of recruits who would have been turned away. Had the tide of war turned so badly now that previously exempted men such as my husband had to be drafted? I thought I was emotionally ready to send him off, but I was extremely distressed. As I prepared for his departure, I tried desperately to keep from crying.
>
> At the beginning of the war, people gathered for boisterous parties to send off the young men. It was

a great honor to be able to serve the country, and it was celebrated with *sekihan* (sweet rice cooked with red beans) and toasts of sake, accompanied by shouts of "*Kampai!*" (bottoms up!) and "*Tenno-Heika Banzai!*" (long live the emperor!). Now we had been told to be discreet. The people being sent to the war were no longer young. There were no young men left. So, there was no lively farewell from neighbors. It was a very sad start for a father of three children.

The time for my husband's departure approached. His olive-colored cloth service bag was packed. I had given him new underwear, which he wore. For me, new underwear was the symbol for new beginning, his new life as a soldier. With all of the necessary preparations complete, I looked at him. He appeared nonchalant, as if nothing unusual was happening. He merely sat at the dining table and used a toothpick to pick small crumbs of food from the gap of our wooden dining table. What was he thinking? Didn't he have any last words for us?

This image of my father sitting at the wooden dining table, picking up crumbs, not knowing what to say to his wife—not because there was nothing to say, but because there was too much—is vivid in my mind. I feel as if I were there, standing by the dining table and watching him.

Mother's notebook continued.

Three colleagues from his office came to say goodbye. One of the three, Mr. Takeda, said to him, "Enokido-san. Don't worry about your family. I will come around to see how they are doing, and I will take photos and send them to you."

His thoughtful words made me feel good, and I appreciated his promise. I had no reason to believe he wouldn't keep it.

The time had come for my husband to depart. With his right hand, he held our younger son, Takashi, who was only one year old at the time, and we went out with his colleagues to see him off. The teacher of our older son, Isao (six years old), who lived in our neighborhood, joined us. My husband bowed to him, and then continued toward the bus stop, walking ahead of us while chatting casually with the other men and swinging his service bag in his left hand. He looked as if he was just heading out to go shopping.

I choked up as I wondered what my husband was thinking. I knew that a husband who shows concern for his wife was considered not masculine, and a wife who demands attention from her husband in public was not graceful. Japanese men of the time were usually non-expressive, but it did not mean that they had no feelings. Rather, it meant they were taught to suppress their agonies and pains. A real man must be stoic. When he does open his heart, he may burst into tears as if a floodgate in his heart has collapsed. That situation was not permitted. Better to be stone-faced with steel determination to honor century-old tradition. He knew I, as his wife, understood. It was my role not to lose composure so as to help keep my husband's dignity. In the face of great emotional struggle, we acted as a respectable normal couple in normal circumstances.

The bus arrived.

My husband released his left arm and gave one-year-old Takashi back to me. "Thank you very much," he said simply to his colleagues, standing straight.

"Take care," they responded by tapping his shoulder lightly. They too observed the taboo against being sentimental even though they knew they might not see each other again.

Without any tender word for us, he boarded the bus. The bus chugged off, and he did not even look back as it started moving. I forced back my tears and stood there until the bus disappeared from sight. I did not want to believe that he was gone, perhaps forever.

I took a deep breath.

"Thank you for coming," I managed to say as I bowed politely to my husband's colleagues. I felt dizzy, but I was able to walk back to our house with steady footsteps. In front of the entrance door, I told the two older children, Isao and Kashiyo, our middle child and only daughter, who was three, to play outside. With Takashi in my arms, I went inside.

The house suddenly looked bare. The emptiness hit me hard. Outside, I had kept my emotions hidden as a proper woman in wartime. But no more. I could not keep my tears from gushing out. Clinging to Takashi's baby bed, I cried out loud without constraint. I cried and cried my heart out. That calmed me down a bit. Now I was exhausted.

On that sad spring day, I was just thirty-five years old.

My mother, and most Japanese in Manchuria, probably did not know that the war looked increasingly bleak for the Japanese well before my father was drafted. Japan had lost several important battles, many of its best pilots had been killed, and the nation's industrial capacity was diminishing. As early as October 1944, Japan sent skilled patriotic young pilots as *kamikaze* (divine wind), for essentially suicide attacks to destroy the enemy's warships loaded with bombs, torpedoes, or other explosives. Their instructions were "never come back alive." It was a repulsive strategy to use brilliant young people as disposable armaments. On the mainland during the war, women and old people had been trained to attack Americans with bamboo spears. Japan's strategy after the fall of Okinawa was to create "human shields" everywhere that Japan had occupied, to delay the advancement by Americans to the mainland.

In November, long-range B-29s started bombing Japan from the Mariana Islands. The nights of March 9 and 10, 1945, saw the single most destructive bombing raid in human history. There were 334 B-29s, and 279 of them dropped bombs. Sixteen square miles of central Tokyo were destroyed, leaving an estimated 100,000 civilians dead and over one million homeless.

The Battle of Iwo Jima, which started in February and concluded on March 26 that year, caused 7,000 American deaths, while Japan lost more than 22,000 soldiers who fought to the death to delay America's attack on their mainland. Then on April 1, 1945, the bloodiest battle of the Pacific War started in Okinawa with the largest amphibious assault by the US. The Battle of Okinawa lasted until June 22, 1945. An estimated 110,000 Japanese soldiers and sailors were killed in addition to approximately 150,000 citizens' lives lost; while American casualties were 45,000, including more than 12,500 deaths. The US gained command of the air, and they were free to bomb Japan anytime and anywhere they wanted. And they did. Trying to escape from the incessant bombings, some Japanese decided to flee to Manchuria even as late as the spring of 1945.

In April, Benito Mussolini was executed by the Italian resistance; and two days later, Adolf Hitler committed suicide by shooting himself in the head. Japan had lost its Axis

Powers partners and became the only remaining country fighting against the Allies.

Any news was delivered to the media by the military, and when a Japanese defeat was reported, the word *gyokusai* (die an honorable death) was used to glorify the soldiers' heroic spirit. Anyone with any questions or criticism of the war effort was labeled unpatriotic *hikokumin* (the worst derogatory label). Regardless, whether they liked it or not, Japanese people still accepted (wishfully) the official reports as true; they, like my parents, had no choice but to obey orders.

CHAPTER 4

TAKE CARE OF OUR HEIRLOOM SWORD

Until that beautiful spring day in 1945 when my father reported for duty, our life had been rather calm, despite great chaos outside Manchuria. My parents got up early every morning. Soft sunlight came in through thick double windows. While my mother chopped tofu and seaweed for morning miso soup, my father got ready to go to work. Shinkyo Meteorological Observatory was located in the suburb beyond South Shinkyo Station, next to a golf course. It would have taken more than thirty minutes to walk there. I don't know if he took a streetcar or a bus.

About two weeks prior to my father's enlistment in May 1945, Germany had surrendered. But Japanese newspapers had discovered that stories about Japanese success on the war front dramatically increased circulation and revenue, so they continued to generate stories based on false information provided by the military. Was media complicit in the falsehoods, or did they believe what they were reporting? The Japanese propaganda machine had been designed to influence soldiers and individuals to heighten a sense of nationalism and to demonize enemies. People like my parents had been led to believe that Japan possessed divine power that Germans did not have.

Everything changed after my father left. No more morning routine of chopping vegetables and preparing breakfast. My mother's lonely and uncertain days were barely comforted by watching three active young children. But even those days came to an end unexpectedly, as she wrote in her notebook.

> There is a Japanese expression, *Nonaka no ippon sugi*–meaning a lone cryptomeria tree in an open field, or someone standing alone with no help. The person whom I wholly depended upon was gone. I was left alone in *gaichi* (land outside of Japan) with no adult family members after Kunimitsu, my husband's brother, died of pneumonia and his wife and children returned to Japan. Every day I felt empty. Only my children, healthy and lively, saved me from complete despair.
>
> Unfortunately, even that barely tolerable situation was about to change. Approximately one month after my husband departed, my daughter Kashiyo, who was four years old, was unexpectedly stricken with severe diarrhea and a high fever. I immediately called a doctor, who came to our house to examine her.
>
> "I believe that her stomach is the trouble," he said solemnly. The doctor had nothing more useful to say, apparently, and he left. He told me to go to the hospital to get some medicine.
>
> A week passed, and her condition did not improve. Instead, she became weaker. I called a different doctor. When this second doctor examined my daughter, he glared at me and demanded an explanation.
>
> "How could you let her get so sick?"

I was shocked and could not say anything. I just stared at the doctor's stern face.

"If you don't do something, she will die soon."

I came to my senses and explained that I had been following another doctor's orders. The new doctor stopped accusing me and continued his examination, a grim look on his face.

"Boil water. I will give her an injection."

I think this must have been some kind of Ringer's solution, with salts dissolved in water to fight dehydration. This second doctor took out a huge syringe with a barrel about an inch in diameter. It was so long and fat, I shuddered. Before I was married, I had been a nurse in a large general hospital in Tokyo and only stopped working when Isao was born. Witnessing the shots given to sick children was a routine matter as a nurse, but when it came to my own child, it was a different story. Seeing my little girl get this injection made me tremble. She was very young, and her thigh was pathetically thin.

"You are going to get a shot," I told Kashiyo. "It will hurt, but be brave. If you don't take this, you won't be able to see your father."

Kashiyo nodded. I told the doctor that she understood.

The big needle went deep into her left thigh, which swelled up right away. The doctor made a similar injection into her right thigh. Her thighs were too thin to take two injections in one thigh.

Kashiyo did not complain. She endured the pain without crying. I was proud of her, but my heart ached.

"She seems to have infantile dysentery," the doctor said. He instructed me how to make sure the other children would not be infected. He closed his black leather bag and left. After I sent the doctor off at the entrance with a deep bow, I quickly returned to Kashiyo. With hot towels, I gently massaged her thighs, which were swollen like balloons. It was clear that we had narrowly averted a serious crisis.

I was determined to treat my daughter like a patient in a hospital. I decided to make one room of the house into a convalescent room that the other children were not permitted to enter. Remembering the infectious disease wards in which I had worked, I arranged the room as best I could. I was afraid the other children might already be infected, but they showed no symptoms. Kashiyo probably should have gone to a hospital, but it was not possible. We were at war.

Instead, I tried to recall as much medical knowledge as I could and focused on tending to my sick child. The new doctor came back the next day and the day after that. He gave Kashiyo a shot every day for three or four days.

"You are an excellent nurse," he told me. The doctor's praise brought a bitter smile to my face.

It would not be the last time I wished my husband was there with me. I missed him terribly. I was put in a position of tackling a serious family crisis alone. But this first encounter with a grave family crisis would be nothing to compare to the situations that were awaiting me. When I faced those horrifying situations later, I would not even have the capacity to think about my husband.

I worked hard and with great determination. Fortunately, Kashiyo survived. When all of the children returned to good health, I started worrying about my husband again, where he might be and what he might be doing. He was supposed to be stationed in Sunwu, near the Soviet border on the bank of the

Amur River, but I did not know that for sure. The only comfort I had was one postcard that had arrived in June. It held a very simple message. "I am fine. Make sure you take very good care of our heirloom sword."

He did not ask about me or his children. I was upset. "What was he thinking?" But I came to understand there was strict censorship in the military; he could not write what I wanted to hear. Instead, he referred to the sword that was his family's treasure. His older brother, Kunimitsu, had kept it before him. After Kunimitsu's untimely death, it had come to our house and was prominently displayed in our alcove.

My mother often repeated, "Take care of our heirloom sword" after we—my brothers and I—were older, and whenever she reminisced about her Manchuria stories in Japan. We were not particularly interested in the origin of the precious sword. The three of us simply accepted that this was one of those episodes that showed our father's character. He was the youngest son in a wealthy family; when he had been drafted, he had not yet been tossed about in the storm of life. Many men of his age had escaped being drafted. Why couldn't he have resisted, like his classmate from Ibaraki who stayed behind with his family in Shinkyo? Without knowing the origin and history of the heirloom sword, it became our family's joke; but my mother was not in a mood to take anything lightheartedly. She was dead serious about everything. Her notebook continues.

I wrote to him often and maintained the demeanor of a brave patriotic wife. I repeated that he should be courageous for our country. I could not tell him how I really felt, and how much I missed him. Anybody could read my letters, and I didn't want them to be able to find fault with me or my family.

There was a group of wives whose husbands had also been drafted, and we would get together to discuss our plight from time to time. Some of them had been told they might be able to see their husbands in August. There was no way to know if this was true or just a rumor. There was no official announcement. Nevertheless, we decided to believe it and waited anxiously for August to come.

CHAPTER 5

DARK DAYS

My mother's notebooks were full of details about her fears and struggles in Manchuria with three small children and an absent husband. They told the story of her world, but nothing much outside of that universe. Was it because she was too busy with her own story, or was it because she did not know what had happened beyond her environment?

It is understandable that ordinary citizens had no idea what was coming, but surely they could sense the dark clouds encroaching.

> While a group of wives were anxiously waiting for August to arrive, unease came over our whole neighborhood. All that people talked about were air-raid shelters and emergency food provisions. Once-kind neighbors were now interested only in themselves. No one cared about anyone else; self-preservation was the top priority.

Neither my husband's colleagues nor our Japanese community members ever came to check on us to see how we were. Mr. Takeda, who had promised he would look after us when my husband left, never visited. Only Ching-kun, a young Chinese man who ran errands around my husband's office, came twice and showed that he cared. My husband had given Ching-kun a chance to work at his office and treated him kindly, and now it seemed he wanted to repay the favor. He had brought my husband's personal belongings from his office at the time of his departure. This small act of kindness meant the world to me. In return, I gave him a pair of my husband's shoes and trousers. I was not sure when my husband would be back to use those things himself.

Ching-kun asked me, "Why should your husband have to go to the war?"

It was true that my husband was older than most soldiers and had three small children. But the war situation was growing increasingly dire. We felt restless and uneasy. Mail from Japan was delivered less frequently and less regularly. People's faces were grave. We had few reasons to laugh. Our next-door neighbor was also drafted. He left two small children. His wife and I shared our worries. We continued talking about August when we hoped we might be able to see our husbands. We shared the joy of anticipation and grumbled about the uncertainty. The dark days went on.

One day, I wrote a letter to my sister in Japan. "This letter may be the last one you will receive, but please do not worry about me. Whatever happens to me, I promise you that I will act as a proud Japanese woman of whom you will not be ashamed."

I am not sure how I reacted as a four-year-old child to our father's departure and our mother's despair. I have no memories; any stories I have from this time must have been acquired from my mother's recollections, or I might have read them somewhere.

During July of that year, the hottest season in Shinkyo, my mother began to prepare for the coming winter. Summer in Manchuria was very short; there was perhaps only a six-week period when the sun blazed overhead into the evening and one did not have to wear a jacket. My mother spent this time making fuel balls by cleaning the leftover charcoal powder from the *pechka*, a Russian brick stove, and placing it in a coal bucket. To this she added some sticky soil from our garden, a kind of red clay. She poured water into this mixture and shaped the materials into balls, then set them out in the sun. These balls were completely dry in just one long summer day. My mother worked at these balls all day long. She made one to two hundred balls every day. Then she arranged them neatly in three or four rows and displayed them to dry at the corner of the front yard. She was satisfied to see that her fuel balls were perfectly shaped compared to those of her neighbors. She was a perfectionist with a competitive spirit; I believe I have inherited this trait from her.

Every day, my mother made these balls, not allowing herself to be distracted. Once they were dry, she placed them in the storage space under the dining room floor. She also leased a vegetable garden of about five tsubo (around two hundred square feet) and started growing potatoes. She had never used a shovel before, but she dug and planted potato seeds. We helped her, and it turned out to be fun watching our crop sprout—a tender moment in a darkening time.

CHAPTER 6

THE SOVIET UNION ENTERS THE WAR

My mother's effort to maintain a daily routine as cheerfully as possible must have worked well. I have no memory of suffering. My older brother, Isao, must have kept going to school as a first grader. His teacher had come to see our father's departure and walked with us to the bus stop where my father stepped inside and we watched him leave. Despite the incessant bombings of Japan's mainland by America's B-29s, our life in Shinkyo in 1945 was not desperate until the end of July.

> One evening around midnight, I was suddenly awakened by the air-raid alarm. People were shouting, "Get to the shelters quickly!" I woke the children, and without changing into proper clothes, we went to the underground shelter in our backyard that my husband had asked a carpenter to build before he left. It was only one *tsubo* (a little more than thirty square feet), but there was electricity, water, and food for one day.

This was our first air-raid drill experience. I shuddered with fear, but I told the children, "Don't worry. Nothing will happen."

From that night on, air-raid practices were repeated every night.

In the beginning, we followed the instructions. But after several nights, these became routine, as even the most loathsome or absurd situations can. I hated to wake the children from their deep sleep. In time, I came to feel that the repeated exercise was pointless and decided we would no longer go to the shelter. I used the excuse that Kashiyo had not completely recovered from her illness. This was not true, but the chief of our neighborhood association who came around to check on us was none the wiser. He granted approval for us to not go to the shelter any longer. I was resigned to our fate; whatever was going to happen, was going to happen. If we were to die, at least we would die together. I sometimes wonder how I resorted to this fatalistic view.

During the daytime, wherever people gathered, all they talked about were the night raids. No one knew what would happen next. There was no television and no newspaper. If we had known what was going on in the larger world, we would have been terrified. But in our isolation, there was only a vague, uneasy feeling, a sense of insecurity that intensified as days went by.

I was envious of families whose husbands and fathers were at home. Only three fathers had been drafted from our neighborhood. How could we have been so unlucky? I got together with these other wives whenever I could. We talked, but there was nothing we could really do to help each other. In the end, each woman was only capable of, and interested in, protecting herself and her family.

One August afternoon when the hot sun was beating down, we gathered in front of our community shelter. The men of the neighborhood were saying–as if it was a clever idea–that they must eat and sleep during the daytime. This made me especially angry. What about the families with no fathers? Who would take care of the small children if I were to sleep during the daytime? Nobody from my husband's office offered me any help. No neighbor did anything for us. The three families whose husbands had been drafted were not in their thoughts. I shed tears of bitterness and resignation, thinking why should I even dream of having anybody to depend on?

Around August 8 or 9 my mother was told by the neighborhood leader to attend a meeting at the usual shelter. There she was given shocking news.

"The Soviet Union has entered the war. Soon this area will become a battleground. All women and children should evacuate. Families without husbands should come to Shinkyo Station by noon tomorrow. The ultimate destination is somewhere deep in the mountains to the south."

At this point, we were at the very end of World War II in 1945. We did not know, but two atomic bombs had been dropped on Hiroshima and Nagasaki (on August 6 and 9, respectively). We did not imagine that Japan's defeat was imminent. But the Russians knew. In fact, they knew more than anybody.

The truth is that the Russians did not want Japan to surrender before they could get involved in the war. Joseph Stalin ordered his troops to invade Manchuria without delay. They crossed the border with tanks and machine guns at two minutes after midnight on August 9, savagely killing Japanese settlers like insects. More than 1.5 million Russian soldiers, five thousand tanks and armored motorcars, and twenty thousand heavy artillery and supply materials were deployed over the Soviet-Manchurian border, which extended more than five thousand miles.

President Franklin Roosevelt, Prime Minister Winston Churchill, and Secretary General Joseph Stalin had met near Yalta in Crimea in February 1945 to discuss Europe's postwar reorganization. At that conference, Roosevelt encouraged Stalin to attack Japan in the North—Manchuria. America needed Russia to divide the Japanese strength by forcing them to fight on two fronts.

The heads of the same three countries met again at Potsdam in occupied Germany in the summer of 1945. Later that same year, President Roosevelt died, and Harry S. Truman became president.

The Soviets knew that Japanese soldiers were fanatically resolute and brave. While Japan's military equipment was inferior to that of the Soviets, Russian attackers would need a fighting force twice as large as those fearless defenders.

If Japan surrendered quickly due to the horrendous casualties caused by the atomic bombs, Stalin was concerned the Soviets might miss the opportunity to defeat Japan. They did not want America to claim all the glory for winning the war.

While actions were being weighed by the Allied Forces, the Japanese government still had sufficient time to notify their own citizens to move away from the Russian border areas during the spring. But if they started evacuating, the Russians would notice. In order to deceive one's enemies, it is necessary to deceive one's own citizens. As Takao Iwami wrote in *Memories of Defeated Manchuria*, "Therefore, the

Imperial General Headquarters decided to let Japanese citizens stay where they were. Keep on living as if nothing was the matter. Thus, 300,000 Japanese settlers were abandoned by their own military."[3] The most important mission, as the Japanese military saw it, was to maintain the national polity, not to protect the people. The military did not serve the people, but the emperor.

Each of those Japanese settlers abandoned by their government had a story. For example, Japanese soldiers from northern Manchuria were ordered to gather at a southern city. They had to walk over three hundred miles through swamps and forests to avoid Russian and Chinese attacks. A former Japanese sergeant wrote that after four or five days of walking, he noticed a woman with three children following behind their group.

> The woman looked to be in her late thirties. She had two boys, one seven or eight years old, and the other four or five. She also had a baby on her back. She was desperate to keep up with us. Sometimes, she stopped to feed the baby and gave food to the two children. We were exhausted and did not exchange any conversation. We sent them silent messages to keep going by looking at each other. She never asked us to help. She just kept on walking quietly on the same path with us for several days. Eventually, they disappeared from our sight. I was struck by this mother's strong sense of determination to fight for life. She probably knew that she could not depend upon the Kwantung army after the government had abandoned settlers. Nobody knew what happened to them.[4]

That could have been us; that essentially *was* us. These tales of a single woman—possibly widowed—and three young children doing whatever they could to survive described our family unit perfectly, as my mother's account of that time made clear.

> The Empire of Japan was crumbling, but we did not know exactly what was happening. It was unthinkable that the invulnerable Kwantung Army could not defend us. All we knew for sure was that winter was coming.
> When I was told by our neighborhood leader that we had to evacuate Shinkyo immediately, I asked him who had directed him to deliver that message and where we were going. He responded that he did not know, but that we had to hurry to get ready. I did not argue. Perhaps we would find out when we got there. Besides, we seemed to have no other options.
> I got ready to evacuate the next day, equipped for the coming cold. Despite the summer heat, I wore winter trousers and a heavy overcoat. I prepared the children the same way. I packed underclothing and food for several days in rucksacks, then we rushed to the train station.
> We arrived at the train station in sweltering heat, but the evacuation train had already left the station. I was dumbstruck. We had not been late. We arrived at the station at the appointed time. I did not know what to do; we were completely lost. We just sat down at the station and could not move. I asked the station attendant when the next train would come. He said he didn't know.
> We waited there for a long time, but, of course, nothing happened. I pulled myself together and decided to return home. The children complained that it was too hot, in part because we were wearing all kinds of extra clothes.

In a rare display of pent-up anger, I lost my temper and scolded them, "Be quiet! We have no choice!"

I was furious, but I didn't know with whom. I just kept mumbling to myself, "We were not late, we were not late."

I started walking to the streetcar station, my children in tow. How could this have happened? We were thoroughly disciplined to follow instructions. Where was the reliable chain of command?

We got off the streetcar near our house. On one side, there was a wide-open space with no buildings or vehicles, just a green field. It was a completely peaceful spot. I collapsed on the soft grass. I was exhausted from our all-day forced march with heavy winter clothes on this searing summer day.

I do not remember how long we were there.

"What happened to you?"

I looked up at the person with the voice. It was a doctor from the Red Cross Hospital, a familiar face, as we had all visited his office regularly for one reason or another. The nurses there joked that we were the hospital's most valuable clients. I often invited the doctors and nurses to parties to celebrate the recovery from illness of our children from one thing or another, so I thought I had found one reliable ally in an enemy's camp. I told him about our experience of the day.

"It cannot be helped. It is all for our country." The doctor's voice was cool and formal. He gave me no comfort.

"What can we do?" I asked him, but he left without answering. I felt a stab of pain. It seemed like another example of the cold reality that we could not expect any help from others. In these last days of the empire, everyone had to take care of themselves. I had to take care of myself.

We pulled ourselves together; a mother and three children dragging ourselves home. Just wearing the heavy winter clothing in the 90°F heat was grueling in itself, but the indescribable disappointment and bewilderment of the day added emotional exhaustion. We must have looked like beggars trudging along under the scorching sun.

Two or three days passed after the time we were supposed to have left, but we were still in our home. Neighbors were disappearing, one by one. Since my husband had worked for the meteorological observatory, our housing complex belonged to the government. There were twelve families in three buildings, four families in each. Each morning when I woke up, I saw that one house had emptied, then another.

By August 12, hardly anyone remained. It was as quiet as a ghost town. My children had lost all their playmates, so they simply played together inside. In the daytime, we could pretend everything was fine, but when night came, I couldn't help but get frightened. As I lay down for the night, I wondered when–or if–sleep would come.

One evening, we had a visitor, a highly unusual event.

"I was sent by the government office. You should join us to evacuate tomorrow. Here is your husband's salary for one year."

The young man handed me 3,000 yen and hurriedly left without asking for a receipt. Three thousand yen was a lot of money. In those days, you could buy a luxury Swiss watch for 10 yen, while an ordinary watch was 3.50 yen.

Our previous experience with evacuation remained a bitter memory. It felt as if I was standing on a crossroad without a guidepost. Should we go or should we stay? No matter what we did, we were not like most people. I was just a wife with no husband at home, and three small children. The youngest was a toddler who had only started walking months before. The oldest was a first grader–smart and responsible, but still only a child, not a man with muscles. Even if my husband had been there, this was not going to be an easy journey. I had no information that could help me decide, but I knew the situation was very grave. I thought hard, and finally concluded that we would not go. If this place became a battleground, as many people predicted, so be it. We would live or we would die. It would be up to fate.

Once I made the decision, my mind became clear. I had no doubts. It was not difficult to convince myself that it was the most reasonable decision under the circumstances.

CHAPTER 7

THE DOLL

In Japan, children were brought up to behave well so that they would not shame their parents. Japanese parents believe their children are an extension of themselves, sharing an unbreakable bond. They emphasize collective values, conformity, and respect for authority. Western parents prioritize individualism, creativity, and questioning authority.

One stark example of this cultural difference is family suicide, or what I was shocked to learn is a crime called "murder-suicide" in America. In Japan, when a family encounters impossible difficulty, parents feel it is benevolent to take their children with them when they decide to end their lives, rather than toss their dear children into stormy lives without them. And this was what my mother contemplated in Manchuria, facing the invasion by Russians during the summer of 1945.

> The next day, I filled the bathtub–something I had not done in many days. After we bathed, we all changed into fresh clean clothes. If our bodies were to be

found, we should at least look presentable. My pride in respectability under any circumstances was still intact. We had been given a ration of poison to take our lives, if need be. It would be more honorable to use poison rather than be killed disgracefully by cruel enemies. I was determined to give a merciful and peaceful end to my beloved children. If our situation became desperate, we should still look placid and brave, even in death.

Calmly, I started putting the house in good order. At that moment, I was ready to die, but I still had the awareness to worry about my reputation.

Another night passed. Our surroundings were eerily quiet. There was no change from the day before. I do not remember what I did all day.

When night fell, someone knocked on our door. "I am from the government office," the man said. "Tomorrow, we will evacuate to Andong. This will be the last evacuation. Be sure to be there. We will gather in the square in front of the Transportation Department building."

I wondered who had been checking on us since we had not followed the previous evacuation order. This time, we were told the destination. Andong (modern-day Dandong) was an important border town between Manchuria and Korea, and it was much closer to Japan than Shinkyo.

My firm determination of the day before was weakened. Still, I wavered between going and not going. Things would be the same wherever I went. It would be a long, treacherous journey. The odds of being able to make the passage safely with three very young children were small.

In the afternoon of August 14, our last remaining neighbor, Mrs. Murata, came to ask what I was going to do. Her husband, who had worked with my husband, had also been drafted, leaving her with their three children, who were older than mine. The oldest was probably in fifth or sixth grade. Mrs. Murata was stunned to learn that I was leaning toward staying. She urged me to change my mind. While we were talking, our children were running around and laughing happily with Mrs. Murata's children. Some sense of the possibilities of the future must have crept into my mind because my determination gradually crumbled.

"Well, then. Let's go," I said to Mrs. Murata. "Let's get ready."

"We are already ready!"

I went into a frenzy, dashing here and there. Our rucksacks were still packed from the last time we had meant to evacuate. I tried to add one of my husband's suits to the rucksack but could barely close it. Then I remembered that we had a box of sugar cubes. I tried to push the box into the rucksack but could not do it. I had to break the box and push the sugar into the rucksack one cube at a time. Even so I could only fit half and had to leave the rest behind.

As before, we had to prepare for winter. We did not have the luxury of feeling the heat of summer. Just before we left the house, I glanced at Kashiyo. She was holding a big doll with a long red dress. This Western-style doll had been given to her by Mrs. Mori a few days before, and it made her so happy. She held her all day long. It was her treasure.

"Leave her here!" I said, but she did not listen. She held her doll more tightly to her chest.

We did not have time to argue. I held Takashi and carried my rucksack on my back. Kashiyo followed with Isao, holding his hand. Again, we walked under the hot sun with heavy winter clothes.

We arrived early at the Transportation Department Square. I could not believe the size of the crowd. Who were all these people and where had they been? The men appeared to be in good physical condition. They looked about the same age as my husband, and some were even younger. Why had my husband been drafted if there were so many younger men still at home with their families? I was incensed by the unfairness of it all.

The throng was very noisy. In the crowd, I turned and saw Mr. Takeda, my husband's associate, with his wife and their daughter. He noticed me at the same time.

"Ah, Mrs. Enokido. How are you? I have not seen you for a long time. It was not easy for me to find the time to visit you."

I thought that was a weak excuse, especially after this man had offered soothing words to my departing husband about the care he would offer to us. I turned away from him quickly.

"Never mind," was all I could say.

One truck arrived. Just one truck.

I wondered how all these people could fit into that one truck. Children went first. In Japanese, we call that kind of crowd "washing potatoes," an expression similar to saying "packed like sardines." Desperate people with big rucksacks were pushing and pulling–it was complete chaos. Children were placed in the middle, and adults stood in a ring around them, holding hands to create a fence to surround them.

The children were crying and screaming, "It hurts, it hurts."

Once we all managed to get on a truck, a man shouted in a loud voice, "The kid with the doll! Throw it away!"

Even one little doll was too much in such a packed space. There was no room to move an inch. Without a word, I snatched the doll from Kashiyo and threw it from the truck. As soon as it hit the ground, it was snatched up by a Chinese girl who looked about six years old. She held it in her arms and smiled happily. Kashiyo looked sad. Her lips twisted, and she fought not to cry.

Dusk was gathering when we arrived at Shinkyo Station. I had Takashi on my back. The three children suffered in silence.

"You were good," I told them. I seldom praised my own children, but I really felt they were extremely endearing despite such trouble. They must have sensed the seriousness of the situation, even if the actions of adults over the past few days were incomprehensible to them. I did not explain what was happening. They never asked questions, and they never complained or cried.

We got onto the train, a flatbed wagon. It was worse than any class of train that previously had held people; even workers with dirty clothes with unpleasant odors rode in more comfort. Everybody grumbled that we were being treated worse than baggage, even though we knew there was no point in complaining.

The crowding was worse than it had been on the truck. On the truck, everyone had stood, but on the train, everybody tried to sit down. It created a terrible uproar. I pulled Takashi from my back, folded my legs, and sat straight with him on my lap. The other two children sat on either side of me, knees to knees.

The train started at twilight. We gazed at the flickering light of the train station as it receded in the distance. What would happen to us next? Nobody knew.

The train ran a bit and stopped. Ran again a bit and stopped–again and again. Would we ever arrive at Andong at this pace?

Night came. It was pitch dark.

To make matters worse, it started to rain. Most of us had no umbrellas, and we became soaked. People on the flatbed started quarreling out of sheer frustration and discomfort.

"Your leg is poking me."

"You elbowed me."

"Raindrops are streaming from your umbrella and hitting me."

The few who had umbrellas stayed dry, but in the totally packed train, they made things worse for those around them. The soot and smoke of the engine made us choke.

I managed to get a large towel from the rucksack and covered the four of us. This protected us from the coal cinders, but not the rain. I unbuttoned my overcoat and held Takashi close to my chest. Then I stretched out both arms to hold the other two children tightly.

The rain became heavier and heavier. There was no mercy. The temperature was dropping. It was cold! I was exhausted, and my children kept falling asleep.

"Don't fall asleep," I told the children. "If you sleep, you will die." It was cold and wet. They lacked body fat, and they were exhausted–the essential elements for hypothermia.

I was desperate to keep them awake, pinching their knees, slapping their faces, but they still dozed off. I woke them many times. Each time, tears rolled down my cheeks. And still the bickering went on all around us.

"You hurt me."

"Your legs are stretched out too far."

The weight of Takashi on my lap began to hurt my legs. I tried to change my position, just a little bit. Instantly, someone shouted at me, "Your legs are in the way!"

"Can't you understand it can't be helped?" I shot back. "I cannot bear the pain."

These were the first words I had uttered in protest. I was determined not to cave in.

When dawn arrived, the rain stopped, and the sun came out. It had been a long and tormenting night. My children were all wearing fur coats, but they were still drenched to the skin. I wanted to change their clothes, but everything in the rucksacks was wet. What choice did we have? It could not be helped. The sun would take care of it.

The train stopped again. We did not know where we were. Manchurian peddlers gathered around the train. Somebody bought cucumbers and handed them out. I assumed the person who bought the cucumbers must be the group leader. I did not know who he was, and I did not even care. I was the last person to receive a cucumber; women without accompanying men were always treated as less important.

The sun was shining, and we were thirsty, so the cucumber was a blessing. I scrubbed the dirt from it with my kimono and we all savored it.

The train station was far quieter and more rustic than Shinkyo Station. We were given an hour to rest. We got off the train, which had been a torture chamber. We stretched our arms and legs and breathed deeply. Everyone tried to dry his or her wet clothes. I opened our rucksacks. Almost everything was soaking wet. I found the few items that were the driest and changed the children's clothes. I had put my crocodile wallet inside a band beneath my obi sash, but despite that, the paper money in the wallet was completely soaked.

    I carefully peeled off the bills one by one and lined them on stones on the train track. Then I placed stones on top of them. While I was trying to dry them, I never took my eyes off those notes, even for a second.

CHAPTER 8

INFERNO IN MANCHURIA

The distance from Shinkyo, today's Changchun, to Andong is approximately 370 miles. Andong means "pacifying the east," reflecting the power that China had over Korea, situated to China's east. The 490-mile Yalu River forms the border between northeastern China, Manchuria, and the Korean Peninsula. We had been packed on evacuating trains like sardines in Shinkyo, and I cannot imagine how long the journey took in 1945. Today, the journey takes a little over six hours by high-speed train. I could only visualize "poor us" from my mother's writing.

> After we arrived at the Andong train station, we were given an hour's rest. Then, we were told to walk. It must have been forty minutes before we arrived at the desolate town that was our destination. On one side were mountains, while the other side was lined with houses–all in a similar style, all shabby.
> I do not know who had arranged for the residents of the town to receive us, but they took families

separately to their individual houses. The family who took us in was a couple in their mid-forties with one son. When we met them, they said to us, "You must be tired." These simple words melted my hardened soul and body. We had fought to get into the crowded truck. We had squeezed ourselves into packed, roofless cargo trains. We had been exposed to coal cinders, and soaked by merciless rain. We had dragged our tired feet to finally meet people with warmth and compassion. I felt like a human again.

"This way." The couple started walking, and we followed. I was still carrying my rucksack and Takashi on my back. The couple did not offer to help me with my load, but I was not offended. I was just thankful. After all, we were not visiting our welcoming family for a joyous vacation.

The couple stopped in front of a modest house with the simple words, "Here we are." We all took off our shoes and went inside.

"I am very much obliged," I sat and kneeled, putting two hands in front of my head; I bowed deeply to touch my forehead to the tatami floor. It was the best I could do to show my gratitude.

In the evening, they offered us warm rice for dinner. We had been told that we had to leave Shinkyo because the Russians were coming. So, we had escaped but we still did not know exactly what was happening or what we would be doing in Andong. But the steaming white rice was exceedingly delicious. Isao's chopsticks moved quickly. He must have been hungry. Both Kashiyo and Takashi were more tired than hungry. They did not show much appetite; instead, they dozed off. All three children soon fell fast asleep on mats on the floor. The woman of the house put the dishes in the kitchen sink, and we three adults sat down in front of a small round table under dim light.

"I have something important to tell you," said the head of the family solemnly. His manner made me tense. Then he said that Japan had surrendered.

I shook my head. I stared at his face. What did he say? I could not understand at first.

"The emperor told us that we surrendered." His lips quivered.

Was this true? Wasn't some spy spreading misinformation? But the mournful tone of the man's voice sounded genuine. The three of us looked at each other without a word. After a moment, we all started sobbing. Once we started, our sobbing turned to bawling, and we did not know how to stop. A thousand emotions rushed through me. We had endured hardship and sacrifice because we had been convinced of Japan's victory. The possibility of our defeat had not even entered our minds in the slightest degree. How could we accept this reality? An awareness of our unfathomable humiliation descended on us. Oh, Americans! Was it possible for them to have beaten us? My hatred toward Americans swelled.

On August 15, 1945, the front page of *Asahi Shimbun* newspaper, with a readership of over two million people, bitterly declared it a day for national mourning in Japan. The reporter of *Asahi* rushed to the Imperial Palace Front Gardens where hundreds of Japanese citizens had already gathered to hear Emperor Showa at noon. Everyone sat on the ground to listen to the first-ever live broadcast by the "living god" whose actual voice had never been heard by his people. The message had actually been recorded on the previous day, and the emperor's voice was not clear. His unique vocabulary, used only within royal circles, was unfamiliar to common people. But the Japanese people understood it. Upon hearing the emperor's message, the *Asahi* reporter grabbed handfuls of gravel and clenched his fists tightly, shouting in desperation, "Emperor! Forgive us!"

Another newspaper, *Mainichi Shimbun*, with a circulation of 1.6 million, reported the same sentiment the next day, apologizing to the emperor for the country's defeat. "Our Tears and Blood Are Dripping for the Pain of the Emperor. Repent of Our Sins!" Such was the reverence that Japanese people had for the emperor—even though Japan had started a war in the name of that emperor, which only ended after approximately three million military and ordinary citizens were killed.

Japan's literacy rate was nearly 99 percent, so people all over the nation had access to the information provided by those nationally circulated newspapers. When the Potsdam Declaration calling on Japan to surrender had been released earlier in July, the headlines of those same newspapers had shouted, "Terms for Japan's Surrender Totally Laughable!" (in the *Asahi*) "Blow Up the Arrogance of US/UK/Nationalist China! We Will Fight Our Holy War Until the Bitter End!" (in the *Mainichi Shimbun*). People wanted to believe in Japan's ability to triumph, clinging to hope against hope.

But that hot summer day of August 15, 1945, changed everything. The truth was revealed. Japan had lost the war.

Today, Japan observes August 15 as Memorial Day, the day the war ended. In an elaborate ceremony, the emperor gives a speech before a giant altar arrayed with hundreds of thousands of yellow and white chrysanthemums. In Korea, it is a national holiday celebrating the end of thirty-five years of Japanese occupation. For Russians, the war did not officially end until September 2, 1945, when Japan signed the formal surrender instruments on the USS *Missouri*.

The fighting with the Allied forces, except for Russia, stopped in Japan. But in Manchuria, the killing continued. Manchuria was an inferno due to the Soviet invasion Stalin had ordered.

Rei Nakanishi, a highly acclaimed songwriter and novelist, remembered the ongoing war in Manchuria. He was born in Botankou (Mudanjiang) in Manchuria in 1938 and died in 2020. His vivid memories of the day when the Soviets started attacking Manchuria were published in the *Yomiuri* newspaper:

> My father was on a business trip to Shinkyo. My mother decided to escape. Through her contacts, she was successful in arranging for us to join the military train headed to Harbin. I thought this was just like a school excursion trip, and we would return soon.
>
> The next morning, the train suddenly stopped. Somebody shouted, "Raid by enemy plane!" Everyone jumped out of the train. Without thinking, I promptly crept under the seat. The Soviet planes repeatedly machine-gunned the train. When the gunning stopped and I came to my senses, I saw a man lying in front me. He was wearing an army uniform and was bleeding from being shot in the head. If the bullet had hit just a few inches away from him, I would have been dead.
>
> Countless dead bodies were thrown out of the train. As the bodies fell in the wilderness, indigenous people gathered around and tore off their clothes, [and] stole the gold teeth from the mouths of the deceased. The Manchuria that had been a heaven changed to a hell in a single day. The trains before us must have encountered a similar situation, because along the rail tracks, I saw numerous naked bodies scattered all around.
>
> We arrived at Harbin around noon of August 15. We were told by Manchurian soldiers of Japan's defeat.

Sobbing sounds spread in the train. My mother and sister were crying too.

The end of the war on August 15, 1945, was just the beginning of a long, agonizing struggle for our family.

When we arrived at Harbin, our baggage was confiscated. The only cash we had was what my mother had wrapped in her obi and wound around me for safekeeping. We stayed in a hotel in the city that night. The next morning, several armed men broke into our room. An interpreter rattled off, "We are Soviet soldiers. Bring the men. (The Soviets wanted to take any able Japanese men to their labor camp.) Bring cash and goods. If you lie, we will kill you."

The Soviet soldiers searched the room. I felt more dead than alive as I had the cash around my waist. They did not search my body because I was only three years old. During the time they were looking all over our hotel room, we could hear shouts, shrieks and gunshots from outside...

Japanese men who were rounded up by the Soviet soldiers were taken for labor. After the Soviet soldiers were gone, the hotel was a gruesome scene. Blood-stained bodies lay scattered around. We moved to a refugee shelter that day.[5]

Regardless of what international arrangements had been made, the Soviets did not stop their attacks. In addition to these Russian attacks, the Chinese and the Koreans started revolting against the Japanese in Manchuria where more than 1.5 million civilian Japanese had been left alone to defend themselves. The fact of Japan's unconditional surrender did not change our reality. Rather, it only created confusion and fear of the unknown. My mother's notebook described a more immediate and personal agony after Japan's surrender. It was about our younger brother Takashi.

The day after I learned about Japan's surrender, Takashi had terrible diarrhea. He was one year and four months old. He had already been toilet trained, so I had no diapers for him. I thought it was just a temporary condition, and I did not pay serious attention. We had just arrived at Andong the day before, and we were then given the shocking news that Japan had surrendered. Our world became chaotic. I could not concentrate on taking care of Takashi's condition. The confusion caused by Japan's defeat was mounting every day. Two or three days passed. Even though I was concerned about Takashi, I could not do anything about it.

For the Japanese in Manchuria, life became hell. The tables had completely turned. Immediately after the declaration of Japan's defeat, Manchurians and Koreans became emboldened and Japanese were increasingly reviled. We were told not to resist in any situation. Farming communities of Japanese settlers in the north near the Russian borders were savagely attacked and their houses were burned down by the Chinese. After all, the Chinese had cultivated and supported their families on those farmlands for generations, until they had been forcibly taken by the Japanese military to provide land for Japanese settlers. When the Japanese settlers had moved to Manchuria as colonists, they had treated Chinese and Koreans as second-class citizens. The Japanese did not think it was discrimination. They simply thought that was the way it should be.

When Japan surrendered, the suppressed anger, hatred, and rage among Chinese and Koreans exploded. One day, I saw a Japanese man being violently beaten by long bamboo sticks by five or six Manchurian kids. I had no idea what they were saying, but I was sure that they were cursing in their language. The man did not try to resist or escape. He just knelt there on the ground. Many Manchurians and Japanese adults were watching, but no one tried to stop them. It was unbearable to witness. I left quickly. I trembled to think of our future.

The sight would have been inconceivable just a week before. And now we were supposed to put up absolutely no resistance? How pathetic. We had to swallow the reality that the mighty Japanese Empire, with all of its enormous power, had collapsed overnight. There is an expression in Japanese, "Like a leaf floating on the big ocean." That is how we felt, as utterly helpless as that leaf.

We had followed instructions from our leaders because we had believed that they had known better, and they had always been right. Hadn't anyone known that Japan could be defeated? Much later, I was dismayed to learn that top military officials had indeed known that the end of the war was imminent. The officers of the Kwantung Army and their families had been evacuated earlier and safely returned to Japan. But not the common people like us. We were left behind.

My mother later told me that she and my father had no suspicion they had done anything wrong when they moved to Manchuria. They did not recognize their own arrogance at the time. "It was the way it was," I heard them say. They wanted to believe that they fit harmoniously into the environment and that there was no friction between the different communities, but it was the Manchurian vendors who came to the house to take orders for groceries every day, and Manchurians did the manual labor that the Japanese did not want to do. Japan had colonized Korea and taken control of this part of China, and my parents were the beneficiaries. The Chinese and Koreans were second-class citizens, and my parents had fallen into a society of privilege.

My parents were far from alone, of course, in a belated understanding of these sociopolitical realities. In his essay, "Mother Killed My Brother—Living Hell in Manchuria," Akira Takahashi described the shifting political and cultural superiority he witnessed with his own eyes in Manchuria in August of 1945. Sometime before Japan's surrender, Japanese colonists sensed that something changed by observing the behavior of the Chinese laborers. They stopped coming to work, and they did not return the horses that they had borrowed from their Japanese employers. In fact, these Chinese laborers must have anticipated Japan's defeat, even though the Japanese colonists had no idea what was going to happen. The local people's information networks were much more accurate than those of the Japanese conquerors, who were victims of their own propaganda. Takahashi writes:

> My father never struck our laborer, named Xie. We had a good relationship. The Xie family invited us for a Chinese New Year, and we used to enjoy eating dumplings together.
> On August 15, 1945, Chinese laborers started attacking Japanese villages with sickles. My family shut ourselves in a room. Our old laborer, Xie, came and told us, "We are not going to kill you, but this place is dangerous. Escape to the south."
> My family was fortunate enough to run away while one in ten of those Japanese who remained were massacred that day.[6]

While the enmity boiled over in Manchuria between the Japanese and the Chinese and Koreans, the Russians were worse. Not only did the Russians continue killing and raping the Japanese, they also ravaged the towns and countryside, taking machinery and anything of perceived value from Japanese factories, offices, and private residences. Because the Russians needed the Japanese to teach them how to operate the machines they looted, they also commandeered Japanese engineers and other skilled workers and transported them to Russia.

Many Russian soldiers wore four or five watches on their arms that they had taken from the Japanese. When the watches stopped, they threw them away because they did not know that the mechanisms had to be wound. The Japanese were frightened by the Russian soldiers but looked down upon them as uneducated beasts. And so, the cycle of cultural derision, defensiveness, survival, and confusion continued. My family found itself in the middle of this upheaval.

> We were told that the Soviet troops were coming, and no woman or child should go outside. Rumors spread that the Russians were as ferocious as wolves.
> On the night when we were notified of the Russian advancement to Andong, my landlord declared, "If you are to be shamed by Russian soldiers, I will help you end your life with this!"
> He drew his sword and swung it a few times. It was a beautifully polished Japanese sword and made me think of the sword of our family treasure, which I had to leave behind in Shinkyo.
> I was not frightened by his sword. I bowed with appreciation and asked him to do so if the time came. I would rather die by his sword than risk being raped by the Russian soldiers. Women prided themselves on absolute chastity during this time. If women

were disgraced, death was preferable to dishonor. However, I learned much later that some women who made a living with their bodies acted bravely and saved ordinary women. They heroically offered themselves to Russian soldiers who demanded women.

CHAPTER 9

MOTHER'S PAINFUL CHOICE

Life as evacuees without money or support was brutal. The 3,000 yen my mother had been given just before the evacuation was the only cash she had after the packed cargo train transported us to Andong, a supposed safe location after leaving Shinkyo. There the evacuees were told Japan had surrendered, but they could not comprehend what they were being told—it was too much to understand. What could they do in that strange place with such extraordinary information?

Judging from the number of abandoned houses, many Japanese families who had been in Andong must have already left town. It was not difficult to find an empty house. My mother decided to move out of our host family's house, and quickly found a small place nearby. The living quarters had just two rooms, one with eight *tatami* (straw) mats (a little bit less than 150 square feet) and the other with four and a half mats (about 80 square feet). It had no furniture. Previous residents might have moved away or had been evacuated—but where did the furniture go? Did they take it with them, or had it been stolen?

We said goodbye to our host family. They had no obligation to take care of us, but they were thoughtful enough to give us one futon, a thin coverlet, one pot, two or three plates, and a few bowls. These were the only things that we–a mother and three children–had in our possession, besides the contents of our rucksacks.

I wanted to give our host family something to express our appreciation, but I had nothing to offer. I could not spare any money; the future was too unpredictable. I decided to give them the crocodile-skin wallet that held my last 3,000 yen. I removed all the money and wrapped it in paper.

"What an expensive wallet," the head of household said. He held the wallet with two hands. He turned it over, then opened the wallet. He seemed very pleased. The wallet had been a gift from my husband before we were married, when he was traveling in Europe. Another link to my husband was severed. I became wallet-less thereafter.

Andong was a rustic town. Unlike Shinkyo, there was no city gas supply or flush toilets. Even Japan itself did not have flush toilets at that time. When my sister visited us in Shinkyo when Kashiyo was born, she was amazed by how many modern conveniences we had. But no longer.

When we moved to the small house, I was prepared for a Spartan standard of living, yet I still needed more than what we had. I purchased some things that were absolutely necessary. In Andong, most Chinese and Koreans seemed to have adopted some of the elements of a comfortable lifestyle from their Japanese occupiers. Clothes, food, and other supplies were freely traded by crafty merchants. These Koreans and Manchurians did not hesitate to take advantage of the newly poor Japanese. Anyone with money could buy anything, but the prices of even basic staples like rice were astronomical–it was as if the sellers were punishing the Japanese by their price gouging. Anything I could obtain without spending money felt like a victory. I picked up three old bricks from the street and created a place to cook by arranging them in a U-shape and digging a pit beneath them. This was how a new life started for our family of four.

At this time, many Japanese men started doing manual labor to earn money. People who had never held anything heavier than chopsticks had to swallow their pride and become cheaply paid laborers at farms, in grocery stores, and as road construction crews–whatever menial jobs the Chinese people did not want to do anymore. Everyone was eager to earn money in order to survive. I could not help wishing that my husband was with me. How could I earn what I needed to care for three small children without a partner? I lamented my circumstances every day.

Two or three days after we moved into our house, I learned that three men were living next door: the head of my husband's office (whose name I don't remember); my husband's immediate boss, Mr. Ishida; and Mr. Takeda, who had promised my husband he would take care of us. I had no idea what happened to their families. They had not come to Andong for some reason. I felt uneasy. They knew my husband had been drafted and that I had been left alone with three children. And they knew I was living next to them. Why did they not bother to come see us? They were not our relatives, but couldn't they have the common decency to check on us and see how we were? Couldn't they be polite, even on a superficial level?

For some income, I decided to make the small room our private space, while I would rent the larger room to the Japanese neighborhood association as a meeting place. It is a funny thing about our people, but it is Japanese nature to form an association whenever more than a few people get together. We have a strong tendency to feel more comfortable when we act as a group. There is always one person who volunteers to be the leader of the group, and those associations always consisted of men only. This group of men who used our second room as a meeting place discussed the affairs of the day, but they never shared any information with women. They were probably trying to figure out what might have happened to Japan after the total surrender by collecting any piece of information here and there that they could find. Had the country been occupied by Americans? Were Americans attacking Japanese women? Would we ever return to Japan? And if so, when and how? In those days, women never thought of questioning why they were excluded. It was not a woman's job to analyze the situation we were in or to make plans for the future. We were trained to follow the leader.

As a single mother, however, struggling mightily to get by in the most extreme circumstances, such questions began to occur to me more and more often. One such time was when all the refugees from Shinkyo were told to attend a meeting.

"We still have some money from the company," the leader told us. "So, we will distribute some to all of you."

I was given 700 yen and about three meters of white cotton cloth. I could not help wondering why they had kept so much money. Instead of holding on to it, couldn't it have been used earlier to improve the quality of our lives? I grew more discontented with these know-it-all men. Nevertheless, 700 yen and white fabric were valuable. I used the fabric to make underwear for the children, dishtowels, and some necessaries for myself. My own underwear had been turned into diapers for Takashi when he had his terrible diarrhea after we arrived at Andong.

In a strange turn of events, the meetings in the larger room of the house where we were squatting turned out to be a source of joy for me. Some of these men had worked at the same office with my husband, and they seemed to have access to a slush fund of office money left in the banks before the evacuation. Those who had been in a position to manage the accounts must have withdrawn all of the cash before the banks had closed for good. That money did not belong to them personally; they were assets that belonged to the organization. Yet the men spent it freely, bringing cakes, snacks, and fruit to every meeting. After their gatherings were over, I cleaned up the room and carefully collected the leftovers to give to my children. Cakes and fruit were things we could hardly dream of having otherwise.

For some reason, these meetings were always held at night. Mr. Takeda from next door made it a habit to visit us the mornings after the meetings. Yet, he did not have anything to say. At first, I was puzzled, but then I came to realize that he wanted some of the leftovers. What a pitiful, shameless man. I despised him and would not entertain him. He came two or three times, but when he received nothing for his trouble—the same courtesy as he had extended to me and my family—he finally stopped coming around.

One reason I had for moving from our host family's house in Andong was because of Takashi's health. His diarrhea that had started the day after we learned about Japan's surrender had continued intermittently. Eventually, he grew so listless I had to take him to a doctor's office. Fortunately, Mrs. Murata was nearby. I asked her to look after my other two children. I made two large rice balls, known as onigiri, for their lunch. Then I took a bus, carrying Takashi on my back the entire way.

The clinic was not an official medical office, but there were two trained physicians who had been evacuated to Andong working there. The clinic was packed with many patients, and I had to wait a long time to talk to a doctor who then only met with me for a few minutes. I had to wait still longer to get medicine for Takashi. And then, of course, there was the arduous return trip home.

I made this trip several times, but Takashi's condition did not improve. He became completely emaciated. He could not stand up. Deep, vertical lines appeared on his thighs. His small chest showed his ribs. I spent a great deal of our precious money on Takashi, with no visible improvement. As a parent, I never wanted to tally what I was expending on my child's well-being; it was terrible to reckon things in this way. Yet, without any income, it was painful to spend any money at all on anything other than the daily necessities for my other children.

Takashi's condition grew worse. He had been largely bedridden for quite some time. It became our daily routine to take a walk after supper. Eventually Takashi could not walk at all, so I carried him in my arms while the two older children walked beside me. We went along slowly. Whenever we saw something of possible interest to Takashi, I stopped and talked to him.

"Look, Takashi. There is a dog." Or I would say, "Oh, there! Can you see the horses?"

These sights cheered him as evidenced by the faint smile that he wore on his thin cheeks. Even these walks were not without agony, however; as we set out each day, I could feel Takashi grow lighter and lighter. The thought that he might die soon brought tears to my eyes, which dropped onto his pale cheeks. How could I explain this to my husband? Would he understand that I did the best I could? Would we ever see him again?

The lightness of Takashi's body made me feel absolutely powerless. What could I do except cry? Yet I could not show my tears to my children. I admonished myself that I had to be strong for my two relatively healthy children. I forced myself to smile.

One day, I picked up Takashi and noticed a huge flea on his neck. Stunned, I removed his clothes quickly. I found the seams were packed with flea eggs. It was the same with my older two children. Good heavens! I wanted to take everybody's clothes and douse them with piping hot water, but we did not have enough clothes to change into. We could only change our underwear. We could not afford the elegant practice of changing into pajamas at night. We wore the same clothes all day and all night.

Instead, I tried to pick out as many fleas as I could every day, patiently and carefully. I could not completely eliminate them, but the constant and tedious work provided me a temporary diversion from my other worries. We had not had a bath since we arrived in Andong. All day long, the three children were quiet. I could not let them die. I needed to do something.

My worries about them occupied me day and night, my whole body and soul, but I could not do anything.

As the days went by, I felt increasingly desperate. We were running out of money. I had to think two or three times before buying even basic foodstuffs. I wracked my brain and tried to think of options. The only thing I could think of was to stop taking Takashi to the doctor. That would save us some money. I hated this idea, but I did not know what else to do.

I am very sorry, Takashi, I thought. *I do not want to do this; but if I don't, Isao and Kashiyo will suffer the same fate as you.* It was a dreadful decision, but I had to protect the two other children by sacrificing the smallest and weakest one.

The next day, I put this plan in action. I stopped taking Takashi to the doctor's office. I stopped spending money for his medicine.

Of all the times when I found myself unable to comprehend what my mother had gone through during the war, these days are the starkest and most unimaginable. What level of pressure and desperation could have existed to bring such a good woman to this pit of despair? The more I learned about the last days of Manchuria, it became clear that she was not alone in having to make such agonizing decisions; in fact, she acted far more rationally than some other mothers who had been abandoned and had to care for several children.

There are far too many memoirs written by Japanese family members who killed their young children when they thought they had no other options. The family of Akira Takahashi, whom we met in the previous chapter, was escaping a Russian attack on the settlement of north

Manchuria, close to the Russian border, when the following events took place.

> Everybody became insane. We killed or were killed. Our minds were totally numb.
> We kept on walking. When we entered a swampy area, bullets came from the front and back. We could not move. There was no water to drink.
> Suddenly, the group leader ordered, "Sick people, people who cannot walk, and children under the age of five should all be disposed of."
> Is this the end of my life? I thought. When I looked back at my mother, I saw she was choking my two-year-old brother to death with a washcloth, and she threw my five-year-old sister into a river. But my mother was not strong enough to throw her all the way into the water. My younger sister's little fingers grabbed a tree branch on the riverbank, and she crawled back up the bank.
> My older sister, who was fourteen at the time, rushed to our younger sister. She hugged the little one and said, "I will take care of her."
> My mother had behaved as if she had completely gone insane. There were many other mothers who killed their small children. It was nothing other than complete madness.
> My older sister carried the younger one and walked by pulling her mother's hand. Five days later, my older sister fell. She could not get up. Her strength was totally exhausted. She was gone. All my mother and I could do was to cover my sister's face with weeds.[7]

This is just one of many stories of mothers ending their own children's lives during this time. I have become convinced that I cannot ever judge the actions of someone forced to undergo such unspeakable mental and physical torment. I can only feel immense gratitude that my mother chose a different path in a crucial moment, and that our family's fortunes proceeded very differently as a result.

> We had been in Andong for a month. We had barely enough food to survive. We were in extreme poverty. Our staple dish was thin gruel mixed with a large portion of *kaoliang* (a kind of cereal usually fed to livestock). I wanted to add something more nutritious, so I bought oil from Manchurian merchants. I also went to their farms and purchased some greens and stir-fried them as side dishes. Those merchants were relatively kind, which brought some relief to my heart. I always chose the cheapest greens. There was no seasoning except for a tiny bit of precious soy sauce for a little flavor.

Tei Fujiwara, whose husband had also worked at the Meteorological Observatory in Shinkyo like my father, although in a much higher position, had evacuated with three small children to a village near the border of North Korea without her husband. She became a best-selling author who published many books about her experience in Manchuria. Her first book, *Nagareru Hoshi Wa Ikiteiru (The Shooting Stars Are Alive)*, was first published in 1949. It was creative nonfiction based on her own experience, edited skillfully, probably by her husband who was a prominent writer in Japan. I have read her original Japanese version many times. It was an extremely moving book.

My mother's memoir in Japanese was not edited, yet I remain in awe of her writing. Each time I read it she becomes alive; I relive her life along with her. How I wish she was still with me so I could shower her with great admiration, like Americans who do not hesitate to give compliments to their own family members. Such talk about your own family was considered indiscreet in our society where modesty and humility are virtues.

That ethos is ingrained in me, and I have struggled to praise my own children. They thought I didn't acknowledge and appreciate their achievements enough, but I cannot recall that my mother ever gave me any words of encouragement. Whatever achievements I accomplished I was made to feel were expected. It is thus more than heartwarming to learn from her writings that she cherished her children and openly expressed how good we were.

> My children were so very young, but even they seemed to understand we were in dire circumstances. They ate quietly, without complaint. We continued our routine of walking after supper, always with Takashi in my arms.
>
> Whenever we met acquaintances in the street, they would say, "You cannot help but sacrifice this young one."
>
> I heard this many times.
>
> "Yes, I am very distressed, but I am doing the best I can," I would say.
>
> Everyone tried to console me, but their words were empty; they gave me no concrete help or any solace at all. Suddenly I thought, if this child is going to die, why not give him as much food as possible? I wanted him to die with a full stomach. As his mother, that was the only thing I could do for my unfortunate child.
>
> From that day on, I gave Takashi as much food as he could consume. If I could even manage an extra treat, I would give it to him. After all, those special treats cost only a fraction of what I had been paying

the doctor. The other children did not ask for the same treatment, but they had to be envious. They stared intently at Takashi's hands. It was pitiful, but I tried to ignore them.

I am sorry, I am sorry, I cried out in my heart.

Several days passed after I changed Takashi's diet. To my astonishment, his diarrhea stopped. He looked livelier, and he became more spirited every day. After a few more days, he stood up and walked. What vitality! I was an atheist, but I thanked all the gods.

CHAPTER 10

•

WINTER APPROACHES IN ANDONG

It seems miraculous that Takashi's life was saved. But was it really? He likely had suffered from malnutrition. Which begs the question—why hadn't the doctor in Andong diagnosed Takashi's symptoms as starvation? The doctors in the Andong clinics had medical backgrounds, but during this chaotic period and in desperate situations, some of them were veterinarians, and others were unlicensed. But the evacuees were all desperate; they could not be choosy.

With Takashi literally back on his feet, my most pressing problem was solved. Now I began to wonder how much longer we would stay in Andong. Would we ever reach Japan? Rumors about our fate circulated and disappeared, bringing us joy alternating with disappointment.

The season started to turn to fall; a refreshing, cool breeze began visiting Andong. The time for summer clothes was over, and winter would not be far behind.

With the approach of the colder weather, I realized once again that we only had one very thin futon cover that our landlord had given us when we left his house. We would place it on the tatami, and the four of us would lie down. Because this thin summer coverlet was no longer enough to keep us warm, we used our coats beneath it. We did not have pillows, so we gathered other clothing to make headrests. The children could manage with this arrangement, but my feet stuck out in the night, and I was invariably woken up by being cold. I knew it only would get worse when winter arrived.

At the end of September, people started saying that Shinkyo was safe, and that our houses there might even be habitable. How I longed to go back home! A man who claimed to be an acquaintance came to visit me. I could not remember where I knew him from, but he had a lot of interesting information for me. He told me that my sister-in-law, widow of my husband's older brother, was now living in our house in Shinkyo.

The news delighted me. Our house was still standing! At the same time, I was troubled. I had normally tried to keep away from my sister-in-law, whom we called "Mama." She had a number of personality quirks I disliked. For one, she was profligate; when her husband was alive and active–and quite prosperous–she complained constantly that she did not have enough money. She borrowed money to buy expensive kimonos, yet she did not care if her children's socks had big holes. She had a habit of throwing things away without trying to mend them.

My sister-in-law was also very unconventional. She frequented bars and cabarets. She smoked anywhere she liked and paid no attention to what others thought of her. She was always beautifully made up and wore her hair in a bob, an extremely rare and modern hairstyle among Japanese women at that time. She let her children call their parents Papa and Mama, which was highly unusual, instead of using the more formal Japanese terms, *Otou-sama* and *Okaa-sama*. When we first came to Manchuria from Japan, we had stayed with them at their house until we found our own place to live, and we started calling them Papa and Mama like their children did.

In addition to her erratic behavior, I did not approve of her decisions. After her husband, Kunimitsu, had died of acute pneumonia at the age of forty-one at the Red Cross Hospital in Shinkyo, she initially went back to Japan. Then she left her three primary-school-age children at the Enokido family home in Ibaraki and returned to Manchuria with her oldest son, Terume, who was in middle school. At the time, it puzzled me that she chose to explicitly favor this one child and placed such a burden on her in-laws with the additional children. Now I understand that she probably did not have much choice. It must have been too much for her to support four children by herself in Manchuria, and it must have been too much for the Enokido family to take care of four children. I also could easily imagine that those children left in Ibaraki did not have a good time under the chilly gaze of the cold-hearted Enokido family.

I had lost contact with Mama during the upheaval in Manchuria, but it was a real surprise to learn that she was back in Shinkyo. I was worried that our house would be ruined if she continued to stay there. Luckily, I happened to meet someone who was returning to our old town. I wondered how anybody could travel to Shinkyo since the Manchurian Railway had ceased functioning for quite some time. I asked this person to deliver a written message to my sister-in-law. "We are fine. We have evacuated to Andong. But we will be coming back soon. Please keep our house in good shape."

A few days later, someone else was going to Shinkyo, so I sent a similar message to my sister-in-law again. I talked myself into believing that the more messages I sent, the better chance she would pay attention to me, and that this would put some kind of curb on her exceptional sloppiness. I still continued to assume that other people would think the same way as I did–upholding responsibilities and honoring obligations.

While I was puzzling about how people could travel, we heard that the Soviet troops would soon march into Andong, demanding wine and women. They were said to be especially interested in women between twenty-five and thirty-five years old who had already given birth. We did not know why it mattered for the Russians if women had had children, but that was what we heard. I was distraught. That definition described me perfectly; I was thirty-five, and I had my three children. What could I do to protect myself?

Frightening stories were rampant. One day, a woman whom I knew ran into my house wearing only socks on her feet. She told me that she had been taken to a Russian cabaret and nearly raped. She had escaped through a bathroom window. We agreed the best we could do was to avoid being seen by Russian soldiers. Soon, all Japanese women vanished completely from the streets. When I peeked outside from the window, I saw only men. But I still had to shop for food. Whenever I went out, I looked around very carefully and then ran as fast as possible, racing back home afterward without wasting even a second. The fear never diminished, and the gloomy days continued.

On one such melancholy afternoon, I suddenly heard an accordion playing a wonderful tune. It had been many years since I heard Western music like this. We had been prohibited from anything Western because such things belonged to the enemy's world. The music penetrated my whole body, and it was such a comfort. I opened the window slowly. The sound of music grew louder.

The song was "The Blue Danube"! I recognized the tune. Without thinking of my safety, I ran outside. A truck was parked nearby in a small vacant lot. A young soldier with blond hair was playing, and three soldiers about his age were sitting nearby. They were all smiling. Smiling Russian soldiers were beyond my imagination. Fifteen or sixteen Japanese women surrounded the truck. Either they were all fearless or the music had proved far too enchanting.

When the tune ended, it was followed by heartfelt applause. The same tune was played again, again to loud applause. For some reason, the soldier repeated only this one tune. Then the soldiers all stood up casually and left, still smiling.

This was the first pleasurable experience I had had since we came to Andong. I am not a musical expert, and I could not judge if the performance was good or just fair. But it did not matter. It was absolutely delightful. The slogan "Ugly Americans, Hateful Russians" had been imprinted into my brain, but that day, I learned that individual people could still be nice, even if their nations were at war.

Unfortunately, those empathetic feelings did not last. One day, not long after, I met a woman near our house. Her clothes were tattered and barely covered her body. Her hair was in total disarray, and she was crying and shivering. She said Russian soldiers and Manchurians had attacked her on a train. They stole everything she had, and then raped her in front of other people. Why was she on a train? It did not matter. The story made me wish even harder to escape from this place and to go back to Shinkyo. But I did not want to take any chance of being attacked on a return trip to our old house. I did not know what to do. One thing was clear—we could not spend the winter in Andong. It would mean just waiting to die of severe cold and hunger. We had to return, no matter the danger. I talked with Mrs. Murata whose husband had also been drafted, leaving her with three boys. She agreed to go back to Shinkyo with me.

    I started collecting information. I met more people who traveled between Andong and Shinkyo, and each time I asked them how they did it. I discovered that many government officials and wealthy business executives who were living in Andong were able to hire trains through brokers who made these arrangements. Whatever might happen, I told myself we should take one of those trains. It was better to take a risk than to wait to freeze and starve to death in Andong.

Winter comes quickly in Manchuria. By mid-October, the cold was so wicked that it cut right through us. Even as I kept my mind focused on our escape, we had to prepare for a brutal season. It was all making me extremely nervous. Takashi had recovered enough so he could play outside, tottering under his heavy overcoat. He was more active than ever, but it was pitiful to see his thin neck, which still had traces of a few thick vertical lines due to lack of food. His tendons and bones were visible under his skin. We could not afford to delay our departure.

I learned that a certain corporation had hired one car of a train going to Shinkyo soon, and I could get seats. The fare would be very high, but it could not be helped. It was a black-market deal. What little cash I had left was enough. We could manage.

We were told that we should be prepared to leave at a moment's notice. The date of departure was not set. My first concern was how to carry my last small sum of cash. What little was left was all the more precious. I decided to let the children carry the cash and sewed paper money into the collars and hems of their overcoats. I put most of the money into Takashi's underwear and pants.

We were ready. I did not know what I would do when we got back to Shinkyo. I just wanted to go back. I had no definite plan. I simply had to go.

CHAPTER 11

THE TRAIN LEAVES TONIGHT

The Japanese government's slogan during the war was "Beget and Multiply." Women were encouraged to marry early and produce healthy children. Not only was it an important duty for mothers to have babies, but they also needed to raise them to be healthy children and eventually good soldiers. To create unity and to facilitate reproduction, marriages were promoted. Arranged marriage was predominant and considered the "proper way" for "proper people."

Other slogans during the war were "We Won't Ask for It, Until We Win" and "Luxuries are Enemies." Those slogans were effective tools to inspire a sense of patriotism among ordinary citizens. Citizens had to be "all together," and it was their pride and honor to be part of the national unity.

I always believed that my parents had married despite their parents' opposition, and that it must have been a love marriage. But recently the idea has come to my mind that their marriage might have been arranged. After all, they met through an introduction by my mother's sister, our aunt, acting as a matchmaker. I do not know if my parents had exchanged personal resumes that would have included their educations, jobs, salaries, and family structures together with formal photographs taken at photo studios, wearing the best suits for him and lovely kimono for her.

Even if it had been an arranged marriage, she must have developed romantic feelings. Many Japanese couples in arranged marriages fall in love with their partners after marriage. They also develop strong comradeships as they share many ups and downs together. But in the circumstances my mother found herself in, she could not keep on missing him and weeping in self-pity. She did not have the capacity to indulge in romantic longings.

In my mother's memoir, there are passages where she longs for the presence of my father after he was drafted, but I did not get the impression she missed him necessarily for romantic reasons. Her top priority was to keep her children alive—feeding them, keeping them warm, and protecting them from violence and illness. It was her responsibility and obligation to take them to Japan, while her husband was exercising his duty and responsibility for the country.

Throughout our evacuation and time in a refugee camp, she missed her husband because she needed another pair of hands to carry heavy rucksacks and help with three small children. She missed her husband because a woman without a husband was discriminated against. It was not her fault that she did not have a husband with her. Nevertheless, she was treated unfairly because she was "just" a woman. My mother did not have a husband who could bring in even pitiable earnings while we were starving and shivering with no money to buy food or coal. My mother envied those families with husbands, and she deeply missed her husband for practical reasons. But I am not saying that she missed him for practical reasons alone. He was her husband, her children's father, and her partner whom she had chosen. He was still the most important person to her, even as her children occupied most of her attention under the constant threat of starvation, illness, and unexpected violence.

Gradually, she was forced to be a decision-maker. She became a sole provider and protector for the three of us because nobody else was. She tried to be a good "follower," but the time had come to make an independent decision that went against the group's leaders. Their priorities were their own welfare, and whenever opportunities arose, they would take advantage of the situation for their own interests. Breaking away from the group demanded great courage. She knew she had to make her own decision. She felt she had had enough.

> Cold winds started blowing. Andong is situated in the south, but it is still part of Manchuria. I crossed my fingers every day, waiting to hear about our train to Shinkyo. I had no idea what had happened to my husband. Was he dead or alive? There was no way of knowing, but I thought that maybe if we were in Shinkyo, we might learn something. I clung to wisps of hope like this as I counted the days that passed.
>
> Mrs. Murata, whose husband also had been drafted, and I agreed that we had to leave Andong for Shinkyo before we starved or froze to death. We met every day and made plans while we were waiting for news of when a train would take us back to Shinkyo. We promised to help each other as much as we could. If one of our houses in Shinkyo had been ransacked, for example, we vowed we would share whatever the other had. To my disappointment, this promise later turned out to be empty.
>
> It was almost the end of October. Soon it would be the season to light fires in the *pechka* (stove made of masonry) for warmth. But in Andong, we had no fuel

to put in the *pechka*. We did not even have a *hibachi*. We shivered at night under the thin coverlet, and I was afraid the children might catch cold. I let them wear all the clothes they had. We each put on several layers of summer clothes in addition to our few winter clothes.

The men in our neighborhood drove me crazy with their self-absorption. I could hear them out in the street talking loudly about getting coal. They even had the nerve to laugh out loud outside my window. What uncaring people! What was so funny? My family would not have any heat for winter! It was hard to restrain my indignation. I wondered whether, if my husband had been with me, would we have been talking and laughing with them? No, I would never have allowed myself to be friendly with this uncaring group!

During a quiet afternoon on an unusually warm fine day, I started to prepare dinner a bit early. I poured *kaoliang* (sorghum grains) into our aluminum pot, the only pot we had, and steamed the grains very slowly to make it as soft as possible. Then I moved the steamed grains aside. Using the same pot, I mixed together half rice and half *kaoliang*. That was all we would have for dinner, but it would have to be enough.

I put out the fire. A simple dinner was ready. I could now relax and enjoy that quiet warm evening. I was breathing deeply—a moment of simple bliss.

Then I saw Mrs. Murata through our kitchen window. She was rushing to our house with her three children. As soon as I opened the door, she blurted out, "I heard that a train is leaving tonight."

Without taking a breath, she shouted, "Let's go right away!"

I looked at Mrs. Murata and saw she was carrying a rucksack on her back. Her three children were also carrying small rucksacks. They appeared to be completely ready to go. This abrupt development threw me for a moment, but then I remembered we had been waiting for this moment, and I was ready.

I let my children go out to play with Mrs. Murata's children. I went back to our small room and picked up the rucksacks I had prepared for a hurried departure. I looked around the house. I wanted to make sure that I would not miss anything. Through the window, I could see the six children chatting noisily and happily, as if they were going on a picnic.

I took our rucksacks and closed the door of this house where we spent such an unhappy short period of time. The three men from next door saw me.

"Where are you going?" they asked.

"We are leaving this place," I quickly answered.

"Where are you going?" they repeated.

"We are taking a train for Shinkyo."

They opened their mouths, but no words came out immediately. They seemed to be dumbfounded.

"Going up north now? That is ridiculous," one of them said.

"This place is farther south, and much closer to Japan," another one joined in. "If we stay here, we have a better chance to get back home."

I grew angry. I wanted to say, "You never tried to help us. You have no right to tell us what to do, and what not to do. Just mind your own business."

But I could not find the right thing to say or the right way to say it, so I kept it all bottled up inside. Trying to make them understand was not worth my effort. Besides, time was pressing. We must not miss the train!

"Let's go," I said to Mrs. Murata. We collected our children. I pulled Takashi's hand, and only then did I think of the meal I had just finished cooking, and the bag with a little remaining rice I was leaving behind. That food was nearly as important as our own lives, and I was abandoning it. The *kaoliang* I had left on the brick oven must be fully steamed by now. All these thoughts were swirling around in my head as I hurried to the train station.

Reading my mother's memoir, I marveled at the details she could recall more than thirty years later. Sitting at her kitchen table in Yokohama, she could still smell the *kaoliang* on the brick oven and see how the red berries were swollen, with the white contents bursting out of their husks. Was it the terrible stress that branded these memories into her brain? Was it the intensity of the drama in which she was the main character? I have never faced such difficult decisions in my entire life—I would wager that most people haven't. Perhaps if I had, I would understand better the workings of the human memory.

Takashi, who was still recovering from his long illness, walked for a while but quickly became exhausted. At first, I pulled him along by the hand, but then I picked him up and carried him the rest of the way. Isao was holding Kashiyo's hand firmly and walking in front of us. It was the same way we had left Shinkyo and perfectly captured the image I had of the four of us, fighting against the fate seemingly assigned to us.

We arrived at the train station. Mrs. Sugita, who had come from a prominent family in Tokyo and was friendly to us in Shinkyo, was peddling *daifuku*, cakes made from sweetened red azuki beans wrapped with sticky mochi rice. Our children always wanted these delicacies, but I could never afford them. This was a special occasion, however, so I decided we would have *daifuku* for our supper.

    I told Mrs. Sugita that we had decided to leave for Shinkyo.

    "That is a good idea," she told me, smiling gently. "Please take good care of yourself. These *daifuku* are on me."

    Her graciousness was so touching. It was like a warming sun coming out from behind the dark clouds. I put six *daifuku* in my coat pocket. I bowed deeply and walked to the platform. The train was already there, yet there was no ticket officer. I went to the designated train car. We had become separated from Mrs. Murata's family.

    A man was standing in front of the entry of the assigned boxcar. He asked me my name. The fare was higher than I had been told, but there was nothing I could do about it now. Anybody could make extra money as they chose. I paid, and we got on board.

    I opened the door to the compartment, and my heart sank. It was totally packed. There did not even appear to be a place to stand. Most of the faces I saw belonged to women and children. No matter how we tried, we could not wedge ourselves in. Finally, I somehow managed to close the door behind us. As I pulled the door, we stood there, but we could not keep standing. I asked some people close to us to at least let the three children sit. At last, a small space was made. Isao and Kashiyo sat, leaning against the door. I held Takashi and somehow crouched in front of them.

    The air was stuffy. The windows were covered by black cloth so that the inside of the train could not be seen from outside. To make matters worse, the train did not move. For many hours, we were stuffed in that unmoving, dark box. There was no air circulation. Finally, when it grew dark, the train lurched into motion.

Good-bye, Andong. You treated us mercilessly for seventy days. We would never come back.

Departing from Andong gave me new courage. Hope sprang in my breast, but that hope disappeared as the train soon stopped. After a short stop, it started moving. This pattern was repeated frequently. The train would run, then cease moving, then start again as if it had remembered its purpose. I was frustrated and wondered when we would ever get to our destination.

One time when the train got going again, a man opened the door and came in to make an announcement.

"This train has hired several fully armed Russian soldiers to protect us from possible danger on the way. However, we cannot guarantee their behavior. Women should be extra cautious. Never let your babies cry. If they know there are babies, there must be mothers. We cannot know what they might do to you."

This situation was so ugly. It frightened me in ways that sheer survival did not–that at least was up to me, the elements, and my luck. But this had to do with the unpredictable behavior of other people who held absolute power.

"Takashi," I told my youngest, "do not cry. If you cry, your mother will be taken away."

It sounded like I was trying to reason with my eighteen-month-old son. And yet, my meaning seemed to get through. For all the many hours we spent in that tight space, this wise child never cried.

The train stopped and started all through the night. The inside of the train was deathly quiet. No one spoke. We heard only the regular clackety-clack of the train's wheels.

Suddenly, a baby started crying. Immediately, someone roared, "Don't let him cry!"

Isao and Kashiyo were exhausted. They leaned against the door, trying to sleep, but had to wake up every time the door opened. Men who seemed to be engaged in some tasks kept coming and going. When the door opened, the children would stand up, woozily, and then would slump back down again.

Eventually, I understood what these men were doing. They were protecting the women from the drunken Russian soldiers guarding the train–because the next thing the Russian guards would want was women. The Japanese men were guarding the Russian guards. Their comings and goings were the changing of the guard.

The long night finally came to an end. As faint light came through black cloth on the windows, people started grumbling. Their hips and legs were hurting. We had been more than just uncomfortable, but at least we had been in a passenger car this time. We were not soaked with rain or covered by coal cinders, as we had been when we evacuated from Shinkyo.

I admired the leadership of this company that had hired the train to send their employees and families home. What did my husband's company do for us? My husband's colleagues used company funds to buy themselves barbecued meats and to spend the winter in Andong comfortably, ignoring people who scarcely had enough food and fuel to survive.

The train stopped again. A man came forward and announced, "The Russian soldiers are sleeping now.

If you need to use the toilet, get off the train and do what you need to do."

Many people scrambled to get out. We had not had even a drop of water since the previous night, but I felt the need, as the train ride was long, and I did not know when the next opportunity might come. I decided to go first, before taking the children out. I got out to a vast open field. There was nothing as far as the eyes could see except for a few houses along one side. I had made several round trips between Shinkyo and Andong with my husband during peacetime, but now I had no idea where I was.

Coming out of the stuffy train, I breathed a sigh of relief. I looked around to find an appropriate place to relieve myself and chose a spot quite far from the platform. While doing what I came to do, I happened to look up. I saw a Russian soldier running toward me.

"Oh, madam," I could hear him shouting in a strange accent.

I stopped my "business" hastily and dashed back to the train. I was gasping with fear as I ran full speed.

The train did not start up again. We had stopped several times before, but those stops had not lasted very long. This time was different. We stayed in the same spot for over an hour.

"Our engine was stolen. Now we are looking for a replacement engine," a man finally explained the reason for the long stop.

Now we understood why the train could not run. We were stunned. How could such a thing have happened? Didn't anyone see the culprits? We could not change trains; all we could do was to be patient. What would happen if bandits found the train and attacked us? Would the Russian guards help us? Worst-case scenarios raced through my mind as

I trembled with fear. The only thing we could do was to hold our breath.

Long hours passed. Finally, news came that a new engine had been found.

"We are saved!" someone shouted. Our joyful voices rose in a chorus of exhilaration. We were united in our relief. We forgot our bickering.

We arrived at South Shinkyo Station in late afternoon. No one had attacked us; everyone was safe. South Shinkyo Station was only one stop away from Shinkyo Station. I wondered why the train was going no farther. But it did not matter. I did not even want to know. My heart was too busy leaping with joy. Our house was nearby. Nothing could bother me any longer. We would be there soon!

There was no streetcar, and it was a bit too far to walk all the way home with small children, so we took a horse-drawn cart with several other people heading in our direction. The cart moved across the open field. The wind kissed our cheeks. The air was crisper than in Andong. The setting sun was a huge red ball and magnificent. Clop, clop, clop–my heart was dancing with the rhythm of the galloping horse's gait. The weeds in the field were completely dried out. Not a soul was to be seen. Our horse cart continued clop, clop, clop in pleasant monotony. The cold wind did not bother me at all, for soon, we would be home.

When our house came into view, I wanted to run. What a slow horse!

CHAPTER 12

•

MOTHER CONFRONTS "MAMA"

Thinking back, I wonder why housing complexes like ours in Shinkyo were spared from the Russian invasion. Were we just lucky? The Japanese military and government had abandoned all their buildings in Manchuria. They burned as many documents and records as possible before deserting their properties. Many buildings built and used by the Japanese military and governments were taken over by the Chinese after Japan's surrender on August 15.

But China was not unified. The Chinese National Party (KMT) and The Eighth Route Army[8] resumed fighting against each other. Amid the chaos and confusion, Russians and Chinese looted Japanese properties freely.

I am not sure if my mother questioned whether the lands and properties the Japanese colonists had taken over by force still belonged to the nation of Japan, much less to the people who had lived in them. After all, the Japanese Empire had lost everything overnight. Upon learning of Japan's unconditional surrender, the Japanese people in Manchuria wondered if the country called Japan still existed. So why would my mother believe that the house that the Japanese government built for us still belonged to us? Perhaps she did not think deeply but simply yearned to get back to Shinkyo—to the place she called home.

>The horse cart took us to the street where we had lived. I could see our house right in front of us. There were no words to express my joy, and I felt my whole body glowing from the inside. I was in an ecstatic state. I forgot everything, I forgave everybody. I was just anxious to get into our house.
>
>We got off the horse cart and ran for a few minutes without stopping for breath. The children ran too. We arrived at the front door. The four of us looked at each other. "*Tada-i-ma-a-a-a!*" (We are b-a-a-a-c–k!) I screamed. After all our troubles, we were finally home.
>
>This was my house. I pulled the doorknob, and it opened without difficulty. Immediately, my heart sank. The *genkan* (entrance) was messy, as if burglars had just left. I knew what I would find might not be good, but I was still hopeful.
>
>On the train from Andong, my mind had at times started churning about what state our house could be in. When I had left the house for evacuation, there were kimonos in our chests with my husband's good suits. By selling those things, I thought we could survive for a year or two until we could get back to Japan. In the *genkan*, I slid open the paper sliding doors, and I was stunned. I did not expect things to be just the way we had left them, but what I saw was beyond anything I could have imagined.
>
>The house was wrecked, a total disaster. There was nowhere even to step. I opened the chest. Not a single kimono remained; all I found was half of a paper

pattern for some children's clothes and one of my silk stockings.

How should I put it? I could not even cry. For a while, I could not utter a word. I was shocked, and then the anger started to swell up.

This must be what my sister-in-law, "Mama," did, I thought. What should I say to her?

I opened three other chests, one by one. There was nothing of any value left. All that remained were the children's things—children's clothes must not have had much cash value, fortunately.

The futons in the closet were there, neatly folded as I had left them. At least we would sleep warmly that night. The image of the thin futon in Andong passed through my mind and vanished just as quickly—no matter what state our house was, I was grateful not to be any longer in Andong in a shabby rental house with only one thin futon for warmth for four of us.

I wondered how Mama had slept at our house if she did not use our futons. I opened the large bag of guest futons. As I suspected, one set was missing. It was just the kind of thing this woman would do. She had come into our house without permission and used the guest futons, which were fancier and more expensive than the ones we used ourselves daily. I was disgusted and loathed my sister-in-law even more than I had thought possible.

When I managed to calm down, I inspected the rest of the house to see if there was anything worth selling. There was nothing that Mama had not touched. All of the drawers of each chest, the woven baskets in the closets, the dressing table, the sewing box—even my small makeup table had been plundered. Did this woman have no shame?

Most of the kitchen utensils were safe, but there was no rice chest–the essential thing. There was not a single scrap of food.

While I was standing there, my jaw agape, Mrs. Ueda from next door appeared.

"Ah, *Oku-sama* (madam)! How wonderful to see you back!"

It had been a long time ago since I had been addressed as *Oku-sama*. I had completely forgotten that I once had a well-mannered life. I had been just an annoying woman with three small children, a burden, at the refugee camp in Andong. Mrs. Ueda's gracious greeting used to be the norm before the war ended. It was so pleasant to hear, and it made me appreciate being back in Shinkyo.

Mrs. Ueda filled me in on what had happened in our neighborhood since I had left. Her family had returned to Shinkyo from their evacuated location right after the war ended. Everybody eventually came back. We were, in fact, almost the last ones to return, except for two other families who never returned at all. The twelve families in this housing unit had all worked for different employers, so everyone had taken a different course of action. Yet it was only my husband's employer that had not helped their employees to make arrangements.

I showed Mrs. Ueda our house. She told me that my sister-in-law had come soon after we had been evacuated. One day, Mrs. Ueda saw her through the window taking my kimonos out of the chests and throwing them around. Then she saw Mama pile them all up in a heap and sell them to a Manchurian.

Mrs. Ueda said she could not restrain herself and burst into my house, saying to my sister-in-law, "You should not do such a terrible thing. Don't you know Mrs. Enokido will be upset when she returns?"

"She won't be back. There is no way she will ever return," my sister-in-law responded, and she simply continued selling everything she could.

A day or two later, Mama came back to my house, bringing three other women who were made up like geisha girls, and they all had a noisy drinking party. I was not surprised to hear about this behavior, but I still could not contain my anger and revulsion.

As days passed, I cleaned up the messy house and visited some friends. I went to see our potato garden, only to find that all the potatoes were gone. Someone had taken every single one—nothing remained. We had worked hard to grow those potatoes. I gazed at the empty garden for a while, seething inside, while trying to comfort myself with thoughts that maybe someone needed them more than us. I knew food was precious, and I was stupid to even think that potatoes in an "abandoned" vegetable garden would remain untouched. But I could not simply give up.

The garden was situated between our government housing and a private company's employee housing. I talked about those potatoes with everyone I met, trying to find the thief. They all said they knew nothing, and I never found out anything. I would not have been surprised to learn the thief was someone I talked to about the theft, and who had played at being innocent.

It was distressing to think we could not trust anyone anymore. With our national defeat, Japanese people had lost all their social and moral anchors. At the same time, with each difficulty I encountered, I could sense I was becoming stronger and stronger. My newfound strength would soon be put to the test.

Several days later, my sister-in-law appeared.

"Oh, you are back," she said to me, as if nothing had happened at all. At first, I was so irritated I could not utter a word. I thought my silence should have sent her a message, but no such luck. She entered the house uninvited and said, "Why don't you go buy me some cigarettes?"

I was angry, but she was the wife of my husband's older brother, so she was senior to me. I went out and bought a pack of cigarettes and handed it over without a word. My silent resistance did not convey any of my unhappiness to her.

"What is bothering you?" she asked as she lit a cigarette. She rested one elbow on the table and looked as if she was completely at ease. She relished the long drags she took on her cigarette. I was overwhelmed by her composure and my speechlessness continued. Finally, I pulled myself together and sat down in front of her.

In truth, her attitude infuriated me, and I could no longer restrain myself. I do not remember what I said, but I blurted out all my resentment and frustration. She remained silent, continuing to puff on one cigarette after another. Her defiance was both repugnant and awe-inspiring.

"You are wasting your time. It could not be helped. When I got here, the house had already been robbed."

"What about my kimonos? What about the parties with the geishas? What about those?"

"Humph. Yeah, something like that happened. But from now on, don't worry. I will work to support your family."

"No, thank you!" I snapped at her.

"Get over yourself! How can you make a living here with those small children? Stop pretending you are not helpless."

"I don't know if I can make it or not. But I can promise you this—whatever happens to us, I will never ask your help. So go away and don't bother us anymore, ever!"

I was extremely rude, but I could not help it. She sneered and said that I could try, but she was sure that I would end up asking for her help. I was determined that would never come to pass, even if I had to die. I did not care about where she was living or what she was doing, but I had to inquire about our guest futon.

"Did you take my futon?"

Mama did not answer me directly. She was not a person who minced words, but her evasive rambling made it clear that she was working at a cabaret. I could not care less what she was doing there with Soviet soldiers. If we were in Japan and not at war, I might be embarrassed to admit my relative was working at a cabaret. But we were in Manchuria, in a desperate time. I just wanted her to return my futon.

Mama had sold everything she could from our house to get cash. She had no sentimental attachment to anything I had owned. Everything went for cash, and she spent it all. And then she had moved on. She was not the type of person who paid close attention to anything.

Just before she left, she casually said, "Oh, I should mention that Mr. Ching (Ching-kun, as we used to call him) came twice to see how you were doing."

How nice to hear somebody cared about us! Particularly a Chinese person. I decided to visit Ching-kun, who had worked for my husband and was kind enough to visit me even after we lost the war.

The next day, I carried Takashi on my back. I told the two older children to lock the door from inside and not to open it to anyone. I had heard that many Chinese families wanted to adopt or even buy small Japanese children to raise as their own. Several Japanese children had been kidnapped by the Chinese.

I walked to the street. All the signs on the stores had been changed to the Chinese language, but I knew where the streetcars ran. I got on a streetcar with a Chinese conductor.

My memory was fuzzy. Where was Ching-kun's house? We had visited him only once, and we had not used a streetcar to get there. He had come to pick us up. As I was leaning against the window of the streetcar, trying to read the street signs, I lost myself in a recollection of that day.

It had been a beautiful day in late spring. A pleasant spring scent from fresh lilacs along the streets had surrounded us. My husband and I had sat in a horse-drawn carriage with a folding top, and Ching-kun took a separate carriage. We rode through the immaculate streets. All electric wires had been buried underground. Roadside trees had been planted in equal distance along the wide boulevards. The mustachioed Chinese coachman was gentle with the whip. The bells of the two carts had tinkled, and white petals of apricot flowers had fluttered down to our shoulders.

Ah, what a splendid spring day that was! I indulged myself in the sweet memory for a moment, daydreaming. Suddenly the noise of the streetcar woke me up from my brief fantasy. I shook my head and looked around. I was standing alone with Takashi on my back surrounded by unfriendly looking Chinese passengers, and I could not help feeling miserable.

The conductor called out the names of the streetcar stations, but in Chinese. Before the end of the war, we had lived in a Japanese community, and we communicated in Japanese. There had been no need to learn Chinese. Even Chinese vendors who came to take our orders every day spoke some Japanese. I had only picked up a fundamental, limited Chinese vocabulary. I could not understand what the conductor was saying, and I was at a complete loss. Whenever the streetcar stopped, I tried to read the faded original names in Japanese on the wooden poles. Having only a vague hunch, I got off the streetcar and wandered around. Was it here? No, not here, and not there. I looked and looked until I finally gave up.

"Let's go home," I told Takashi who had been quiet, and we returned home, heartbroken.

That night, my thoughts and memories were racing. I felt I had been betrayed by everybody and everything. I could not fall asleep.

Suddenly, it hit me. I was still hoping that someone would help us. I needed to let go of my sense of dependency. Hadn't I gone to look for Ching-kun, hoping he would provide me some assistance? I needed to take charge of looking after my family and myself. Wasn't I the one who had made a grand speech to my sister-in-law?

All right! I said to myself. Then that is what I will do. I made up my mind I would only rely on myself from now on, and that commitment centered me so that I almost felt calm.

CHAPTER 13

FURNITURE MAKES THE BEST FIREWOOD

If it were not for my mother's notebooks, I might never have believed just how terrible the final days of Manchuria were, or understood how hard she fought. My mother had no reason to exaggerate. She was simply pushing her pen as she recalled the past while sitting at a kitchen table in Yokohama thirty years later, recording fragmented memories as they came to her mind without consulting any source materials. These experiences must have been stored in her head and heart for a long time. If anything, she might have downplayed events that were too gruesome for words. I am not sure if it is a blessing, but translating my mother's vivid memories brought home to me the grisly realities of the time. It was like I was living it myself all over again, but this time with the ability to both applaud and pity this courageous woman—all the while realizing that our experience could have been even worse.

Throughout this period, Japanese settlers who had gone farther north to farm started arriving in Shinkyo as refugees. Their appearance was shocking. Many had no shoes, and their ragged clothes hung loosely on their emaciated, skeletal frames. From their stories, I learned that these were the lucky ones. Their journey to Shinkyo had been a long, ghastly escape from their homes close to the Soviet border. To escape to the south, they had to walk through rugged mountains, rapid rivers, and thick jungles, all while avoiding the unrelenting gunfire of Soviet soldiers and gruesome attacks by Chinese mobs. Mothers killed their own children and then themselves, or sold their offspring for money, while still others were given up for adoption to Chinese families so they might have a better chance of survival. Old people were left to die, or if they attempted to make the trip and stumbled along the way, they were left behind where they fell, half dead. Everyone braved extreme hunger and exhaustion.

We were only seeing the survivors in Shinkyo.

The food they had in Shinkyo consisted solely of *kaoliang* and salt supplied by the Japanese Association, an organization that accommodated refugees in an abandoned school. We were asked to donate food and clothes, so I gave some of the children's clothes, feeling sorry that I did not have more to give. Others gave blankets, sorghum, and millet, but even these were not enough to save lives when the winter's cold reached its peak. Small children died on nearly a daily basis. Even adults who survived the winter could not walk because of extreme malnutrition. I felt their pain keenly, as I imagined how that might have been our fate if we had stayed in Andong. We were destitute, but at least we had a roof over our heads and a little money. These people who survived the harrowing journey from the north had nothing except the clothes they were wearing–some did not even have that much but wore hemp sacks, as their scant clothes were stolen along the way.

One day, a woman refugee carrying a small baby on her back came to our house to peddle. The baby was all skin and bones with no weight left to lose. Its eyes were so big. The woman was weeping as she told me she had lost all her other children.

"Only this one has barely survived because I was nursing. But my breast milk has stopped for some time. The only thing I could give to this baby was the corn chewed in my mouth."

The baby looked like a skeleton. I bought things from her that I did not need and gave her food. I told her to come back again. As she went away, she bowed deeply many times.

Several days later she came back. There was no baby. I invited her in. She ate, saying she did not remember the last time she had eaten rice. Tears were streaming down her cheeks. Again, I sympathized with her plight. True, she was like a beggar, but if my path had been just a little different, I might have been there in her place. She was from Hokkaido and was two or three years older than me. I gave her a little money before she left. She thanked me and asked for my address so she could send me salmon when she returned to Hokkaido. I jotted it down and gave it to her, but I never heard from her again. Perhaps she did not survive.

Nearly half the Japanese refugees who lived in that refugee camp in Shinkyo died from the cold, starvation, typhus, or dysentery. Settlers that remained in the northern territories as the war wound down might have thought that the

Kwantung Army would still protect them, but the privileged officers had long since fled to safety, abandoning their countrymen and women. These northern settlers were given only one tangible kind of aid—potassium cyanide to kill themselves. It is truly impossible to fathom. By this time, it was mostly women and children who remained in those villages, along with a handful of old men. Most of the younger men, like my father, had been drafted in the last months of the war. In her memoir, my mother often reflects on this cruel twist of fate and how, when she needed her husband the most in her entire life, he was nowhere to be found, through no fault of his own. At the same time, if he had been there, would she have grown into her own the way she had?

> The weather was getting colder every day. I could not afford coal, so I had nothing to burn in the *pechka*. I got a small wood-burning heater and had to pay five Japanese workmen from the neighborhood to install it for me. The stove kept us warm, and I managed to cook our meals on it. We had some firewood because we had torn up the air raid shelter behind our house.
>
> When that wood ran out, we used nearly all the charcoal balls that I had stored under the kitchen floor; nobody had stolen them. Spring was still far away. Our fuel supplies had dwindled to practically nothing. I had to do something. We still had furniture—and all of it was made of wood. We could never take this furniture back to Japan with us, but still, I could not bring myself to destroy it with my own hands. I had a great sense of attachment to it because most of it had been part of my trousseau. But finally, I overcame my hesitation and decided Takashi's bed would be the first to go. It was made-to-order and very solid.

When it came time to chop up the bed for firewood, I remembered the day my husband left, and how I had clung to that bed as I cried. Then I swung the ax as if to chase away the sentimental memory.

Furniture made the best firewood ever.

I also bought a little bit of coal for the first time. High-quality coal would glisten, while low-quality coal was dull and somewhat grayer. I bought low-quality coal, but there were some small shiny bits mixed in, like black diamonds.

There was a saying that went, "In Manchuria, you never die from lack of rice, but you can die from lack of coal in one night."

That cold grew more severe as the days went by. Snow fell, and never seemed to stop. One day, I was summoned to shovel the street. One person from each family was supposed to participate. I, who had no husband, represented our family. Mrs. Ueda, Mrs. Higuchi, and I were the only women who participated.

It was hard to scoop up the snow with the heavy shovel. We worked diligently, but we had to rest frequently. We women were not as fast as the men. We stopped, huffed, and panted. Suddenly, the booming voice of our neighborhood chief nearly knocked us over.

"Wake up! What are you doing? You are not getting anything done!"

His words made my blood boil.

"Damn it! What are you talking about? We have to be here because our husbands are gone. They did not choose to go to war."

Once I started, I found it impossible to stop. It was as if a dam had broken.

"Do you think they are not here because they wanted to be away from their families? If you think we're so bad at shoveling snow, why don't you let your own wife come out and show us how she does it? I'm sure she is staying nice and warm under the *kotatsu* (foot warmer). What right do you have to criticize us?"

I was shouting in men's words—I did not know I had such a vocabulary. But I could not stop; I was not thinking. After I let my anger and frustration explode, I wonder what kind of repercussions might befall me, having broken a cultural norm. But the situation was too dire, it seemed—no one could afford cultural norms anymore. The chief shut his mouth. I, having finally challenged injustice, felt relieved.

When we finished shoveling and were on the way home, Mrs. Higuchi leaned in and whispered conspiratorially in my ear, "Enokido-san. Thank you. I wanted to say that too."

Reflecting on the day's events later that night, I amazed even myself. How did I manage to utter such bold words? After this incident, people's attitudes toward me changed. I was encouraged by this, and my determination not to be pushed around became stronger.

At this point in our time in Shinkyo, my mother had nothing more to sell. Banks had been closed a long time ago. Who knows what happened to people's savings at the banks? Nobody expected anything from collapsed institutions. Many women joined the workforce as peddlers to make very small amounts of money. My mother also started peddling.

FURNITURE MAKES THE BEST FIREWOOD

Several days after I returned to Shinkyo, I started peddling miso, hand-rolled cigarettes, and *pon senbei* (popcorn-like rice crackers) that were made by the neighbors who had little, if any, culinary training. The income from peddling was small; it was something, but it did not really bring in enough money to support the four of us. I searched all over the house, trying to find something I could sell. Manchurians seemed to think anything owned by Japanese people was a prize and were happy to buy anything I offered, but I did not have much left I could part with. I had to think of some other way to make money. We had no idea when or how—or even if—we would ever get back to Japan.

One day during a severe blizzard, I was asked to deliver a large amount of *kaoliang*. I had added a delivery service to my peddling business; I would do anything for a little money. I had to carry the big order, on foot, to a house in Shinka-Gai, near South Shinkyo Station. I bundled myself up completely, wearing my husband's old trousers over my own loose pants. I put on my thickest socks then wore *tabi* (Japanese split-toed socks) over them. My husband's old big shoes fit my feet after I covered them with layers of socks and *tabi*.

I carried a rucksack with twenty-two pounds on my shoulders, and an eleven-pound bag in each hand. I staggered a bit getting started. Could I carry all of this? Never mind. I just had to do it! If there was any chance to make a little money, I was not in a position to refuse.

I crossed the street and came to an open field. It was over a half mile from there to my destination. The world was blanketed in white. There was not a house in sight; not a single soul was outdoors. I walked carefully, one step at a time, so as not to lose my balance.

Snow battered me mercilessly. Hold on, I told myself, hold on. You can do this; you can do this. To encourage myself, I pictured my children's faces. I planted my feet carefully and firmly, one in front of the other. I could not see even a few steps ahead. I lowered my face and pressed on.

What might this scene look like to a painter or a photographer? In a vast, empty universe–a huge, white, open field–there was one black spot, me. Would the title be "Peddler Woman"? "Through the Blizzard"? "One Black Spot"? I could visualize the completed artwork. When my reverie was over, I smiled wryly. In the real world, the rucksack was heavy and both my hands hurt from the weight, but I had made quite some distance.

My destination was in sight. I was close! And then I finally arrived. Ahhh! I was so happy.

I knocked on the door and stepped inside the house. I wondered why this household would need so much *kaoliang*, but I was in no position to ask. All I needed was to get paid a little money for the delivery. The residents of the house offered me hot tea, and it was delicious. Their children were eating boiled potatoes the size of ping-pong balls. Beside them, the wife was handling a huge number of frozen potatoes. I wondered what she was going to do with those potatoes. But again, it was none of my business. The wife offered me one boiled potato. I was a poor woman, but I still maintained certain standards of taste. I was exhausted to have carried their food stuffs and the hot tea was good, but I could not say the potato was any good, even just to be diplomatic.

With all of this *kaoliang* and the huge number of potatoes, I thought they must be wealthy, or at least much better off than me to be able to stock up so much food. But I thought they had to be thrifty as well because they paid me very little money for my delivery service. We knew we all had to be thrifty unless you were Chinese or Korean profiteers.

The husband was a colleague of my husband from work. We exchanged small talk, reminiscing about the good old days and complaining about the current uncertainties. Then I left for home.

The blizzard was still strong. It took longer than I expected. Dusk fell, and it grew dark. Again, I imagined my children's faces. The fire in the stove must have gone out by now. They must be cold.

Hurry, hurry, I admonished myself. Yet, try as I might, I could not run in the deep snow. My footsteps from my outbound trek were completely covered with new snow. I did not feel cold at all because I was so anxious to get home.

When I finally arrived home, I saw the children sitting huddled together inside the cold tatami room. They stretched their legs, each covered by a corner of futon. They must have thought they could keep each other's feet warm this way.

Isao looked at me and said cheerfully, "*Hi-no nai kotatsu* (foot warmer without heater). This is supposed to warm our feet and bodies, but it was not working well because we did not have heat inside."

Isao smiled innocently, and rather proudly. He must have been pleased with his clever "invention." I felt a lump in my throat and could barely hold back my tears. I saw Isao was chewing sunflower seeds. He told me he had opened the package for Takashi to keep him happy while they waited for me to return.

The further I got in translating my mother's story, the more I realized what a hero my older brother Isao had been. I wouldn't have been able to see it clearly at the time, of course, being just a toddler. I knew other, later stories of my brother's inner resilience well, but the seeds of his stoic commitment were planted even earlier, as I now saw. My mother's account continued, illustrating the hardships of winter.

> That winter was severe. Every day, it was between -5°F and -13°F. Sometimes it got as cold as -22°F. It was cold beyond cold; it was painful. I had read a newspaper article describing the cold as "murderous." I felt that was apt. Nobody could stand still outside even for a moment. One had to keep moving. Without a *pechka*, even inside the house was like being inside a freezer. The walls were almost a foot thick, and all the windows were doubled, but this was not much help. The water pipes froze and never thawed, so we could not use the water from the faucet in the kitchen or the flush toilet. The only water we could use was in the bathroom, but we had to keep the water running through day and night so the pipes would not freeze. This meant the bathroom floor was covered with a sheet of ice because we seldom heated the bath.
>
> I continued to peddle foodstuffs every day. Isao looked after his younger siblings while I was away from home. He was only seven years old, but he was my right-hand man. Without him, I could not go out, and I would never have accomplished half as much as I did.
>
> One day, I came down with a very high fever. It was evening. I was in pain, but I made an effort to prepare a meal for the children. Then I went to bed. As I was dozing

off, I heard the noise of cracking ice. Isao was chopping ice in the bathroom, and he brought me a water pillow stuffed with ice chips to lower my temperature.

I was filled with gratitude toward my young son. With his little hands in that freezing place, he had managed to make an ice pillow for me. I was touched beyond words by his sweetness and thoughtfulness.

It was by now pitch dark outside. Takashi said he was sleepy. Isao removed Takashi's *hanten* (Japanese-style padded jacket) and slipped his young brother into my futon. I fell asleep again, exhausted from pent-up fatigue. I must have slept for a few hours. When I woke up, it was very late at night. I looked around me. Isao was sitting and looking at me. Kashiyo was asleep on the futon.

"Isao, your mother is okay," I said. "You must be cold. You should go to bed now."

He took off his own *hanten* and slid next to Kashiyo without a word.

When I woke up the next morning, my fever had subsided. I felt so good. Was the previous night's incident just my imagination? I got up quietly and looked at the children; they were all sleeping soundly. I started to make a fire in the stove as quietly as possible. I pushed in papers, then small twigs for kindling, and struck a match.

"Feeling better?" Isao asked as he opened his eyes.

"Yes, I feel much better. Why don't you stay in bed? You did not get to sleep until very late."

"No, I am not sleepy anymore."

He got up, and he was ready to help me. The kitchen sink was clean. He must have washed the dishes. Was this a job for a seven-year-old child? In times of peace, a little boy like him would never face such hardship. If only my husband were here.

"I am sorry . . . and thank you." I could not think of what to say. My heart was too full for words.

On another day around this time, I went out right after breakfast to do some chores. As always, I came home for a quick lunch. It was way past noon by this time.

"Mother, I am warming our rice now," Isao said.

I saw the pot was on the stove. Isao had added water to the leftover rice from breakfast and smoothed it all down flat in the pot. I was amazed to see how much Isao had learned by watching me and imitating what I did.

"You don't have to do this. I am afraid you might burn yourself. How did you manage to lift such a heavy pot?"

"Don't worry. I am careful."

Isao's daily life must not have been easy. He had to keep a close eye on his two siblings, especially Takashi who was always toddling around. He even worried about me and tried to be helpful. Another evening when I came home, Isao was wearing a heavy overcoat and chopping firewood at the front entrance with all his might.

"I chopped wood for tomorrow morning. Will this be enough?"

The logs were the same size as those I had chopped, and he had chopped quite a few of them. The ax was bigger than his arms. How did he do it?! I was amazed. He had to make many trips outside to get that much firewood. He was wearing gloves because it was -4°F outside. Even the front entry area was not much warmer than outside.

"Thank you, *onii-chan* (big brother). I can go to work because you are so good at looking after the house."

I told him of my appreciation without reservation.

He warmed my heart, and he made me forget all the terrible events that were taking place.

When my peddling business started picking up, my revenue finally exceeded my expenditures, if only by a little. Occasionally, I would even buy sweets on the way home as a treat for the children. That gave me great pleasure, too, but I knew I had to concentrate most of my efforts to saving money. I had to be prepared to spend another harsh winter here if we could not get back to Japan, and we needed money to survive. There was nothing left to sell in the house. Fortunately, it appeared that people appreciated my work. Through word of mouth, people started coming to our house to give me business opportunities and more things to sell.

After dinner, when the children had gone to bed, I enjoyed counting the day's income. Occasionally, Isao got up and watched me do this.

"Mother, did you make money today?"

"Yes, I made money."

"Oh, that is good. Then we can buy rice again."

This was the kind of conversation that a mother and her seven-year-old son exchanged.

By the time the air started sparkling, I had several thousand yen. In those days, even 1,000 yen was an enormous amount of money. The starting monthly salary for a government official was about 75 yen. I was relieved that I no longer had to worry about day-to-day needs. I was able to relax a little.

We had survived the winter safely. The children started playing outside, and they grew more cheerful again. I found it hard to believe that before the war ended, we had made trips to a hospital almost daily for one reason or another. I might have been overprotective because we could afford such frequent visits. Now, except when I had had a high fever, the four of us were all quite healthy.

    Once we had attained a certain level of comfort, I needed a safe place to hide the cash. I had to be exceedingly careful. Japanese people had become extremely skillful at hiding money, but looters had become equally skillful at searching. One family's rice chest was emptied, and another family's tatami mats torn up by thieves. I decided to hide the money in four different places. That way, if thieves did come, they would most likely find only some of our money. But that made it harder for me to remember exactly where I had hidden each stash, and how much was in each. Before I went to bed, I formed the daily habit of reviewing in my head how much money I had in each place.

    As my business skills improved, I no longer needed to go out to peddle every day. Sometimes, I worked only every other day. There were times, however, when I had to go out after supper. I would catch Isao's eye and give him a wink just before supper was over. He would nod wordlessly and take the two younger children outside. As I stepped out the door, Isao would crane his neck around the corner of the house, keeping his siblings behind him. After he made sure that I was gone, he took his brother and sister back inside. He invented this process because Takashi, who had turned two years old, had begun to hate to see me leave.

    It must have been very difficult for Isao to look after the house while soothing his younger siblings. I deeply regretted that the failed evacuation had resulted in so much difficulty for our children. In other families with fathers at home, children were able to play innocently, without responsibilities. I didn't know how I was perceived in the community–did people think I was single, or available now? A few different events showed me the precarious status of a mother living without other adults in a time of post-war desolation.

The first incident came when I was asked to take in a tenant, one of the refugees from northern Manchuria. The person who brought me the request said that this man had been separated from his wife and children, was in his mid-forties, and appeared to have quite a bit of money. In return for a place to stay, he would take care of the four of us. The person making the suggestion emphasized what a good arrangement it could be. I was interested, but I decided not to accept because for the first time in a long time, I thought of myself as a woman. What would I do if this man tried to make advances toward me? Would I be tempted to give in? My inner voice warned me of danger. At the same time, I realized the idea of dependence still appealed to me, if only for the time being.

The second incident occurred when one day, I did not feel like going out to work to peddle and decided to rest. I heard someone knocking on the door. Who could it be? I opened the door, surprised to see the Manchurian grocer standing there. This man used to come every day to take orders before the war ended, but now he had changed almost beyond recognition. He had much better clothes; he must have made a lot of money. He had become arrogant and kept talking as he pushed himself into the house. I was too dumbfounded to speak. He had never been inside our house before.

I was obliged to follow him into my own house. I sat down in front of the stove. The Manchurian sat behind me, keeping his distance. He kept talking about nothing in particular. I gave only vague answers, hoping he would leave quickly. He looked at the firewood and the charcoal balls, and said, "Don't you have regular charcoal? I will buy some for you."

"Of course we have," I lied.

I felt something touching me. I looked around. The Manchurian had come up very close behind me. He was grinning lewdly, his hand on my buttocks.

You fool! I screamed in my mind. I stood up abruptly and left that room. Totally ignoring him, I joined the children who were playing. With them around, there was nothing he could do, so he left, dejected, mumbling something to himself. I immediately slammed the door loudly and locked it.

I was mortified. I exploded with all the foul language in my heart. "Stupid fool! Who do you think I am? Do you think I would give in to a man like you! Even though we were defeated, I am still a proud Japanese woman."

I shuddered. I could not keep from thinking what might have happened if I had been alone, without my three children present. After this frightening incident, I decided I would never open the front door again. We would enter and leave the house through the windows of the next room, facing the garden. I put steps both on the inside and the outside of those windows for the children. The area around the front door became a storage space for firewood.

It wasn't only in my house, however, where I experienced the danger of being a woman.

At the time, the town was filled with fear. There were many Soviet soldiers on the street, always armed with small machine guns outfitted with bayonets slung over their backs. Whenever I encountered them, cold sweat ran down my back. Plundering was nothing new, and you were considered lucky if that was all they did. Nobody would help you even if you were about to die. At night, we often heard the sound of gunfire. "Ah, someone is being killed." We became so accustomed to such incidents; we became numb. Of course, we never went outside at night. In the midst of such chaos, it took all my effort every day, just for us to stay alive.

CHAPTER 14

THE MENACE OF RUSSIAN SOLDIERS

Worrying about how to secure daily food for one's children was dreadful enough in the chaos of Shinkyo. Mothers did anything to keep their children alive and healthy. And if they had to worry about their own safety from possible rape or being killed? It was more than ghastly. My mother describes some of that danger.

> The Soviet soldiers' behavior grew more outrageous. We heard that someone's house had been attacked, things were stolen, and the wife had been abducted. We were enraged by hearing stories about soldiers forcing themselves into people's houses and taking whatever they wanted. If the husband was at home, they ordered him to get into the closet, and they did as they pleased with his wife. They wanted to take watches and fountain pens. When they entered Shinkyo, many Russians were barefoot; most were poor ignorant criminals, we heard. Now they were wearing shoes taken from Japanese soldiers.

I did not know if all of these stories were true, but in our rage, we could not help but dehumanize those Soviet soldiers.

Women cut their hair very short and wore dirty clothes to make themselves inconspicuous and unattractive, like beggars. I sternly told the two older children, "If you see Soviet soldiers, cry out as loud as you can. I will pinch Takashi to make him cry. Otherwise, your mother will be taken away." The two older children listened intently. I did this because I had heard some woman was saved from Soviet soldiers because her children cried. After all, perhaps there were some soldiers with human emotions. I remember one incident when Isao came home, beaming. He stretched out his arm with a cup filled with sunflower seeds.

"When I said 'hello' in Russian to a soldier, he smiled at me and gave these," he proudly reported.

To take advantage of the possibility that I might be saved by a soldier's softer side, I often carried Takashi with me when I left the house. His innocent presence helped me get through situations that were potentially dangerous. For instance, a camera that had been stolen from our house was found under the floor of an abandoned house and returned to me. It was prohibited at that time to possess a camera, which made it particularly valuable. I wanted to sell the camera to Mr. Yamashita, my husband's classmate. To prepare to visit him, I wrapped the camera in a *furoshiki* (cloth wrapping) and tied it at my waist. Then I put Takashi on my back with a padded nursery coat to cover him and the camera. I walked carefully, as if I were treading on thin ice. Along the way, I encountered many Soviet soldiers and Manchurians. I forced myself to stay calm, but inside I was trembling with fear. Takashi was a perfect prop on such occasions.

When I read this portion of my mother's account, I was frightened for her. She was bold to walk with a camera on her body. It was also astounding to learn that the stolen camera had been returned to her. My father had been an avid amateur photographer. I saw several photographs of my father, snapped in some exotic places, so it was not surprising that he had a camera in Shinkyo. I hope my mother got a lot of money by selling that camera!

> Other women had different ways of handling the situation, of course, some of which I would never have permitted myself. A prime example of that was my sister-in-law, Mama, who came back to see me twice more while we were still in Shinkyo.
> On her second visit, her eldest son, Terumi, was staying with us. When Terumi-kun was fourteen years old, he had been recruited as a student laborer under the "All Student Mobilization Act" just before Japan's surrender. Young people, even girls in middle school, had been sent to farms for settlers in the north to help the families because all of the men between the ages of seventeen and forty-five had been drafted. The young people's mission was to take over manual labor in place of household heads who were absent from farms.
> After the war ended, those young students were released from their duties, but they had to find their way back home on their own. Terumi-kun walked for over two months with no money or guidance. When he arrived at my house in Shinkyo, he looked no better than a beggar. He had a terrible skin disease. We were poor, but I sent him to a doctor, got him treated, gave him food and clothing, and a place to live for a while. Those were hard days to add even one extra dependent child.

My sister-in-law did not give me one cent for her son's medical bills. She seemed not to care. After Terumi-kun recovered, he moved out and started working at a tofu shop, and his mother came around to our house, nonchalantly as always.

"You are doing well. Not bad . . ." she said.

"I am a better-made human. Not like you, Mama."

She made a face and lit another cigarette. I thought she had an iron will. She did not care what other people thought.

"How can you stay in such a miserable business?" she asked me.

She was referring to my peddling. I did not know exactly what she did, but I had a pretty good idea. "I could not possibly do business like you, Mama. It is impossible for me."

"It cannot be helped."

I disagreed and I told her so. "I could absolutely never do anything I would hesitate to tell my children about when they are grown."

Mama's son, Terumi, is my cousin, but I didn't see him after his stay with us in Manchuria until 2019 at his home in Japan. The bad blood between my mother and his mother had kept us apart. I visited Terumi in a suburb of Chiba approximately fifty miles northwest of Yokohama, as I learned that he had published a book in Japanese about his experience in Manchuria. He was extremely friendly and resourceful. He provided me with a lot of writing materials and guidance.

He also told me his story. When he had been sent to the northern border of Russia as part of the "student work force," the Japanese military predicted the Russian attacks. Despite this, they sent the children anyway. Terumi was furious, but as a fourteen-year-old, he did not have any choice but to follow instructions. One hundred and twenty-six middle school children had to take over jobs done by the farmers who had been drafted. Young children were trained to plant rice, go to distant pastures to cut grass for cows, and take care of farmers' horses. They even had training to fight the Russian soldiers should they be attacked.

On August 9, 1945, their instructor told them, "The Russians are coming. You, guys, leave! Go to the south. Hurry!" So, these young children started out on the long, treacherous trip back to Shinkyo by themselves. Some did not make it; Terumi did.

In his book, published in 2018, he described his mother as a beautiful, courageous, hardworking, dedicated mother. According to his account, his mother loved literature from a young age. During the time when girls were told that they did not need to read newspapers but should concentrate instead on helping with household chores, she wanted to have a career. She enrolled as a full-time student to become a beautician. She met my uncle, Kunimitsu (or "Papa") during this time, and they fell passionately in love. The parents of both families rejected the idea of their marriage. They eloped and Terumi was born. The Enokido family did not permit Terumi's birth to be registered in the *koseki tohon* (a family's census register that includes all family members' histories).

In Japan, we are required to present our *koseki tohon* to establish our legitimacy on many occasions, such as when we apply for school, a job, a change of address, marriage, divorce, and for birth and death. Terumi needed his *koseki tohon* when he applied for a driver's license, and he found a questionable date.

According to Terumi's book, he discovered that his *koseki tohon* showed that he had been born seventy-two hours after his parents (Papa and Mama) married on March 22, 1931. Then his sister was born on December 30, 1931, fewer than ten months later.

"You must have been an extremely busy woman, having two children in one year," he said to his mother. She lit a cigarette, leaned against the *hibachi*, and gave a small sigh. It was September 1949 in Tokyo. The room was gloomy, with one naked electric bulb hanging from the ceiling. It could hardly be called a house. It was a shack under a railroad track.

"I was not ideal bride material," she said. "I indulged in reading a complete series of Japanese literature instead of engaging in household matters to train to be a good wife. I wanted to have my own career, and I was attending beautician's school as a full-time student in Tokyo. During that time, I met your father and fell in love. But our parents furiously opposed our marriage. I moved in with your father, and I became pregnant. You were actually born on May 18, 1930," she explained while inhaling tobacco.

According to Terumi, Mama loved the game of GO, an abstract strategy board game for two players. She used to tell Terumi, "GO is a wonderful game. It fosters the abilities to see a broad view, intelligence, and good foresight. It is different from Shogi," which is a distinct kind of strategy board game—the game of generals. "GO is a game with dignity."

My mother's antagonist was not the same person that her son remembered. The only memory they had in common was that she smoked.

CHAPTER 15

"WE ARE EQUAL HUMAN BEINGS"

When I think back on the things my mother endured, I am not only struck by the severity of her situation but also by how unpredictable it was. It was literally one disconcerting event after another. The return to Shinkyo had been accomplished, but what would happen next?

She joined her neighbors and friends in speculating about when the authorities—whoever that might be—would allow them to repatriate. Everybody thought it should happen soon, because that was what they wanted to happen. In the meantime, her account describes in a sometimes almost offhand manner moments of intense fear and anxiety for members of her community. It was as if the scale of traumatic events had been reset, and only the most personally dire experiences warranted her full apprehension. For many of her extreme hardships, she would simply make an accommodation.

I'm sure my mother had never imagined that she would be in such precarious circumstances. Could she ever have thought, for example, that she would be in the middle of a Chinese Civil War not far from her own home? Perhaps she did not know that China had been in chaos before Manchukuo had been established. Or maybe she assumed that Japan had saved China by invading Manchuria, as had been promulgated by Japanese leaders. She did not learn Chinese history in school. I was never taught it either, except superficially about the series of various dynasties.

Chinese history, particularly its modern history, is complicated. The rise and fall of various imperial rules lasted for two thousand years. In 1911, the Qing Dynasty was overthrown by Sun Yat-sen who had returned from exile. The last emperor of the Qing Dynasty, Puyi, abdicated at the age of six, and Sun Yat-sen became a leader for China's Nationalist Party, Kuomintang (KMT). He eventually set up a government in Ganzhou (Canton). In the meantime, a former warlord, Yuan Shikai, assumed the presidency and formed the Republic of China in Peking—thus there were two governments.

In 1921, the Chinese Communist Party (CCP) was founded by the help of the Russian Communist Party (Bolsheviks). The Soviet leadership initially supported both the KMT and CCP in response to the request from Sun Yat-sen to counter the Japanese. Sun Yat-sen died in 1925, and Chiang Kai-shek took over the KMT leadership.

In 1931, the Japanese invaded and occupied Manchuria, and Chiang Kai-shek decided to pursue a strategy of appeasing Japan. He is reported to have said, "Communism was a cancer, while the Japanese represented a superficial wound." His priority was to eliminate the CCP first, then build strength to fight against the Japanese.

The KMT in 1927, at Chiang's direction, purged members of the CCP in Shanghai, the headquarters of the party. This campaign was unpopular and created a widening gap between the CCP and KMT. When the second Sino-Japanese war—which led to World War II—started in 1937, the CCP was supposed to fight in alliance with the KMT. However, the CCP acted independently and seldom engaged the Japanese in conventional battle. Mao Zedong of the CCP sold intelligence about the KMT to the Japanese in return for huge rewards, according to Homare Endo's book, *Mao Zedong: The Man Who Conspired with the Japanese Army*.

Dr. Homare Endo was born in Shinkyo in 1941 and lived through the Chinese Revolutionary War with her family. She is a director of the Global Research Institute on Chinese Issues in Tokyo. She wrote that Mao Zedong never once celebrated the day commemorating victory over Japan, because he was grateful to the Imperial Japanese Army who weakened the KMT forces and subsequently made the CCP victorious over the KMT.

She further states, "[Mao] was loath to mention the Nanjing Massacre" because when the Nanjing Incident happened in December 1937, Mao Zedong and his supporters were nowhere to be seen. They "had fled so deep into the mountains ... it was the KMT forces led by Chiang Kai-shek who fought on the frontline in Nanjing."[9]

Mao Zedong's strategy was to let the KMT fight against the Japanese and thereby preserve the CCP's power to destroy the KMT later. Mao's strategy worked. The Japanese Empire surrendered in 1945. Chiang Kai-shek and Mao Zedong tried to engage in peace talks, but that effort failed. By the end of World War II, the civil war between the KMT and the CCP had resumed with ferocity.

My mother likely had no idea of any of these intrigues. But one day, she heard gunfire. The Chinese Civil War came to our neighborhood in Shinkyo in 1946, and I was there.

> One day, we suddenly heard the sound of gunfire close by. We looked out the window and saw several soldiers running around our housing complex. They were shouting, but I couldn't understand them.

I was shaking. After an hour, the shooting stopped. I wanted to ask someone what was going on, but I could not leave the house, and we had no telephone. And we had neither newspapers nor radio, so we had no way of learning about the situation on the following day. A few days later, I learned it had been a fight between Chinese soldiers of the *Kokufu-gun* (KMT) and of *Hachiro-gun* (CCP). I could not understand why the Chinese would be fighting their own countrymen; but from that day on, similar scenes were repeated every day. It was strange to have those battles raging within the bounds of our housing complex.

The two armies advanced and retreated, advanced and retreated. One day, it appeared the Nationalists had the upper hand; the next day, the situation might be reversed. We learned to recognize their uniforms, although it was often far from clear who had gained control on any given day. Japanese men who had been conscripted into service would often carry injured Chinese soldiers to a hospital. At first, I was relieved that the two armies seemed to be simply interested only in each other and paid no attention to us or our homes. They never stormed in to take any of our things, for example, nor was our house damaged. Then, even though I was truly scared, my curiosity grew until I could no longer contain it. Through the windows, I observed the soldiers. There were days when I simply watched them shooting at each other all day long. Sometimes, the fighting continued into the night; I would peep through a narrow opening in the curtains and see the soldiers or their black shadows passing by, so close to our windows that I could almost reach out and touch them.

After each round of battle was over and the soldiers had left, the children went out to pick up used rifle shells. They cheered noisily whenever they made a discovery. Isao was happy to collect these new treasures and play with them as his toys. I could not understand why the soldiers used only rifles and not any other weapons, nor why they were fighting in a housing complex. There was a lot I didn't understand in those days. Perhaps no one did.

One day, when I looked out of the window, fifteen or sixteen Chinese soldiers were resting near the house. One, who looked like an officer, was seated in a chair. The others were sitting on the ground, each reclining in his own particular posture. Approximately ten Japanese adults and children were also there, so I went out to join them. The seated officer seemed to be in his early thirties, and he was smiling and speaking fluent Japanese.

This sight was so thoroughly unexpected, I got up and walked close to where I could stand right in front of him. I greeted him with a nod. He returned my greeting with a nod—which was also unexpected—as he continued his discourse. He said that Japanese soldiers were brave, and that he liked the Japanese. At the end, he said, "We will do nothing to harm you. We do not look down on you. You and I are equal human beings."

I had been fearful of communism, but I was deeply touched by these words. For the first time, I felt that I could understand the Manchurians' attitude during the occupation by the Communist Eight-Route Army. I had noticed that when the Communists were winning, the Manchurians would be nice to the Japanese. But when the Nationalists were in charge, the Manchurians became very rude. As a result, we Japanese were rooting for the Communists. I had noticed that the Nationalist soldiers seemed to be very slow and lazy, while the Communist soldiers acted briskly. The Nationalist soldiers took their time walking, while the Communist soldiers marched in perfect order, just like the Japanese army. Mrs. Mori told me that she hoped the Nationalists would win, because no matter how good the Communists appeared to be, if they triumphed, we would never make it back to Japan. I thought perhaps she and her husband had access to special sources of information. Yet listening to this young Chinese officer gave me a very favorable impression of the Communist army.

Mrs. Mori was right. It was the Nationalist Party, backed by the United States, that ensured the eventual repatriation of Japanese in Manchuria. My mother was so cut off from any and all reliable sources of information, she did not know that the Nationalists were supported by the United States, while the Communists were assisted by the Soviet Union. I try to imagine being in that situation, where one could only see what was in front of one's eyes. Perhaps it wouldn't even matter very much who won a war in a country from which one was determined to escape. My mother was just eager to return to Japan, regardless of who would arrange the repatriation.

The Chinese Civil War lasted another four years after Japan's defeat, until Mao Zedong's Communist Party chased the Nationalist government leader, Chang Kai-Shek, to Taiwan in 1949. In the meantime, my mother's logistical situation in Shinkyo ranged from dangerous and deprived, to almost bleakly comic. For example, most of the money circulating in town was "military payment certificates" (MPCs). Each side in the civil war issued its own certificates. When one side lost, its MPCs became worthless. Some days, my mother would use one side's certificates in the morning, and they would be worth nothing in the afternoon.

As the MPCs were increasingly unreliable, my mother tried to spend them but accept only national notes in return. The Manchurians were doing the same thing, which became a sore spot and caused small troubles. As a result, my mother's business ran less smoothly.

Then, at some point, the local warfare stopped, and calm returned.

> Even in such violent times, spring eventually arrived. Nature had not forgotten us. There was still snow on the ground, but the weather grew milder. Life returned to normal. No more gunshots. Security improved dramatically. The warm sun returned, and I opened our windows. We started using the next room and unblocked the front entrance. The thick ice in our bathroom melted, and we began to use the entire house freely.
>
> Spring had been late in coming to Shinkyo. By the time we began to feel the warmth of the sun, we were surrounded, all at once, by white blossoms of pears, pink flowers of apricots, and yellow and purple wildflowers. The open field where I had suffered in the heavy blizzard turned green. In the past, we would have gone shopping in a horse-drawn carriage, but that was no longer possible. Japanese people worked for Manchurians now. But at least it was a great relief that we no longer had to fight against severe cold.
>
> In addition to peddling, I started doing laundry occasionally for injured soldiers. I would wash the sweaty, dusty, and bloodstained clothes. Of course, we did not have a washing machine. I squatted on our blue tile floor in our bathroom and scrubbed

dirty clothes on a washboard. It was hard work. Still, I worked carefully and thoroughly. I even mended torn clothes. The soldiers I worked for were pleased and gave me small amounts of money, an added source of income.

One fine afternoon, I was sewing torn clothes, sitting at the window. The light was streaming in brilliantly. A Chinese soldier brought several articles of military clothing under his arm. He even had his own soap with him. He came back the next day to pick them up, but I was still working on them. I asked him to wait. While he did, I let him come into the house.

He was very shy, but he played with my children. He spoke Chinese. My children responded in Japanese mixed with some Chinese. They chattered and laughed. It seemed that no communication problem existed among them. When I finished, I folded the clothes neatly and presented them to him. It was then when I got a good look at him for the first time. He had firm features with smooth skin and thick, dark eyebrows. He looked like a young valiant soldier, probably about twenty years old. I thought he had an air of elegance.

"What happened to your husband?" he asked, while massaging his leg gently. He must have been injured.

"My husband was drafted," I responded.

"You must have suffered a great deal of hardship. Your children are very young." His voice was so tender.

These were the first comforting words spoken to me by a Chinese soldier. He handed me a large sum of money, 200 yen. He walked away, carrying his clothes under his left arm, dragging his right leg. I watched his back; the setting sun wrapped his white clothes in bright red.

CHAPTER 16

•

ESCAPE FROM SLAUGHTER

For so many years, I'd taken our survival for granted. Reading my mother's notebooks, I realized the miracle of our existence in this world. It is astounding to learn after so many years how often luck played a role in our family's survival.

> The days grew longer. As the weather became more pleasant, neighbors would come outdoors and chat.
> One day, I joined the group. The men were doing all the talking. One man said casually, as if he had just remembered, that a group of evacuees had all perished on their way to Tonghua, in the mountains on the border with Korea. I gasped! Tonghua was the destination of the train we had missed when we were first ordered to evacuate to the south. I shuddered at the fate that might have awaited us had we taken that train.
> I felt deep resentment toward the man who kept talking without any emotion as if this was nothing

serious. Three thousand Japanese people had been slaughtered by the Chinese Communist Army and the Korean People's Army. How he could discuss such a catastrophic incident so callously was beyond me.

In time, I learned how the atrocious slaughter that we had narrowly escaped had happened. The decision as to how and when to transport 140,000 Japanese in Shinkyo to the south had been made hurriedly, creating confusion. The original destination was Pyongyang, but the route had to be changed, and managing huge and desperate crowds only created more confusion. A woman with three children and without a husband had no priority. Nobody had a responsibility to keep my mother informed. Only well-connected people knew about the latest new arrangements of the trains.

That August afternoon, when we arrived at the train station on time as had been instructed, we found the train had left before that promised time. My mother felt we had been completely abandoned. She was distraught. No other trains were coming. We could only go back home from Shinkyo Station. And so, we returned, dragging our feet, wearing our heavy winter clothes on that hot summer day. On the way, we stopped on a wide green field and stretched our legs. My mother sighed at how miserable we were. We children were exhausted, but we did not complain, watching our all-powerful mother look so helpless.

While we were sitting on a field covered by thick weeds, Chinese mobs with sickles were rushing into what would have been our train, raiding Japanese evacuees. They barely escaped a total slaughter that afternoon, but the same train met another attack in the evening. By that time, we were safely home, dog-tired, and distraught. We had no idea how lucky we were. The train we missed met armed mobs at the entrance of a tunnel that evening. They forced the train to stop. When the train stopped, they immediately burst into the train and killed the security guards. They dragged women outside and gang raped them. Anyone who resisted was shot to death. They threw babies from the windows. More than a hundred Japanese women committed suicide by jumping from a nearby cliff. One thirteen-year-old girl was injured but survived. She walked three miles to the next train station and reported the incident. Six hundred Kwantung Army soldiers arrived at the scene early the next morning. They found Chinese attackers sleeping, holding Japanese women beside them. The attackers were all shot or arrested.

How close had we come to being involved in these kinds of atrocities? The truth is that our survival was not due to my mother's wisdom alone; even times marked by bad fortune proved to have elements of good fortune.

> In the midst of everything, we started to hear the word "repatriation." The word spread like wildfire among the Japanese. We did not know when it would happen, but we were happy to think that it might not be far off. It must be happening, right? Eventually, in the not-too-distant future?
>
> All my time was taken up with preparations for returning home. No room to think of anything else. No more time for washing bloody uniforms. Besides, by then, I had saved a fair amount of money. I could even buy clothes for myself and my children.
>
> About this time, I bought a pearl brooch. I did not give it much thought; I just wanted to have something nice. It was probably in the back of my mind that after I'd returned from Andong, I discovered that all my jewelry had been stolen while we were away. When we had hurriedly evacuated from Shinkyo to Andong, I had completely forgotten that I had stashed my

jewelry deep in my closet. Nobody wore rings during the war and, in our hurry to leave, I had not thought about them. If I had been able to take and sell some jewelry when we evacuated, our life in Andong might not have been so miserable.

This time, I would not repeat the mistakes I had made when evacuating to Andong.

The repatriation date was set for mid-July 1946. We were given strict rules as to what we could take.

- Cash, only 1,000 yen per person
- One watch per family
- Two kimonos, one for summer and one for winter
- Absolutely no valuable jewelry

If anyone broke these rules, as joint punishment, the entire neighborhood group would not be allowed to return to Japan. I felt strongly I had to obey these rules, in order not to cause trouble for others. But I later learned that many people violated these restrictions, and they were able to eat whatever they wanted, while we rule-abiders could only look on in envy and hunger.

I made three rucksacks. One was huge, much too big for me. The two others, for Isao and Kashiyo, were right for their size. As instructed, I took just two kimonos for myself. But I did something clever. I took apart other kimonos to make three large *furoshiki* (cloths for wrapping parcels). These *furoshiki* could later be converted back into kimonos but meanwhile would not be counted as kimonos. I was proud of my invention.

Two kimonos were not enough, but I had no wish to disobey orders. There were many things I wanted to take, but ultimately, I decided to take only high-quality items–an expensive Nishijin kimono for special occasions, Haori with thick embroideries, and *naga-juban* (underwear for kimono) in silk crepe, given to me by Mrs. Mori. I had handled numerous clothes in my peddling trade, but it was rare to see a kimono as splendid as Mrs. Mori's. She had two large trunks packed with kimonos with basting threads untouched, yet she had never worn them. Young, beautiful, and reserved, she never let herself stand out. During the peaceful time before the war, she used to wear clothes equivalent to my dinner wear as everyday clothes. After the war, though, she wore simple clothes just like we did.

When I finished packing, I started to clean the house. I decided to burn our letters and furniture. I stripped photographs from their albums. One by one, I threw them into the fire. Each one brought back a unique memory and I had to struggle against an impulse to save them, but we had no room in our rucksacks, and the repatriation of the first group had started.

The first to go were the refugees who had been farming settlers in the north. We stood on the street in front of our houses and waited for them to arrive. When they came, they were not marching boisterously as we customarily do. They walked unsteadily, in silence. Hardly any small children were seen; they were almost all adults. We applauded and shouted words of encouragement, "*Ganbare-Yo!* (Hold on!)" as if we were cheering on courageous soldiers or sports teams. Two or three people responded by feebly raising their hands, but most remained expressionless. I thought it strange, but it did not take much time to understand their apathetic attitude.

Most of these people must have lost their children. Thousands of small children had been killed by gunfire, starvation, or illness. Some had been adopted by Chinese families, and some had been kidnapped. How painful to leave children, dead or alive, behind in a foreign land while they headed home to Japan. Those sad days in Andong when I had decided to give up on hopelessly undernourished Takashi came back into my thoughts. Their sorrow stabbed my heart.

I grew ashamed of our thoughtless cheers and clapping, just because we were happy to see these people going back to Japan. We were not thinking what kind of treacherous journeys they had experienced to get to this point. I walked back home with a heavy heart. Our days passed slowly until we were notified of the date of our departure.

Bank passbooks, bonds, and all securities were to be deposited at the *Nikkyo Zengo Renraku-jo* (Japan-China After Care Communications Office). I had zealously guarded those assets, but now I exchanged them for a simple piece of paper. The deposit slip was dated July 15, 1946, and I still have it. After more than thirty years, it has turned brown and would look to anyone else like just an old piece of paper. Not someone's worldly savings, the sum total of everything he or she owned.

Our repatriation was a few days later. While we waited, I packed and repacked the rucksacks. I crammed them with sugar cubes and dried bread until not an inch of space was left. Kashiyo had just turned five, and it was pitiful to make her carry such a heavy pack, but it could not be helped.

We were repeatedly reminded not to take embargoed items. I wondered what to do with that one pearl brooch I had recently purchased; it was the only nice item I had. I decided to make a tear in Kashiyo's clothes and use the brooch as a safety pin. Then, I did not need to hide anything. It was a legitimate use of the brooch.

Another problem was my husband's business suit. I had carried the suit to Andong and back to Shinkyo. It was precious to me, and all this time I had refused to sell it because I kept hoping my husband would come back to wear it. Now, as a woman, and under the repatriation restrictions, I could not hold on to a man's suit. Besides, there was no room for it.

Leaving my husband's suit behind seemed to me as if I was deserting him. Even if I could obtain an exception to carry it, should I? Should I make room somewhere for an uncertain hope? Wouldn't it be wiser to keep as many necessities as I knew we were going to need? Then I talked to Mr. Sugita, my partner in the peddling business–his wife had been the one to give us *daifuku* (mochi with sweet red beans) at the train station in Andong when we were ready to leave. Mr. Sugita was fit, and he hardly had any baggage. He agreed to take my husband's suit. It did not occur to me then to question what Mr. Sugita did during and after the war. Now, however, I wonder why had he not been drafted like my husband?

After I finished packing, I swung the huge, heavy rucksack onto my back, but it hung below my waist, and I could not stand up. I tried placing it on the table and strapping it on that way. I practiced walking around the house with the pack on my back. I kept up this training until the day we left.

When that day came, I stashed 4,000 yen under my clothing around my waist, separate from the purse of cash for expenses during the trip, which was in my chest pocket and tied to the string of my *monpe* (loose cotton trousers). It was summer, and we all wore lightweight summer clothes, not the layers and layers of heavy clothing we had worn for the last evacuation. When we were ready, I placed the rucksacks at the front entrance. Then I started cleaning the house. Doing so was not due to my consideration for whomever might come to this house after us; it was just my ingrained mode. My mother used to say, "Flying birds leave no droppings."

Unexpectedly, I felt a great sense of attachment to this place. Memories flooded me of the time when I had first moved in with my husband. So many things had happened during the past six years. I sat on the tatami and took a last look around. Tears rolled down my cheeks. Were they tears of happiness or sorrow? Even I could not tell. I just let the tears pour down.

The time was drawing near. My children were already outside. The furnishings that remained in the house said "goodbye" to me without a word. I stood up and stroked each piece of furniture gently one by one and said, in my mind, "*Sayonara.*" I stroked the stove last. "Thank you for your good work," I told it. "Because of you, the four of us survived the cruel winter."

I could hear my children's cheerful voices through the window. I opened the futon closet and touched the last remaining two sets of futons, saying, "*Sayonara.*"

I stood at the door and looked around one final time. This time I raised my voice and said aloud for anyone to hear, "Good-bye forever. We will never meet again. Be good."

I wiped my tears and resolutely shut the door. No need to lock it anymore.

I collected my children and walked to the meeting place. There, all the people in our large group from

Kangxijie Street were already gathered. I was told that there were sixteen hundred people, faces I had never seen before.

Mr. and Mrs. Mori were there. They had a small rucksack that appeared to be only half full. Mrs. Mori's head hung low. I did not see their dog.

"What happened to Chibi (Little One)?"

Mrs. Mori choked up and said, "We had to leave Chibi behind."

Their dog was like their baby to them. They had no children.

CHAPTER 17

JOURNEY OF REPATRIATION

We did not know and we did not care, but our repatriation had not been initiated by the Japanese government. In fact, the Japanese government was not functioning after August 15, 1941. We were saved by Americans—not because they wanted to save us, but because they wanted to pursue their China policy. According to Paul Maruyama's book, *Escape from Manchuria*, Harry Truman made clear that "repatriation of Japanese was not a matter of humanitarian concerns but rather to get rid of any Japanese influence in China whatsoever."[10] America was trying to build a strong united democratic nation under Chiang Kai-shek during this period. They were afraid Japanese in Manchuria would be brainwashed by Russians to become communists.

Our repatriation point was the village of Huludao on the Liaodong Bay, 320 miles south of Shinkyo, where repatriation ships awaited. It had the only harbor deep enough to be able to anchor the large ships required to repatriate over one million stranded Japanese. It was also the only port free from Russian control.

Formerly proud Japanese colonists were now miserable refugees. Many were loaded almost to the breaking point with everything they owned strapped to their backs or in front, hanging from their necks.

I don't remember any of the events that took place until we got off the train from Shinkyo. What I remember very distinctly then was the scene of all of us trotting through a wide-open field. I was desperate to not to be left behind by our group with my three children (by then seven, five, and two years old). Under the glaring July sun, amid thick clouds of dust, I was the last person, trailing everyone. Isao was holding Kashiyo's hand, and I was grasping Takashi's hand. Holding tightly to one another, we ran and gasped for breath. Takashi, at two years, could not keep up, no matter how hard he tried. Sometimes he fell, and I dragged him behind me, on his knees until he could get back on his feet.

"Get up quick. Stand up quick!" I scolded him.

I could not bend to help him up because I was carrying the big, heavy rucksack. When he could go no farther, I did pick him up and carried him in my right arm. After a few minutes, I would tire and have to put him down again. We repeated this maneuver many times. Somehow, we kept going and Takashi never cried. He just kept running for his life. His knees were bloody and gravel was ground into his skin. It was awful, but there was nothing I could do to help him.

Occasionally our group rested under trees. Even the adults seemed exhausted. Some took short naps, leaning against their rucksacks. I cannot remember how far we walked, for how many hours, or even exactly where we were. We fought as hard as we possibly could, just to keep up with the group as a cloud of red clay dust surrounded us. Finally, we arrived at our destination, Koroto Island, called Huludao in Chinese.

I threw my rucksack from my back and sat flat on the ground. I could no longer think. I was out of breath, and for an instant my mind went totally blank. I quickly came to my senses, though, and stared to my right and left. I could not believe my eyes. I stood and took in the sight of the surging crowd. An enormous flood of people surrounded us in human waves; this was the gathering place for everyone who was repatriating. People were dressed in all manner of clothing, and everyone was noisily talking.

Just about ten feet away from me was Fujiwara-san's family. Fujiwara-san's wife was holding her baby firmly and gently wiping the baby girl's forehead. Fujiwara-san had gone to high school with my husband in Ibaraki. A husband and a wife with one baby. I had three small children without a husband. I was envious, but I was still happy to see their familiar faces. I shouted, "Fujiwara-saaan!" and approached them, elbowing my way through the crowd. We were surprised to see each other and shared the joy that we had safely made it this far.

As it turned out, we had plenty of time before boarding our ship. We had to limit our cash on hand to 4,000 yen or 1,000 for each of the four of us; no excess cash. There were many Manchurian vendors who knew of these cash limits for the evacuees. Some of us had to spend excess money to meet the restriction of 1,000 yen per person, and many simply needed something to eat. I bought delicious food for my children; if we couldn't take the money with us, at least we could eat. We ate with gusto.

It came time to depart.

The water's edge appeared to be five- or six-hundred yards away. I stepped forward, leaving my group, and came to the wharf. There, I saw a big gray ship across a dreary space with nothing to obstruct my view.

A ship!

My heart leapt with joy. I walked to the red clay square, my mind completely blank. I simply put one foot in front of the other, in a state of spiritual nothingness.

When I looked up, there was the huge Hinomaru, the Japanese flag painted on the side of the ship, a vivid red circle on a white background. I was beside myself; the joy, exultation, and emotions I felt in that moment can hardly be described. I could not stop my tears.

Finally, we boarded, walking over a swaying gangplank with our heavy load. I had to be very careful to steady myself with Takashi. I heard that some old people slipped and fell into the water, and nobody helped them. No humane response remained for us in a situation like that, only self-preservation.

We were directed to a hot, stuffy, crowded lower compartment of the old ship.

After the ship left the wharf and had sailed for a while, someone said, "We are still in Chinese territory. Please behave yourselves."

I have often noticed that when a group of Japanese people get together, there is always a self-appointed leader. But this entire ship was occupied only by Japanese. So, what was this person talking about?

I wondered. I lay down. We were leaving behind the place where we had lived for six years, but I no longer felt any sense of attachment, only great relief.

Later, the same voice said, "Now we have entered Japanese territory. We are in Japan! You can say whatever you want."

I still had no feeling. I must have left all my emotions behind on the wharf when I saw the Hinomaru. All I could experience was an enormous sense of relief. I remained lying down with my eyes closed, yielding to the ship's movement for a while. Even though my eyes were closed, I made sure that my children were sitting next to me. All three children had made it out alive.

I opened my eyes and looked around. People on this ship had come to Manchuria with big dreams and ambitions under the banner of the powerful Empire of Japan. Some of them might have attained their goals; and even if they did not accumulate an enormous fortune, they may have enjoyed a privileged life, even fleetingly. Now we were diminished, refugees. We all looked shabby, wearing *monpe* (loose cotton pants), worn-out workmen's blue overalls, rubber-soled footwear, broken sandal slippers, and shoes with holes. There were sick people, old people who could barely walk, and pregnant women. We were finally heading to Japan, but there were people who would not make it. Even after they made it on board the ship at long last, some people breathed their last before reaching Japan. When evacuees died, their bodies were wrapped with blankets and thrown into the sea. The ship blew a long, sad whistle, "Boo-hoo," and circled around the bodies. There were many such sea burial ceremonies during our passage.

After about a week, people went up to the deck.

"Now we can see Japan!"
"What a beautiful sight!"
"It is so green!"

I heard their jubilant shouts. They sounded like somewhat distant echoes.

CHAPTER 18

•

UNWELCOME

I don't recall anything about our arrival in Japan. I should have asked Isao, my older brother who was seven at the time, before he passed away in 2019. Did he remember? I did not even ask my mother how she felt when we arrived at Hakata in Kyushu.

The story she used to tell me was not pleasing. I was told we were showered with white DDT powder from head to toe when we landed at Hakata. DDT was a poison hazardous to children who might ingest it accidentally, causing temporary damage to the nervous system, and had a possible carcinogenic effect. The United States banned the use of DDT in 1972 due to its adverse environmental effect on wildlife as well as its potential human health risk, but during WWII, it was used to control malaria, typhus, body lice, and bubonic plague. We did not have the energy or knowledge to question anything the authorities did; we just blindly submitted ourselves. We might not have objected even if we had been led to a slaughterhouse like animals.

After the DDT treatment, we were given a Certificate of Repatriation. Anyone who had more than 1,000 yen per person had to give up their extra cash, but if a person had no money, the Repatriation Aid Office gave them 100 yen as train fare. Women who had "special needs"—an unfortunate euphemism for those who were victims of rape by Russian soldiers or revengeful Chinese—were taken to a clinic. The rest of us were taken to a camp that had been a horse stable.

We were more exhausted from our long, horrendous journey than pleased to have finally arrived at Japan. Happy to be at a horse stable?

Hakata was one of the eighteen ports of return for approximately 6.6 million Japanese military personnel and civilians who had lived outside the country. These Japanese came from Manchuria, the Soviet Union, China, North and South Korea, Taiwan, Sakhalin Island in Russia, Southeast Asia, the Philippines, Vietnam, and the Pacific Islands—but the largest number of civilians were from Manchuria. Our family had miraculously survived while approximately 250,000 Japanese died in Manchuria.

Every day, approximately four thousand new repatriates arrived in Hakata. Among them were women who blackened their faces with charcoal to repulse attackers, whose hair was cut short, who were wearing men's clothes, and whose stomachs were swelling. A young pregnant woman jumped from the ship to her death despite surviving the dreadful journey to Hakata. She had been raped by a Russian soldier. Perhaps she did not know there was a special place to provide support for women like her in Hakata.

A medical doctor, Seishiro Tanaka, had created such an institution. Dr. Tanaka was an assistant professor at the Keijo Imperial University in Korea. An evacuee himself, he returned to Japan through Hakata where he coincidentally met a former student of his. She told him her story between her tears. She was pregnant and wanted to secretly have an abortion. Later, Dr. Tanaka learned that both she and the baby had died. He was shocked by this incident and decided to create a facility to care for women like his former student. With support from an affiliated association of Japan's Minister of Foreign Affairs, he, together with his colleagues from former Keijo Imperial University's medical team, established Futsukaichi Health Center to conduct abortions. Two doctors and ten nurses worked in an operating room made out of a converted former bathroom. Abortion was illegal then, but the government closed its eyes to allow this facility to open for Japanese women who found themselves in this terrible circumstance.

The health center distributed notices to inform those women repatriating.

> To Women Who Came Back from
> *Gaichi* (outside of Japan).
>
> For those women who were suffering from unfortunate incidents you could not confess to your husbands, parents, siblings, we offer you help. No fee. Completely confidential.

Patients were taken to Futsukaichi Health Center by truck from Hakata Port, a forty-minute ride. Masako Muraishi, a nurse now in her eighties, remembered her work at the center.

> There was no anesthesia. Women lay down on an operating table. The operation started only with a blindfold. The women endured extreme pain. Everybody clenched their teeth, squeezing the nurse's hand so hard that the hand felt like it might be crushed. Nobody screamed. No tears were shed, and no words were uttered. After the operation, they rested in our upstairs tatami room. They closed their eyes, and just lay down. Nobody talked. They did not want to be seen, so they avoided being seen by others. There was no

conversation. The extracted fetuses were buried under cherry blossom trees.[11]

No official records remain, but it is estimated that between four and five hundred abortions were carried out at the center, which closed in 1947. The former site is now a nursing home attached to a hospital. A special mass for departed souls was held ten years later. It has been carried out every year in May since that time.

It was nearly impossible for a young woman to go home with a baby whose father was a rapist from a foreign country. Not only would it be gravely difficult to raise a child financially in now war-torn Japan, but it was unthinkable that a woman would be accepted by society with such a child. It was not the women's fault. But the women could not escape being looked down upon and feeling humiliated by the perception of having done something dishonorable and immoral.

An American anthropologist, Ruth Benedict, wrote in *The Chrysanthemum and the Sword: Patterns of Japanese Culture* in 1947 that Japan was—and still is—a country of shame culture. The US Office of War Information had requested that Benedict assist in understanding and predicting the behavior of Japanese citizens in World War II and after. Her book was influential in shaping American ideas about Japanese culture during the occupation and popularized the distinction between guilt cultures in Western countries and shame cultures of the East. *The Chrysanthemum and the Sword* was translated into Japanese in 1948. After over seventy years, her book is still considered essential reading for students of Japanese culture.

Benedict has been criticized because her research was limited to published articles and stories written by Japanese Americans who had lived in America; she herself had never gone to Japan. Nevertheless, I believe her observations were quite accurate. We Japanese people do not fear God or Buddha, but we are fearful of other people's eyes and mouths. We pay more attention to how we are perceived by others than to whether we are right or wrong. We always avoid being laughed at by others, of being shamed, or of giving a bad name to our families. As a result, we place emphasis on *giri*, or duty, and *ninjyo*, or benevolence. We value honor. At times, we are even willing to give up our lives for the righteousness we believe in, and this high-mindedness receives admiration. The brave actions by Kamikaze pilots during World War II may be explained this way; praise for these pilots also extended to their families. They brought great honor to their families, and grieving parents had to at least pretend they were proud and happy of their sons' gallant patriotism.

My mother was lucky enough to have avoided the circumstances that could have sent her to the Futsukaichi Health Center. Instead, she found herself in a horse stable with three children.

> At the stable, there were wooden partitions every six feet and a wooden floor covered in straw mats. Each family had one six-foot section. As I looked around, I found familiar faces in our camp. I had not noticed that an enormous number of people had somehow been divided into much smaller groups. Our stable building was occupied by my old neighbors from Shinkyo.
>
> We placed our rucksacks on a straw floor and breathed a sigh of relief. I found the situation bearable because it was only temporary. Soon, we would go back to our family's house, where we would sleep on a tatami floor. Then bad news was announced. We had to be quarantined because a child in another building had contracted a contagious disease. We did

not know how old the child was or what kind of disease the child had, maybe dysentery. Rather than sympathizing with the family, I lamented the added inconvenience. We were stuck where we were for two extra weeks.

We were hungry all day long. Two meals were delivered to us, in the morning and evening, but each consisted of just *zosui* (thin rice porridge)–one bowl per person. Between those so-called meals, we gathered grass, boiled it, and ate it with salt. We had not seen green vegetables since we left Shinkyo, so we thought of weeds as wonderful food. At first, we picked soft grasses, and then gradually we had to pick tougher ones. By the time we were ready to leave the camp, there was no green grass left anywhere nearby. Lunch was dried bread, which we had to buy. Once in a while, the distribution center offered us dried bread for free.

The days were long and boring. Occasionally, a group of entertainers came and sang the "Apple Song." It was a simple song, but it cheered us up. The song was uplifting and joyful. It expressed the lovability of a red apple, and suggested that if two people sang the song together, it would be merry; but if everyone sang, it would be even more delightful.

"The Apple Song" captured everyone's fancy at the time. It symbolized both brightness and newness in the demoralized darkness of postwar Japan. Michiko Namiki launched her young singing career with this song, which sold three hundred thousand copies in the first two years of its release. Namiki's wartime experience resembled the shattered lives of many of her admirers. Her mother had been killed in the devastating firebombing of Tokyo on March 10, 1945, and she herself had to be rescued from the Sumida River after the raid. Her father and elder brother had not returned from the war. By her own account, she never forgot the taste of an apple she ate at a movie location where she was working—at a time when apples cost five yen and a young performer's monthly salary was between 100 and 300 yen. John W. Dower, a professor of history at MIT, wrote this about Namiki in his 1999 book, *Embracing Defeat: Japan in the Wake of World War II*.

> Namiki's sudden success made her a symbol of escape from hard times. At concerts, she threw apples to her audience while singing and they, it was suggested, tried to catch them as if reaching for happiness ... Beyond intimations of deliciousness, however, the song lightened people's heart with its frivolity, while its unforgettable red apple, blue-sky imagery gave palpable color to a drab psychic landscape ... For tens of millions of Japanese, the past was dark, the present grim, but the future brighter.[12]

My mother did not need to know this profound analysis of a popular song and the Japanese people's psyche. All she needed to know was "The Apple Song."

> Over one month had passed since we left Shinkyo, and we were finally on Japanese soil, but life in quarantine was not easy. Singing "The Apple Song" provided a little escape from continuous misery but was far from the physical comfort I craved.
> As the time passed in this holding pattern, we realized it was almost *Obon*, the summer festival when we show respect to our ancestors. Our camp decided to perform *bon odori*, the Japanese folk dances, during

the evenings of this traditional festival. Someone had a violin, which was accompanied by percussion on empty cans and barrels.

I volunteered to sing because the musicians were rewarded with two packages of dried bread each. There was just one other singer, and we kept singing for two hours; that was not easy to do on an empty stomach, but the idea of extra bread was enticing. When the two hours were up, I hurried with two bags of the hard bread back to the stall where my children were waiting. The four of us had a late-night snack. Takashi and Kashiyo were happy enough with the food rations, but Isao and I were hungry every day. People whose families lived near the camp in Hakata were able to receive *onigiri* (big white rice balls). Watching them eat, we stared at them in envy.

I had not had a good night's sleep, not even once, since we had left Shinkyo over a month ago. I was worn out. Although I was young, I was exhausted, and the lack of food was not helpful. When we were told that we could finally leave the camp and take a train at Hakata station, I could barely lift my rucksack.

I was sure that the hardship I experienced would not leave me for the rest of my life. When the train pulled out of Hakata Station, however, a small uplifting feeling greeted me. I felt we had come back to Japan at last. During the crowded train ride from Hakata to Tokyo, I imagined what it would be like to meet my husband's family. My heart started jumping with expectation. There was no way to know what actually was waiting for us.

I can imagine my mother experiencing a moment of hope in the last leg of her journey. That feeling of hope did not provide her much respite, unfortunately. The country to which she returned was not what she and many of her fellow repatriates had been dreaming about.

According to Professor Dower, the ravages of war could not be accurately quantified. He explained:

> The first American contingents to arrive in Japan after the war—especially those that made the several-hour journey from Yokohama to Tokyo—were invariably impressed, if not shocked, by the mile after mile of urban devastation they encountered... the first foreign journalist to enter Tokyo, recorded that "everything had been flattened."... The first photographs and newsreel footage from the conquered land captured these endless vistas of urban rubble for American audiences thousands of miles away who had never really grasped what it meant to incinerate great cities... Close to 9 million people were homeless when the emperor told them they had fought and sacrificed in vain. In every major city, families were crowded into dugouts and flimsy shacks... or on sidewalks... The streets of every major city quickly became peopled with demoralized ex-soldiers, war widows, orphans, the homeless and unemployed—most of them preoccupied with simply staving off hunger.[13]

Not all repatriates were welcomed to the devastated land either. Most returning veterans, many of whom had been sent off to the war with parties and parades by their communities, were ill-prepared for the shock of returning home. They represented "losers," and their unkempt appearance seemed a mockery of the heroic ideals and imagery that had saturated wartime propaganda.

War widows, ennobled in public rhetoric, often endured neglect and discrimination. Japanese society, generally speaking, was not kind to women without men. We escaped from hell in Manchuria, but we did not come to a welcoming heaven in Japan. In fact, my mother never dreamed how excruciating it would be to visit my father's parents' home in Ibaraki, approximately sixty-two miles northeast of Tokyo, bordering the Pacific Ocean.

> According to my old train schedule, I could see it took twenty-seven hours to go from Hakata to Tokyo, and an additional ten hours from Tokyo to Ibaraki. But I had lost track of how long it had been since we left Hakata. How many times had we changed from one packed train to another? Even though the crowding was intense, we could still see from the window that Tokyo had been leveled to a scorched plain.
>
> We had to change trains at Ueno Station in Tokyo to get on a local train. Each time I had to disembark from a train, going up and down steps on the train platforms was a struggle with heavy rucksacks and three children. The train stations themselves were also a sight–filled with orphans, homeless people, and injured soldiers, all begging.
>
> When we finally arrived at Iwase Station in Ibaraki Prefecture, it was nighttime. No one was waiting for us in the pitch black. Two weeks before we left Hakata, I had sent a telegram to my husband's older sister who lived near the station about when we might arrive. Our message must not have reached her, or maybe we were late or early, I did not know.
>
> What I did know was that we arrived by freight car. It was difficult to get the baggage and the children off that kind of train during our brief stop. People helped me by throwing our baggage off the train to the platform–and we followed, hurriedly jumping from the train.

I did not know how we would get to Inuta, where the Enokido family lived, on such a dark road. I hated to bother my sister-in-law, but the only thing I could think of was to go to her house to borrow a lantern, so the children and I could find our way down the long unpaved country road.

Her house was dead quiet. I called out, and my sister-in-law came to the door. She looked startled. I asked if my husband, Masayoshi, who was her younger brother, had returned. She said no. Then I asked if I could borrow a lantern. She responded by inviting us to stay at her house, but I could sense that we were not really welcome. I didn't want to trouble her, and I didn't want her to be scolded by her mother-in-law.

In those days, the social rules in Japan were formal and rigid, especially in old-fashioned rural households. When a woman married, she belonged to her husband's family. The husband's mother had all the power in the household. Daughters-in-law had to obey their mother-in-law. My sister-in-law was not in a position to let us into her husband's home without her mother-in-law's permission.

However, she was insistent.

"It is very late, and the old woman (her mother-in-law) is already in bed. So, I cannot ask her permission. It cannot be helped."

My sister-in-law was a kind person. In my heart, I earnestly wanted to stay at her house. We were extremely tired.

"How did you manage to carry this much baggage?" she asked, trying to comfort me. She quickly prepared some food for us, a delicious pumpkin soup with rice. After we finished eating, Kashiyo said, "That was so good." She said it with a smile. I felt as if my heart was going to break. She had endured an extremely long and excruciating trip without any complaining, yet she still gave me an innocent smile with genuine appreciation. What a sweet child!

My sister-in-law gave the children a bath. She was amazed at how dirty they were, describing them as "deep black." We had not bathed for many months.

The next morning, her son volunteered to accompany us to Inuta where the Enokido family's main house was and where my husband had been born. He took Kashiyo, Takashi, and our baggage on a bicycle cart while Isao and I walked behind. I was so grateful! With no baggage, I felt light as a feather. I appreciated my sister-in-law's hospitality and kindness, and that she had raised her son to be so helpful.

We came to the grove of the village shrine. The area surrounding the shrine was densely wooded. In the center, there was an imposing stone monument with my father-in-law's name prominently carved along with a few other major donors to the shrine. From that spot, there was nothing to obstruct the view of the Enokido estate. The estate was nearly a mile from the shrine, but we could see the fine estate over the wide and flat rice field. As we advanced down the narrow road across the rice field, I remembered how my husband talked about the shrine. How he dashed to a train station, going through the woods, to go to school. One day, he found out he did not have a train pass at the station. He simply said, "I am Enokido." The ticket collector just nodded and let him go. I imagined my husband's young student days and wondered where he was now.

As we came close enough to see the long, black wooden fence, I could see my father-in-law, plowing in the field in front of the fence. My heart started beating hard, in great anticipation. He straightened his back. He looked at us, and he seemed to be trying to figure out who we were.

My heart leapt with joy, and I was ready to run to him. I thought he would come out of the field and greet us warmly. But an unexpected thing happened. He started plowing again as if nothing had happened, as if we were not there. He was pretending not to recognize us. With his whole body, he was telling us he would have nothing to do with us. I felt as if I had been doused with a bucket of ice water. I instantly regretted that we had come. We should have gone to my parents' home in Yamanashi Prefecture instead, despite my duty to report to my husband's parents first.

As we approached the field, he did not look up again. Even when we were within ten feet from him, he made himself busy working with his hoe, and did not look up at us. I wanted to cry, but I decided to put on a good face, and exercised strong self-control.

"We are back," I said, bowing deeply to him.

"Ah," was all he said. Still, he did not lift his face. He never stopped plowing. What a cold heart!

Finally, he started walking slowly to the gate, and we followed him. We passed the long, grand gate. The gate looked grand from the distance, but a closer look revealed the sad-looking damage. I remembered the story about the fire that had destroyed a large portion of the estate. The somewhat rundown gate that had never been reconstructed was like a symbol of Japan's defeat. But there were still enough remnants of the prewar era. We walked through the garden with big, gorgeous stones and well-pruned pine trees. We did not exchange a word as we entered the house.

I do not remember what my mother-in-law said to us, but she was as cold as her husband. It was all

I could do to hold in my anger and regret. After I formally greeted my parents-in-law, we went to the main house where the oldest son lived as head of the family. After my husband's parents retired, their oldest son became the head of the Enokido family. There we received the same chilly reception. With my whole body, all I wanted to do was cry, but I could not.

As a wife, I was an outsider who had married into my husband's family, but our children were their grandchildren—true blood relations—even if they had never met. How could this family be so cold and cruel? I was no longer just sad; I became extremely angry, but I kept it inside. I was busy thinking of my next actions, developing a better plan.

I decided we would go to Yamanashi Prefecture the next day. But I had to take care of our dirty clothes. After breakfast, I set about doing our washing. When my sister-in-law in Iwase had given my children a bath the night before, she had changed their clothes. Now I had a mountain of dirty laundry.

I borrowed a washtub and went to the well of the main house. I pumped water until I was out of breath. I was totally exhausted; my body and soul were utterly worn out. It was hard for me to get all of the wash done, and nobody helped me. I just wanted to get to Yamanashi as quickly as I could so that I could rest to my heart's content. My own sisters wouldn't have let me do this chore in my current condition. Fortunately, it was a fine day, and all the laundry would be dry by the following day. My children must have felt that we had come to a strange place because they never left my side, not even for a moment. No one spoke to them.

When I finished the wash, I walked slowly toward the separate house where my husband's parents lived, as was customary for the retired couple. My heart was heavy, and I almost dragged my feet through the spacious Japanese garden with carefully arranged rocks and moss. I was depressed and did not know what to do about it.

Suddenly Isao asked, "What school will I go to?"

"How should I know?" I snapped. "I have no idea!"

Isao was surprised by my harsh response. He became silent. I was sorry I had responded so sharply; it was just my frustration. I thought about it and realized it was nearly the end of August. The second semester would begin soon.

Quickly, I added in a far gentler tone, "You may end up going to school in Yamanashi."

Isao nodded wordlessly.

"Let's go to Yamanashi tomorrow," I said firmly to both Isao and to myself. We both wanted to leave this horrible place as soon as possible.

At lunchtime there was a big iron pot with plenty of white rice. The rice was cold, left over from breakfast, but it tasted delicious. When was the last time we had had white rice? It had to have been a month or more.

I practiced common-sense etiquette in front of my stone-faced in-laws, but I could not resist asking for a second serving. I knew it was not graceful to shovel food into my mouth, so I tried to eat slowly. After the second, I still wanted to eat more, but I stopped. After lunch, my father-in-law said there was not sufficient rice even in the countryside. There were people who had nothing to eat. Food was very precious. He kept droning on and on. He seemed to be hinting that he would rather not have to feed us.

I shrank smaller and smaller in my place. I stopped my children from eating too much. I was more ready to leave than ever, but the next morning, my whole body ached. As anxious as I was to go to Yamanashi, my exhausted body wouldn't budge.

After breakfast, my father-in-law said, "We cannot take care of you. You were the one who did not send us a monthly remittance."

What a chilling attitude. I had never dreamed of staying there for very long. I struggled to hold back my tears.

"Sometimes we sent you spending money. We sent you some gifts." I was not supposed to refute my father-in-law, but I could not help.

He did not stop. He continued by saying that he was not talking about spending money. He was talking about a regular monthly remittance.

I was so overwhelmed I could not open my mouth.

"You must have had a very luxurious life in Manchuria. We cannot take care of those who did not take care of their parents."

It is true, of course, that living conditions for Japanese in Manchuria were generally much better than for people in Japan until the end of the war. But unlike my husband's older brother, Kunimitsu, who had worked as an engineer for a Japanese government agency, my husband had not been well paid. I tried to tell my father-in-law about our life in Manchuria, including details about my husband's salary. My husband was young and did not belong to an elite class. But my old-fashioned father-in-law had no desire to listen. He probably just remembered his grand visit to Manchuria in 1939 when Kunimitsu had invited his father to visit Manchuria.

That visit took place during the height of the stupendous development of Manchukuo, when tourism had become very popular among the Japanese. Travel facilities in Manchukuo offered opportunities for hunting, fishing, mountain climbing, horse racing, golfing, visits to archaeological sites, touring memorable battle fields, a ski resort, a hot spring, and even praying at many Shinto shrines. The cost of continental travel made it impossible, however, for most Japanese to consider the journey even at second-class or third-class group rates. A university graduate who worked for the Tokyo metropolitan government would have to save for two months to be able to afford the transportation, accommodations, and meals of a two-week trip to Manchuria and Korea.

My father-in-law must have been deeply impressed by his trip–which was probably "all expenses paid" by Kunimitsu–and he must have believed that our daily lives were always filled with extra luxuries like the kind he had experienced during his visit.

I lost all interest in saying anything more. I just wanted to leave for Yamanashi without delay, but I begged him to let us stay one more day.

When my father-in-law left the room, I was attacked anew by my sense of misery and humiliation, and this time, I could not stop my tears.

The Enokido family was the most prestigious and wealthy household in the area. At least, that was my understanding. They owned a lot of farmlands; they had to be well-to-do. The oldest son was managing the household with a firm hand. Why should their eighth child, who was their youngest son, have to send money to his parents? To add insult to injury, my father-in-law had scolded me for not having brought any gifts. We did not come to Ibaraki for pleasure! How could anyone have expected gifts from me? Just getting ourselves there had been a life-or-death journey. Nonetheless, I decided to obey the old ways.

I searched our belonging for something suitable for gifting.

I found an *obi-dome* (sash clip), a *han-eri* (a replaceable collar lining for kimono), and a pair of *tabi* (traditional Japanese socks worn with *geta* that resemble flip-flops). The yellow and orange *obi-dome* was so beautiful that, at first, Kashiyo refused to let it go. Of course, it was also my favorite, and I had gone to great pains to bring it back with us. To my father-in-law, I gave knitted underwear I had purchased brand new with money from my dangerous work in Manchuria. All of these items were priceless to me. Instead of helping poor family members who had just been repatriated, my in-laws took precious things from us. We would have appreciated even such a small item as a towel from them.

It was as if we were sitting on straw mats over sharp spikes. My intention in visiting Inuta was to show respect to my husband's family. I had suppressed my desire to go to Yamanashi, my parents' home, thinking that it would be a violation of proper etiquette. I understood my position was inferior to the Enokido family members. In the end, though, they treated us so rudely, thinking we had caused them trouble, that I realized we had made a dreadful mistake in going to see them.

Traveling the long distance to Yamanashi would take at least an entire day, and we would have to change crowded trains several times. I had no other choice but to wait one more day. I needed more rest. I had to be strong and patient.

The next morning after breakfast, my father-in-law stood up abruptly.

"Oh, I just remembered," he said. "There is a letter from Yokohama."

He took a postcard from the top of the chest and handed it to me. It was a message from my sisters. It said that the American bombings had destroyed their two houses, and they had moved. They were living together in the same house now in Yokohama, and the postcard bore their new address. They had wanted to come to Hakata to welcome us back, but they could not make it because of some misunderstanding. I did not know what they meant by "misunderstanding," but I knew it was very difficult to travel the long distance from Yokohama to Hakata. It would take at least two days in crowded trains, and it was not easy to get train tickets. Besides, it was expensive to travel.

"Please hurry to Yokohama," the card read. I burst with joy and wanted to jump and dance. Yokohama was much closer than Yamanashi. My sisters were anxiously awaiting our return! Why had my father-in-law neglected to give me this pleasant and important letter sooner? I grew even angrier with him.

At the same time, I was encouraged by the postcard. We would go to Yokohama! My heart leaping inside my chest, I organized our bags. I knew food was extremely scarce, so I bought enough rice and potatoes from the Enokido family to last us for a while.

Takashi was playing outside, and he came rushing in to tell me something important.

"*Okaa-chama* (honorable Mommy), the chickens are laying eggs! I saw eggs!" he said excitedly.

Eggs! To eat? I knew they were raising chickens in the corner of their backyard, but they never offered us any of the eggs to eat.

"Don't say things like that," I reprimanded Takashi.

My in-laws were nearby, and I was sure they heard Takashi. If they were ordinary people with natural human emotion, they would be embarrassed that they had not offered us any eggs. They were not embarrassed, but I still wanted to avoid any chance that they might be ashamed by their outright stinginess as they saw the excitement and anticipation of an innocent child. How I wished they would give at least one egg to little Takashi!

I glanced at my in-laws. They were puffing on cigarettes, pretending not to hear anything. Their skins were too thick to feel any embarrassment.

"Cruel beasts!" I wanted to scream. Oh, how I longed to give them a piece of my mind!

CHAPTER 19

DAYS OF SLEEP

I am a faithful daughter, and I adored my mother unconditionally. Her story was my story. I believed every word my mother wrote, and her resentment toward my father's parents in Ibaraki was deeply rooted in my heart for years. Even now! Imagining how we had been received by the Enokido elders stung sharply. I did not remember much, so my hurt was more on my mother's behalf. How dare they have treated my mother so cruelly?

My mother was a fighter as well as a very clever person. She found humor even when she was in a miserable situation, as her memoir demonstrates as she prepared to leave the Enokido estate.

I was ready to leave.

About ten feet away from my in-laws, I kneeled straight and placed both hands on the floor. I bowed deeply to show the utmost politeness. My forehead touched the tatami. It was not an expression of my gratitude. While it was a gesture dictated by etiquette, my intention was to show sarcasm. I was acting out my resistance against their coldhearted behavior over the past two days. I was not sure if those old people understood my one-woman act. They might conveniently ignore my sarcasm and only accept my superficial politeness as the proper etiquette. Still, it gave me some satisfaction along with a bit of fun and made me feel better.

I was sure that my in-laws were well aware of the time and distance involved for our trip from Ibaraki to Yokohama. They would know we would not get to Yokohama until late in the evening. As we finished breakfast, I hoped they would give us lunch boxes for our journey, but no such luck. We departed the estate that still retained remnants of its old glory. The four of us walked the long distance to the train station without any additional food, wearing heavy rucksacks on our backs. No one saw us off on our journey.

It was by now mid-August 1946. The trains were packed with desperate people, overwhelming hordes, without any manners whatsoever. It was all I could do to keep my children with me. The throngs kept pushing, heedless of the smaller ones among them, but we somehow managed to make our connections. When we arrived at Omiya Station in Saitama Prefecture to change trains, it was already afternoon.

Our next train arrived, but there was no way to board that train for Yokohama. The crowd rushed to the train, almost violently, and there was absolutely no room for us. We decided to skip this train and wait for the next one, standing at the front of the line. Takashi said he was hungry. The platform was relatively empty because the train had just left. I ran to a station kiosk to try to find some food, but the shelves were empty.

"Be patient," I told him. "When we arrive in Yokohama, I will give you some rice."

The two older children must have been hungry as well, but they were better at hiding it. My heart ached for my poor children, and my resentment at the cold-heartedness of my in-laws welled up again; they had not even given one rice ball to their innocent and hungry grandchildren.

The line for the train got longer and longer. A man behind me kindly warned me, "Make sure you stay safe. People will push you."

When the train arrived, I held Takashi under my arm and let the other two children get on the train. I was shoved hard from behind and staggered, pushing Kashiyo against the train, but to my relief she quickly recovered herself and boarded along with the rest of us. It felt like a rough sport to ride these trains.

We changed trains at Yokohama Station and took a streetcar from Sakuragi-cho. When we finally arrived at Isogo, we were lost. I had never visited my sister's new house. The only thing I had was the address on the postcard that she had sent to my parents-in-law. I asked people along the way, and finally we arrived at Enoki Square. I knocked on the door of a house around the square and asked again. I could sense that we were not far from our destination.

We put down our rucksacks, and I asked the children to wait. I would look for the house by myself. As I left the square for the street, by luck I spied my nephew playing with his friends. I asked him to take us to his mother's home. I quickly went back to the square and picked up the children. With our heavy rucksacks on our backs, we followed my nephew.

We arrived at a house that was small, although it had a proper gate in front.

My nephew opened the sliding door, and we stepped in. My two older sisters saw us and screamed loudly in extreme joy. None of us could speak, we were crying so hard.

"Welcome home, welcome home!"

"How lucky you have made it!" They repeated over and over again.

I felt the weight of the past several days lift from my shoulders. My sisters set steaming bowls of white rice on the table for us, and I gobbled mine up. Nothing could have been better. What a wonderful feeling to be with family members who were warm and kind. I tasted genuine happiness at long last. We had canned salmon, too, and I could not believe such delicious food existed in this world. My sisters had held on to some precious white rice for our return.

After we satisfied our hunger, all I wanted to do was sleep. I tried to drag the rucksack into the room from the entrance hall, but I could not. I had been carrying it for so long, but now I couldn't even move it another inch. My energy had vanished. My sisters laughed as they tried to help.

"How could you have carried this heavy bag?" they asked with amazement.

Amid the warm welcome, I could feel my total exhaustion. I cannot remember what I did for the next two or three weeks. My sisters said I did nothing but sleep and eat. I woke up when meals were ready, and as soon as I finished eating, I would collapse again. Since the day after we left Hakata, I had been suffering from stomachache and diarrhea. My body and soul had reached their limits. I must have arrived in Yokohama by sheer willpower.

Fortunately, my children had held up. I could barely have made it home safely without their support. I was not powerful, but they trusted me completely and unconditionally. Their eyes were so sweet and endearing. Their smiles gave me enormous strength and hope. I was especially grateful for Isao's great cooperation. He was my reliable helper, despite his age. I could not thank him enough.

For the next several days, I slept and ate virtually around the clock, day and night, to a point where my sisters started to worry if there was something wrong with me beyond my exhaustion.

One day, I was awakened by a loud chorus of "*Wasshoi, wasshoi*" ("Heave ho, heave ho!"). It was so noisy that it disrupted my "vegetable-like" deep sleep. I got up and looked out to see what was happening. A crowd of people were carrying a portable shrine; several young men and women in festive costumes were shouting and laughing. I could not believe my eyes. What were they doing? My life in Shinkyo flashed through my mind.

Had these people had such parties while those of us in Manchuria faced death every day, fighting extreme hunger and danger, yearning to return to Japan? So many had perished in misery, while waiting. Even on the ship, on the way to being repatriated to Japan, people had died, their bodies thrown into the sea. And on the bottom of that same sea, there must have been bodies of thousands of young soldiers. When I had been in Manchuria, I imagined that people in Japan struggled as we did. So, what was this?

I felt they must have no concern for what was happening even now to those who had been left behind in Manchuria. They thought it was not their concern. Weren't they Japanese just as I was? Or was I an alien? I felt a deep bitterness. From that moment on, I came to hate festivals, and I still cannot enjoy them to this day.

It took years for me to recognize that everyone has their own way of living their lives. Some people celebrated festivals with joyfulness, even after the war. It might have been their way to escape from misery. Some may have helped to carry the portable shrines even though their stomachs were empty. Just because I could not recover from the shock that I felt at the contrast in our circumstances did not mean that was the way that everyone else would process things.

We had finally met with a heartfelt welcome by my mother's sisters. Unlike the huge and cold house in Ibaraki, my aunt's house was small, crowded, and warm. My mother was trying to consider things from other people's point of view, to create the room to see the other side of the picture. Even with my paternal grandparents, she eventually made an effort to modify her hostile feelings toward them. When we become older, we often become wiser and more forgiving. Over time, she persuaded herself to understand my grandparents' situation during that unfortunate visit. It was more tolerable when she thought through the pain her in-laws had experienced. My father's younger sister, the eighth child of eight, had died when she was young. His older brother Kunimitsu, the brilliant second son and the family's favorite, had eloped with an undesirable woman and died at the age of forty in Manchuria in 1944. And their youngest son, my father, had been drafted in the closing days of the war, and was missing. All this must have broken my grandparents' hearts. Perhaps their life in Ibaraki was not as comfortable as she had thought, my mother later contemplated. But I was different. I had no idea about our grandparents' misfortune, and my sense of resentment lingered.

Weeks passed. One day, I was awakened by my sister who wanted to discuss Isao's schooling. The school year in Japan starts in April and has three terms. After a vacation in summer (one month in August), the second term starts in September. Isao had finished only one term of first grade, and he had not been in school since then. According to his age, he should be in the second grade. I had to think hard about what grade to enroll him in, and eventually chose the second.

My sister must have taken care of the paperwork at the ward office for his school enrollment. I spent days sleeping, leaving my children's care entirely to my sisters. I gradually recovered consciousness, but still acted like a semi-invalid.

As time went by, it seemed I had made the right choice to place him in second grade. Isao's marks were not quite as good as I hoped, but he was in the middle of the class. After getting acclimated, he improved remarkably and quickly reached the top of the class, which made me very happy.

CHAPTER 20

FAILURE IN FILIAL DUTIES

Our neighborhood in Yokohama was middle class with small, cluttered houses. My mother's two best friends, however, were both clearly from the upper middle class. Her friends had daughters the same age as me. I became good friends with them, and I visited them in their homes. Their houses had escaped bombings and were surrounded by grand fences, with the trees of their gardens trimmed by professional caretakers. Our garden was tiny with low-growing bamboo hedges. Our standard of living was clearly far inferior to theirs. They never came to my house.

When we started elementary school a few years after the end of the war, we were under American occupation. Japan was in a chaotic state. Our neighborhood public school had six grades; one grade had eight classes. The school did not have enough classrooms. From first to third grades, students were grouped into two divisions, half in the morning, and the rest in the afternoon, usually fifty students in a class.

There were not many things a very young child could do to bring honor to her mother. I was not living my young life thinking about my grandparents in Ibaraki often, but I wanted to demonstrate how good we were. "Do you see that my mother is doing so well? Look at us. You should be ashamed that you treated her so badly." I repeated this in my heart like a mantra. I cultivated the idea of becoming rich and powerful to get back at them so they would pay due respect to my mother. Even though they might never know that they were the fuel for my desire to shine, I worked diligently. This thinking was just like my mother's deepest sarcastic bow in front of my grandparents when she was ready to leave for Yokohama after our painful two days in Ibaraki. She knew it was an act that might not have any direct effect on her tormentors, but it gave her a certain satisfaction.

I began my quest to get even with my perceived enemies. I was elected class president every year. My middle school posted test scores in English and math, showing all 150 names in descending order from the highest achiever down to the lowest. Today, I think that practice is cruel. The public schools at that time were not gentle to everybody, and their goals were not to enhance diversity and equality. We all stood in a hallway in front of the huge lists of students' names. I always beat my two rich friends, a fact that I proudly reported to my mother. Did I do this for my mother or for my own satisfaction? It was certainly the reward I could give to my mother, and in my young heart, it was a kind of revenge on both my rich friends and my grandparents whom I felt had written off our family and underestimated us. My mother's fierce determination not to be defeated must have cultivated my competitive spirit.

> The house we lived in belonged to my older sister. My second sister's family had come to live with them because, like tens of thousands of people in Japan

during the war, both my sisters' houses had been incinerated by American bombings.

The house in Yokohama had three bedrooms with one toilet—which was not even a flush toilet! Before our arrival, eleven people were living there—six members of my older sister's family and five members of my second sister's family. My children and I brought the total to fifteen. It was more like a commune than a family home. Despite the house bursting at the seams even before our arrival, my sister and her husband took us in without any question. My second sister had one more child, their oldest daughter, who had gone to Yamanashi at the time of our arrival. She, like many school-age children, including children of the royal family, had evacuated to the countryside to avoid the bombings by B-29s.

The house, with ten children laughing, crying, and fighting, was noisy and lively all the time. We divided the children into three groups. Four were in the "school-age group," three were in the "kindergarten group," and three in the group we called the "small ones." I had one child in each group.

Grouping the children in this way was very helpful. When we needed them, we would call them by their group name, and the whole group would come. Food was shared according to group. If we had only enough snacks for three children, they were given to the "small ones," and Kashiyo and Isao's groups would not get any. If we had snacks for six, Isao's group would again not get any. The mothers of the children who did not get snacks sometimes felt resentful. But we had to follow this system if we were going to carry on our communal living with so many people in such tight living quarters. The cooperative system would not work if anyone got preferential treatment. It was okay as long as the pluses and minuses balanced out, but at some point, the system was bound to collapse.

When the second term of the school year started for the older children, Kashiyo went to Yahata Kindergarten with two of her cousins who were a year older. I went with Isao to school and met his teacher. It was against my philosophy of fairness to ask for any special consideration from our children's teachers. But this time was an exception. I explained our situation and solicited understanding and support from his teacher. My children were smart, and I was proud to be their mother. Nonetheless, I felt that Isao, who had attended only one semester of the first grade and had not gone to school for a long time, needed extra attention.

The children went to school cheerfully and enthusiastically every day. Once the seven school-age children and my two sisters' husbands were out of the house, there was some quiet time for the three sisters and the group of three "small ones."

I felt like it was the first time I had lived with my sisters. I had only fragmented memories of them when we were younger. When I started elementary school, my sisters were already in higher grades. We had not spent much time together, so my memories of them from that time are vague.

After I graduated from the village school, I had gone to Tokyo right away. Sending a young girl to Tokyo was a big event at that time. Whenever people in Japan cannot expect to meet again for a long time, or ever, we use the expression that we "exchange farewell cups of water." I understand that this custom originated from a fable. The historical Buddha, Buddha Shakyamuni, had requested water just before he passed away; that developed into the custom to wet a person's lips with water at his or her last moment so that the person would not be thirsty after death. During World War II, Kamikaze pilots exchanged "farewell cups of water" to bid a similar kind of last farewell. Then those soldiers smashed their glasses to show they would never use the same glasses again. They could not, because they were determined not to come back alive.

For a young girl from the village to venture into the big city, she might as well be entering the jungle. Such an act would have needed a great sense of determination from both parties—the girl who departs as well as the parents who send her out.

Twenty years had passed since I had left for Tokyo. After many twists and turns, I was living with my sisters in Yokohama. Life had its ups and downs. Overnight, fate had turned my situation from affluence to misery. But my sisters were kind, and they did nothing to make me feel inferior. My eldest sister was particularly warmhearted. She was genuinely considerate of my children and me, although she never overtly expressed her fondness. She had come to Manchuria with her one-year-old daughter to help me out when I delivered Kashiyo. My eldest sister had inherited something of my father's character. When she got angry, she could be fierce, but she was extremely tender inside her heart most of the time. My second sister, on the other hand, was calm and easygoing and openly showed affection to her husband and children. Each of us had our own personalities.

In the mornings, after everyone else had gone out for the day, the three of us would sit around the hibachi and talk. Mostly I would talk, and my sisters would listen. I had a million things to tell them about our lives in Manchuria and the end of the war. We all cried over the story of the evacuation. They were angered on my behalf by the story of my in-laws in Ibaraki.

"You are our sister," they would say. "And of course we are taking care of you. But your parents-in-law are outrageous. You might be an outsider, but your children are their grandchildren, their blood. How could they have been so cold? It is beyond comprehension!"

I cannot remember how many days we spent like this, but eventually I regained my composure. With my sisters' kindness, gradually I was able to physically and emotionally recover after many months of agony.

Around this time, I was also told something that caused me great shock and sadness—my father had died. He had passed away in February 1944 at the age of sixty-nine. I knew my mother had died earlier because I had been notified while I was still in Manchuria. However, I had spent eighteen months unaware of my father's death. I was stunned and just let my tears roll down my face. I adored my father, and I missed him terribly. I felt I had lost my last refuge, leaving me totally helpless. I had great respect for my father, who supported me under any circumstances.

When he died, it had still been possible for the Japanese to exchange letters with Manchuria. I wondered why no one had told me about his death. My sisters had probably not wanted to add extra anxiety while I was living in a foreign land amid a raging war.

After I regained my strength, I wanted to visit my parents' home in Yamanashi. Unbeknown to me, during my near-vegetative state, I had received two letters from my younger brother, urging me to visit him as soon as possible. While I waited for the right time to return to my parents' home, my younger brother unexpectedly came to Yokohama, since he had received no response from me. He wanted to see me and to celebrate my safe return from Manchuria. He brought winter underwear as a gift for my children, which I greatly appreciated, as we had very little clothing. Even though he had his own children, he had saved the underwear for my sons. I was deeply touched.

All essential items were rationed at that time. The government established the Rice Control Law in 1939, and it completely regulated the price and quantity of rice distribution. People were hungry and marched in the streets in 1946 chanting, "Give us rice!" Each family received a Rice-Ration Book that included the names and ages of all family members; in that way, the book also worked as an ID. We would go to the government-sanctioned distribution center to collect our ration by showing our Rice-Ration Book. It didn't matter that we had enough money; we could not buy rice freely until 1969 when a Voluntary Rice Distribution System was introduced, but government restrictions still existed. It was 1972 before rice became freely available without any restriction.

Those were the days, however, when no Japanese had enough food or things to allow us to have a comfortable life. My brother's visit with precious underwear for my children moved me so much it prompted me to visit him in Yamanashi. Just a few days later, I took my children to my dear old home.

Seeing the house without my parents made me feel more lost than I had anticipated. After my parents passed away, the house now belonged to my younger brother, as he was the only son. This meant that every domestic household matter was now under the control of my brother's wife, and I could do nothing there without her permission. There were no written rules, and my brother's wife was not demanding, but we all obeyed traditional customs and norms. While my parents were alive, I could go to any chest, cabinet, or food storage and pick out anything I wanted. I could use my parents' things as I pleased. No longer. Remembering those old days, I could not help but feel constrained and uncomfortable.

One thing that had not changed, however, was the beauty of the natural surroundings of my old home. The grandeur of Mt. Fuji and the mountains all around my home welcomed me even in my impoverished state.

This was the home I had never forgotten, even for a moment, wherever I had been. More fond memories came back to me, and I appreciated my parents all the more keenly. I then went to the cemetery to pay my respects to them. The giant weeping cherry trees at the temple, whose blossoms I had enjoyed as a child, were still there, their branches hanging gracefully.

At the cemetery, I climbed some stone steps. At the top was my parents' small tombstone. It was covered by soft green moss, a visible sign of the passing of time. Next to the stone was a slightly elevated mound, my father's grave. It was so pitiful. What a contrast to the powerful, proud father he had been in life. I knelt down and cried.

"I am very sorry, Father, for failing in my filial duties."

I put my hands together in prayer, and then could not resist the impulse to dig down, thinking he was under this mound. I remained kneeling. I could not stand up for a long time. I only repeated one word in my heart, "Father, Father."

Later when I related this experience to a friend, she dismissed my deep sentiment with a laugh and said, "You are not a dog."[14] I was determined never to tell anybody about it ever again.

I returned to Yokohama filled with nostalgia for my childhood, a deep longing for my parents, and memories of the peaceful and soothing natural surroundings of my old home. But I was also somewhat dejected. My sister-in-law in Yamanashi had kindly given me a brand-new *furoshiki* (cloths for wrapping parcels) and a long piece of white flannel cloth. If my father were still alive, I could have asked him for a new futon and other necessities such as a set of dishes and kitchen utensils, but I could not ask my brother's family for anything.

Somehow, that was the end of Yamanashi for me. But I would always remember that, when my parents were there, my life was blessed like fully blossomed flowers.

CHAPTER 21

AN ARROGANT GIRL

One vivid bitter memory from my childhood still hurts me. My aunt (my mother's older sister) was our benefactor. We could not have survived without her kindness. My mother described her as a woman with a tender heart but blunt expression. I don't remember the occasion, but she simply said to me in front of my mother, "Kashiyo, you are an arrogant girl." I must have been a first grader. Did I understand the meaning of that word? Probably not, but I was more hurt by my mother's shocked reaction than the words. I felt I had brought dishonor to my mother. My aunt's remark has never left me and I have carried it all the way to Walpole to this day. She must have been right; she was a keen observer. How had she known me so well? If I did not need to admit I was an arrogant girl, I could have dismissed my aunt's comment and forgotten it quickly.

After several months in Japan, the children of our household started calling me *Okaa-chan* (a common form of addressing "Mother"), rather than

Okaa-chama (a more polite and graceful address made by children). It was natural in that new environment. Our life did not belong to the upper middle class any longer.

One day while the children were playing happily, Kashiyo turned to me and said suddenly, "Let's go home. I am tired of living in this dirty house." I did not know what to say. My oldest sister jumped in, "This is your house. You have no house in Manchuria anymore."

"Yes, we do. We have a much more beautiful house, and it is ours."

My oldest sister laughed out loud and said, "Kashiyo is innocent, but what an arrogant attitude. She is completely unaware that she is just a sponger." Recalling our time in Manchuria, I held back my tears. It was painful. Even if she did not mean to hurt me, it stabbed my heart to hear my sister utter the word "sponger" so blithely.

When I read this portion of my mother's writing, I recognized how much my innocent and honest comment hurt my mother. At the same time, my aunt's reaction to her niece's arrogant attitude had given my mother the determination to get out from our dependent situation. Mother was working all day long; and at night, she was mending the holes of our socks under the 60-watt bulbs. She inserted a Japanese teacup into a sock so that she could easily target the hole. I could not recall ever seeing her in bed.

We were struggling, and we did not have money to buy books. I had never dreamed of going to a bookstore to buy books, but there was a small book rental shop near our house. A husband and wife converted their *genkan* (front porch) into a shop, and we could take books for small fees. I was devouring Japanese translations of children's books from Europe, such as *A Dog of Flanders, Heidi, Pollyanna, A Little Princess, The Blue Bird, Anne of Green Gables,* and *Daddy-Long-Legs*. They provided me an escape from our meager living condition in Yokohama as well as a way of becoming acquainted with the Western world. Under the American occupation, we were eager to learn and absorb anything about Western practices—their food, their culture, and their manners.

When my aunt called me a sponger, my mother was terribly wounded and resolved to work hard and earn enough money to buy our own house. I had read somewhere that people in England called their house their "castle." The house we initially shared with the two families of my aunts was a far cry from a castle. These experiences must form the psychological roots of how I view where I live now. My home *is* my castle. We designed our house and three architects refined it; we built it in a forest from the ground up. I treasure my house for its design, comfort, and convenience, in a peaceful environment where we enjoy the dramatic changes of four seasons. I had never lived in the countryside, so when my mother told me that she wanted to go back to Yamanashi to live out her old age, I could not understand her. But I have grown to be attached to country living; how I wish my mother could be here with me.

> I had used up much of the money I had brought back from Manchuria and knew I would have to find work. I could not waste any more time, even though my sisters told me that there was no need to hurry. I felt strongly that I had to contribute at least the cost of the food the four of us ate.
>
> After discussing various options with my sisters, I decided to take up sewing. Fortunately, my second sister had a sewing machine. I could already sew

simple dresses because I had taken sewing lessons before we had left for Manchuria. It was part of the training to be a good bride. Now I would use those same skills to make my living to support my three children. To do that, I would have to find a dressmaking school. I had to be professionally trained.

Before I did that, however, I would have to change my hairstyle. In Shinkyo, after Japan's surrender, all of the women cut their hair very short. Some had even shaved their heads bald and smeared their faces with black charcoal; this obscured their femininity in order to deflect any attention from the rampaging Russian soldiers. In Japan now, my hair was still unusually short compared to most women; my bob cut attracted attention, particularly whenever I rode the streetcar. In those days, the bob cut was reserved for elementary-school children and must have looked odd on an adult. There were times when such a haircut was extremely fashionable. But those days were long gone. I was not ashamed by the attention I received from people; rather, it caused me to grow more defiant. Still, it was not a pleasant experience to be stared at all the time.

I decided to get my hair permed. I had not been in a hair salon for a long time. After my hair was done and I looked in the mirror, I was pleased to see the transformation to an ordinary woman. I had gotten rid of the virtual signboard I wore that identified me as someone who had been repatriated to Japan from Manchuria. I started wearing dresses and a pair of buckskin shoes instead of pants and sneakers and was quite satisfied with the way I looked, after so many years.

Now I was ready to look for a dressmaking school. M stopped by and was startled by my transformation.

He commented, "You really look like a young woman!" It was a sweet compliment. He said he would go with me to look for a school. My conscience bothered me a bit, but I was delighted to be in the company of a handsome young man. It was the first time since my marriage that I had been accompanied by a man other than my husband. My sisters encouraged us and asked M to take good care of me.

When my mother mentioned M, she was referring to a man she had met when she traveled back one more time to my grandparents' house in Ibaraki. Even though she had resolved never to return, she was desperate. She decided to go in order to retrieve some things she had left behind that she had brought from Manchuria: a kimono, overcoats, and other winter clothes. But these things were less important than the more critical mission to bring food from Ibaraki to my aunts' home. Government food rations were not sufficient, and people were forced to buy food from the black market at outrageous prices. Many city people took long trips to rural areas, but often such city dwellers were treated unsympathetically by farmers who refused to sell food to them.

The *kaidashi ressha*, or shopping trains as they were called, were extremely crowded. People hung from the windows and even squeezed onto the roofs of passenger and freight cars. My mother, who had recovered from the exhaustion of repatriation, now courageously took those awful trips, battling the overcrowding. On the trip that she thought would be her last to Ibaraki, she bought chestnuts, rice, and potatoes from her in-laws. The trip took her until late in the evening, as she tried to make the round trip to Ibaraki and back in one day, a seventeen-hour journey. By ten in the evening, she was dog-tired but relieved to be almost home. As she held her rucksack on her knees, she listened absentmindedly to the sounds of the streetcar. Suddenly she was startled by a strange noise. When she opened her eyes, she saw potatoes strewn on the floor. They had broken out of a bag held by a young man, and were rolling all over the streetcar.

The eyes of all the passengers were fixed on the scattered potatoes. The young man was embarrassed and tried to gather them. But his *furoshiki* (cloths for wrapping parcels) was worn and tattered. My mother could not just sit idly by. She untied her *furoshiki* loaded with chestnuts, poured the chestnuts into her potato bag, and then handed her empty *furoshiki* to him. He managed to wrap up his potatoes and thanked her again and again.

The man, who is only ever referred to as "M" in my mother's memoir, said he would like to visit her the next day to return the *furoshiki*. They exchanged addresses and realized that their houses were only six hundred yards apart. At that time, even one *furoshiki* was a valuable item, and it hadn't even belonged to my mother, but to one of my aunts. When my mother returned home and told her sisters what had happened, they laughed and said, "How exciting!"

As promised, the young man came the next day to return the *furoshiki*. He talked with my aunts and was surprised to learn that my mother had three children. He had thought she was single. After that, he started visiting her often. He had also lost his parents and had lived in Manchuria as a military officer; he was now living with his stepmother, whom he disliked. My mother and her sisters saw the shade of loneliness in his face. He was quite handsome and well-proportioned; he had long, narrow eyes. I noticed that my mother had a tendency to make much of good looks.

> M was polite and sincere. My sisters adored him. His graceful behavior surprised me. He was sophisticated

and treated me like a real lady. I was self-conscious and a bit embarrassed but forced myself to be composed. My husband's face flashed in my head briefly. I must have been feeling somewhat guilty.

M and I visited two or three dressmaking schools, but none of them met my expectations. We returned home without success. The afternoon ended as if we had been on a date. I had done nothing to be ashamed of, but I still felt a bit embarrassed. I also felt guilty in front of my children.

A few days later, I heard that a former sewing teacher of mine had come back from the countryside where she had been evacuated. I immediately went to visit her at the house she was renting that stood a little back from the road in Okamura.

I had been her student before I left for Manchuria. Seven years had passed, but she had not changed. As beautiful as ever, she said she was not yet prepared to take any students. However, when she heard about my desperate situation, she changed her mind and agreed to take me as her first student.

I started the next day and worked from morning to evening. I brought my lunch. When I had been a student before, sewing was just a hobby. This time, I was very serious because our livelihood depended on it. Fortunately, my teacher had only two students—me, and the daughter of her landlord. We worked with secondhand fabrics such as my sisters' kimonos and remnants. With so many people living in our house, there was always someone who could use something new to wear.

After a few months, the materials I used to test my sewing skills were exhausted. My teacher's mother suggested that I put out a signboard to attract clients. I was very nervous that I wouldn't attract any, but I decided to put a very small wooden board (of about five inches) at the gate saying "Tailor for women's and children's clothes."

Right away, people started coming, one after the other. There were more requests than I could comfortably deal with. On any given day, I got five or six jobs. People brought me all kinds of fabric–all used. New fabrics were exceedingly rare. Even the so-called "new" fabrics were not really new but had been put away before the war started. The materials brought to me included kimonos, sheets, curtains, small scraps, and sometimes US army blankets. I would turn these pieces of cloth into skirts, dresses, shirts, and overcoats. My clients were delighted, and I earned some money while continuing to hone my skills.

I attended sewing classes for nearly a year and learned as much as ordinary students would learn in three years. By the end, I had learned enough to tailor men's suits.

It was very hard work to get to that level of skill. My teacher was much younger than I was, but she was a perfectionist and extremely strict. She would scold me about my work if it was not perfect, and that caused me to shed tears many times. How mortifying it was to have to undo a finished product that I had poured so much effort into because it bore some imperfection. But in the end, I became competent enough to be independent and did battle with the sewing machine day and night while my sisters did all the household chores, grocery shopping, and even childcare.

Mother's perfectionist attitude annoyed me. I once tried to learn sewing from her because she was like a magician, and I was in awe of her work. She forced me to learn to make patterns using old newspapers; it was not easy. And when she found any small imperfection in my work, she ordered me to do it over again. I did not have patience for that; I did not need it to be perfect, as I was not making dresses for clients. So, I quickly gave up taking her lessons, but the desire to do things perfectly has stayed with me.

I had a close relationship with my mother. She was everything to me. I never questioned her intent. For example, one day she took me to a kindergarten. Neither of my brothers had gone to a kindergarten, and none of the neighborhood children did. It was not required in the late 1940s and early 1950s; it was little more than a glorified play group, and it was considered a kind of luxury for common people like us. Another time she took me to a ballet school because my posture was bad. When she deposited me there, I do not remember questioning what she was doing. I simply accepted her intention. I ended up enjoying lessons every Saturday. We danced at a studio that was part of a Buddhist temple while neighborhood kids watched us, probably with envy, through windows. I felt very special. One day, she took me to a dentist office to pull my crooked double tooth out. In Japan, such a tooth used to be considered to be "cute." We did not have a professional orthodontist for a long time, and nobody had a habit of going to a dentist for checkups. It was not a necessity and not many families had resources to do so. We only visited the dentist when something was wrong. I believe I must have been in the third or fourth grade by then because the dentist was the father of a classmate. His family appeared to be wealthy. So, I was happy to be in his office for the first time in my life. I felt like I had been admitted to their social class.

At the end of the fourth grade, my mother arranged to transfer me from one public school to one known to have a better reputation, and that my younger brother attended.

The classwork was harder than at my old school where I had been one of the top students; in my new school, I was just average. One day, my mother took me to a nice, old house. I remember we went through a large, dignified gate. She had given no explanation, so I did not know what we were doing. Soon I realized that it was a place for private tutoring. I sat at a big Japanese table on the tatami floor with several students my age.

Looking back, I am amazed how resourceful my mother was. How did she find a ballet school? How did she find a tutor? How did she know that pulling out a crooked tooth was a good idea while she was busy sewing every single day to support the family? And how did she find extra money to give me those things?

My husband, Tom, used to marvel that I had all those lessons and ski trips even though we were citizens of the defeated nation, while he did not have any of those privileges when he was growing up in America. To which I say to him, "But you had a victory garden, with rabbits and chickens to eat, and we did not have any of those!"

I am still in awe to think of my mother, who did everything to allow us to live as fully as possible even as her notebooks chiefly describe her sufferings.

CHAPTER 22

THREE CUPS OF COFFEE

Our mother kept busy with sewing, cooking, washing, and cleaning, but she found time to take me to ballet lessons while thinking of other ways to improve our lives. She even found a little time to entertain us by having a sushi party. She was the chef, and we three children ate what she prepared in front of us. I am sure it was simple and inexpensive sushi, but it was fun.

When we had a power failure due to a typhoon, we sat in front of the small wooden table. She told us a frightening story of Cinderella. My mother edited the fairy tale to create a thrilling story, probably considering the two boys in front of her. The flickering shadows from candles helped to create a terrifying atmosphere.

We had no awareness about what was on her mind. We hardly talked about our missing father. She was cheerful in front of us, but she expressed her deep loneliness by composing a short poem in her notebook.

> Pouring out my whole heart, I pray,
> But you have not returned,
> Yet, spring has come back again.

Our life was an ongoing struggle, but we were not alone. The entire nation was fighting a scarcity of food, clothing, and shelter. Everyone was doing their best to survive and improve their lives.

It was now the second spring since my husband had left, drafted in 1945. I was not as excited this year to welcome spring. The willow trees beside the river were turning green, but I had nothing to look forward to. Spring had come, but it left me cold.

Around this time, I began to loathe the evening. My sister's husbands would go to work in the morning, but nighttime was family time. My second sister's family all got along well with one another. Watching the children play with their father, laughing happily and climbing up into his lap and onto his shoulders was unbearable to watch. My eldest sister's family was more reserved. Was this due to my sister's personality? Did they not like each other? Or did they act differently out of consideration for us?

My own children did not seem to react to these family interactions. I wondered how they felt with their father missing. It had been a long time since they had asked about him. Their memory of him might have faded. Just a year old when my husband was drafted, Takashi had never even known his father. He was now welcoming his third spring. Growing up among many children, he somehow learned to read long before he went to school and could easily read books for kindergarteners. His spoken language was clear, and he used adult words. Before we knew it, he was an independent child, no longer a toddler. I was very pleased to have such a bright child.

What would my husband say if he could see how this child had grown?

When I could no longer stand to see my nieces and nephews playing happily with their father, I would go out for a walk in the misty moonlight, although I walked only on brightly lit streets. I would stand on bridges, lean against the railing, and absentmindedly gaze at lights reflected in the river or at the occasional passing streetcar. In those days, there was no automobile traffic.

On one such night, I was approached by a man.

"What's happening?" he asked.

I looked at him with astonishment and replied, "Oh, nothing."

"Okay. I hope that's the case," he said and left. He must have thought I was going to jump into the river. What a crazy misunderstanding. I smiled bitterly, realizing that I might have looked suicidal. This incident made me resolve never to stand on a bridge alone. The street beyond the river was perfect for walks.

Spring passed and summer arrived. One day in June in 1947, after all of the children were in bed, the old clock chimed nine. Only we five adults were chatting around the *hibachi* with no fire, when there was a voice at the front gate.

"Excuse me. Good evening!"

All of us turned toward the voice, wondering who could be visiting us so late. I stood and went out the front door and walked to the small gate.

"Who is it?"

"Me. It's me."

A shabby-looking man was standing under dim light. It took me only a second to realize it was my husband. I felt weak in the knees. I could not utter a word. He looked right past my astonishment, entered the house, and greeted my sisters. He started chatting with them. It may have been only a few seconds, but I felt I had fainted. Recovering, I closed the gate behind him quietly. We had had no communications from government agencies or authorities that this event might be coming.

In the living room, everyone was talking noisily, but I could not understand what they were saying. I wanted to say something, but words would not come out of my mouth. I could only cry. My two sisters were talking while wiping away their own tears. Finally, everybody calmed down, and my second sister's husband made coffee. My husband drank a cup without pausing for breath, and then he finished a second in an instant. After a third cup, he said, "Delicious!"

Everyone had been focused on my husband as if in a trance, their eyes watching his hands that held his coffee cup in silence. After the third cup, everybody started speaking at once.

"What made the third cup delicious?" someone asked.

He responded that with the first cup, he did not taste anything. With the second cup, he thought, "This is coffee." It was not until the third cup that he could finally taste the coffee.

My eldest sister said, "Is this really you? Are you real, Maa-chan? You have legs, don't you?"

In Japan, ghosts are typically depicted with no legs. Everyone burst out laughing. My oldest sister used to say that she would never let my husband into this house because of how cruelly his parents had treated us in Ibaraki. Now, however, she had completely forgotten ever having said that. She was simply happy, crying and laughing.

I was in a state of shock and still could not say a word. My husband did not speak to me. He just kept talking politely to everyone else. He seemed remarkably aloof for someone who had not seen his wife for over two years, although giving me hugs and kisses with tears would have been considered a vulgar expression of overt affection. So, I was not offended, although I was one big bundle of emotion. I wanted to say something, but I did not know where I should start. So many questions, so much to communicate. I was simply overwhelmed and just looked at him as if he was a glorified, mysterious stranger. He was answering everyone's questions courteously. I was paying attention with my whole body. It was really hard to believe that my husband had returned, and he was in front of me.

"How did you find this address?" my sister asked.

When he had landed at *Maizuru* in Kyoto, he went to his sister's house in Tokyo. They knew we were doing fine, but they did not know our address. He quickly went to Yokosuka where his favorite brother, Saburo, lived; it was he who told him where we were. In less than one day, my husband traveled from Tokyo to Yokosuka and from there to Yokohama–a very long distance to travel, more than seventy miles in a straight line. Trains during that time were slow, packed, and even dangerous to ride because people had to fight to get on trains. Anxious people pushed and pulled violently. He had to change trains several times, fighting to get on madly overcrowded trains each time. I knew how hard it was for a physically exhausted body to be pushed and shoved on jam-packed trains. This was all the proof I needed to know how eager he was to see us. I was moved. He had wasted no time to reunite with his family.

He told us that he had been taken to Siberia for hard labor. Food had been extremely scarce; a whole day's rations were less than a single normal meal in ordinary times, and many people starved to death in the severe cold. My husband was finally released when he contracted pneumonia and could no longer work. I felt extremely grateful for that pneumonia. I thought he must have had a Russian guard with a sense of humanity because it was standard practice for Russian guards to simply throw away weak or sick Japanese detainees when they judged them to be useless. In truth, my husband did look extremely worn out.

The next day, when I saw his clothes and belongings, I was shocked. His uniform was torn, and his shoes were not a matching pair. In his rucksack, there was only one rag of a blanket and some worthless rubbish–nothing of any value. The Russians had immediately confiscated his watch and fountain pens. He had come home with his body and nothing more. But I was very content and truly happy.

My husband spent four days with us in Yokohama, and then went to his parents' house in Ibaraki on his own to recuperate. We did not have enough food to help him recover. My sisters and I agreed that his parents' joy at seeing their son again must have been no less than mine.

Our children were puzzled by the sudden appearance of a man they were supposed to call Father. Isao was eight years old and seemed to remember his father clearly, but Kashiyo's memory was vague, and Takashi made everybody laugh by calling him *Ojisan* (uncle).

CHAPTER 23

•

IRRESISTIBLE EGGS

My father's unexpected return must have been a dramatic event, but it did not leave a sharp memory in my mind. In America, we hug and kiss when our children visit us. We practice those rituals when we meet friends too. Hugs are okay for me, but kisses are difficult. Being a parent in America has given me opportunities to learn about American culture and what we are expected to say and how to behave. Knowledge helps, but some things are difficult to do naturally. I hate opening gifts in front of the people who give them to me. I feel so fake when I must say "How beautiful," or "Oh, this is just exactly what I wanted." I am embarrassed to pretend to be Americanized. I feel that part of me departs my body and watches myself from above, telling me "You are phony. You are Japanese, and Japanese don't say or do things like that." Many of my friends, and even my own children, think I am distant. I feel connected to my biological family deep inside; it is not necessary to overtly express our emotions. I am sure I knew my mother was very happy with my father's return. It was not necessary to witness them hugging and kissing, and I am sure I would have been embarrassed to see them overtly display their affection.

About two weeks after my husband went to his parents' home, I wondered how he was. We did not have a telephone, so calling was not an option. It was July. *Obon* was approaching, the five-hundred-year-old custom of honoring the spirits of our ancestors and one of the biggest holidays for family reunions. I decided to bring him back to Yokohama.

When I arrived at Ibaraki, my heart was lighter. As I walked into his parents' well-arranged Japanese garden, I saw my husband picking weeds. He stood up and smiled at me. He seemed to have gained weight. Inside the house, I saw his *futon*, which had three layers, laid out on the tatami. As a son who had returned, he was well treated. My mother-in-law told me how they had fussed over him to enhance his recovery. "Masayoshi has had eggs for every meal—breakfast, lunch, and dinner."

My previous visits to Ibaraki had always been day trips, but this time, they invited me to stay overnight. In the morning, there was an egg in my miso soup. I gazed at the egg, remembering that, when I had arrived with their grandchildren, totally exhausted, they had not even given an egg to our two-year-old Takashi. Still seething with resentment at their previous treatment, I thought about refusing this egg as a protest, but I could not resist the temptation and put it in my mouth. The soft yolk burst lusciously as if it had nothing to do with my complicated emotions. When was the last time I had had an egg? The taste vanquished my resistance.

Days later, my in-laws sent a set of *futons* from my mother-in-law's trousseau to Yokohama, covered with cotton in an old-fashioned arabesque design, along with two bolts (about twenty-four yards) of white, hand-woven, silk cloth for my husband's use. While I appreciated these gifts, they underscored the different attitudes toward a son compared with toward his bride.

With the return of my husband, there were now seventeen people in our household, which was not unusual at the time. The lack of housing was serious, as many people's houses had burned down during the war. Reconstruction was slow. Many people from overseas continued to return to Japan–one report stated that almost six million people were returning to Japan from various foreign shores (countries that Japan had occupied and/or controlled), and many of them had no place to live. More than four million houses would be needed to accommodate those "homeless" people.

As a head of the household, my husband had to find a job, but first he had to have some clothes. I withdrew some money from the bank where I had been depositing yen when I had extra and bought him shoes on the black market. I made him a suit jacket and trousers from the white silk my mother-in-law had sent, which was thick like *tsumugi* (pongee, a soft fabric woven from raw silk threads). I also made a dress shirt from sheets we got from the American military through an acquaintance.

Two years had passed since the end of the war, but it was still not easy to find a job. All my husband could find was a part-time job at an American military camp, as he spoke English. After hopping through two or three temporary jobs at American bases, he finally found a position at the American Military Service Club for a salary of about 2,300 yen a month. Then he was offered a position as a section chief at the local government office, but the pay was only 2,000 yen. Weighing the long-term prospects and the current conditions, he decided to take the job with the higher salary. As we say in Japan, "Fifty today is worth more than one hundred tomorrow."

    After my husband started working, our life became a bit more comfortable. Our dream was to have our own house for just the five of us. And for that dream, I worked as hard as I could.

CHAPTER 24

DYING ON YOUR OWN FUTON

My father's homecoming brought great joy and comfort to my mother. But none of my brothers nor I remember anything special concerning his return. I do not think that our father was unimportant to us. I assume we had not missed him as much as people expected we might.

Memories seem to work differently in the minds of very young children. Our four-year-old granddaughter has moved from Berlin, Germany, to Walpole, New Hampshire. Her mother is German and speaks six languages. Her English is perfect, and her daughter can remember the day when she took a streetcar to visit a zoo in Berlin, and she petted a giraffe when he bent his long neck. She must have been less than four years old. I was four years old when our life underwent catastrophic changes. I wonder why my memories are so slight. Probably all our mental and emotional energy was focused on our mother, who was fighting tooth and nail for our well-being. That narrow focus was our world.

When we had arrived at our aunt's house, we lived with seven cousins with similar ages in a crowded small house. Life was busy, noisy, and stimulating. My mother did not grumble much about our father's absence. If she had repeated with a sigh, "I wish your father were here," I would have remembered, because we would have shared her pain. We, particularly my older brother, Isao, offered as much help as possible, and we did not feel inconvenienced, as far as our memories are concerned. We must have been hungry and cold, but we had been protected by our mother. We had complete trust in her.

My father's return in 1947 did not change our life. My mother had been in charge, and it stayed that way. As we grew older, we developed the habit of talking to our mother when we wanted answers from our parents. We rarely spoke to our father directly. Our mother was the message center and coordinator of our family's discussion.

I later saw a similar pattern in Takashi's family. Takashi had been a reporter at *Asahi Shimbun* newspaper and spent most of his early working years in branch offices in different prefectures, leaving his wife and two children in Tokyo. His children always talked to their mother, Taeko, who then discussed matters with her husband.

This pattern was common in Japan. When husbands got assignments in long-distance locations such as overseas, they often went by themselves, leaving their wives and children in Japan. In this way, husbands could concentrate on their jobs, while their children's education in Japan would not be disturbed. Often, Japanese jokingly describe parents' roles; mothers make small decisions, such as where the family should live and which school their children should go, while fathers make big decisions, like what Japan's China policy should be, and whether Japan should re-arm or not.

At our home, we developed total dependence on, and closeness to, our mother, particularly after we had gone through such extreme circumstances together. It may have not been fair to our father, who had been detained in Siberia. The time he had spent there was beyond our imagination;

we did not know anything about his experience as a soldier in Manchuria and a detainee in Siberia, until much later, long after he had quietly passed away.

I am sure that moving out from our aunts' house was a decision made by both my parents, not by my mother alone.

> Even though our house was extremely crowded, we were lucky to have a house to live in, a roof over our heads. At some point, though, I noticed the relationship between my two sisters began to sour. My oldest sister sometimes quietly complained about my second sister.
>
> "She lets her children eat chocolate at night," she would say. Or "She is hiding candy and sugar."
>
> I, too, had my suspicions, but I did not say anything.
>
> My oldest sister did not like our other sister's husband and disliked their open displays of affection, which were considered indecent and vulgar. I tended to think more like my older sister, but I tried to remain as neutral as possible. As time passed, things got worse. Ultimately, they decided to eat meals at separate tables. My family and I ate at my oldest sister's table.
>
> To help us all, my husband often went back to his parents' home in Ibaraki to get food, which we shared with everyone in the household. My eldest sister appreciated this. The second sister kept saying she wanted to have her own house, and finally she and her husband bought a two-family house. For legal reasons, they used my husband's name as an owner. But the houses were not empty; there were tenants. Those tenants were asked to leave, but they had nowhere to go. Negotiations with them dragged on for months and eventually broke off all together. The situation

was at a stalemate. My sister and her family were unable to move until the situation was resolved.

I was frustrated by the standstill, and I found it intolerable that no one could do anything. I took the initiative to discuss the situation with a friend whose husband had legal training. He suggested that we should go to court. He was very kind and came to our house many times to advise me how to file the documents. There was no question that I should be the one to appear in court. I was the one who did not mind taking actions instead of being complicit. But I was terrified, because I had never been inside a courtroom. I spent days worrying that if I was this nervous, I could not beat my opponent.

The day came and I tried to calm down, but I was trembling all over. To prepare myself before I left home, I went to the toilet, the only place in the house with any privacy, and pleaded with my deceased mother.

"Mother, please help me. Let me win."

Oddly enough, that helped to give me strength and courage. My two sisters looked dead serious as they saw me out the door.

I arrived well before the appointed time. Entering the imposing court, I was overwhelmed but composed. My opponents were a married couple; I was alone. I sat down next to the couple, in front of the mediator. These two people talked incessantly. I refuted their statements, succinctly. They complained about my second sister and her husband (their landlords) and shed tears. They were expert actors. I had been prepared to have a heated discussion, but instead I became increasingly calm.

In the end, the mediator decided in my favor. The couple was ordered to vacate the house by a certain date that gave them some time. My second sister and her family were eventually able to move to that separate house, while we continued to live with my oldest sister and her family. We spent the next half year with no troubles at all.

My mother clearly had a great degree of inner strength. I wonder if she always had those reserves of energy and calm, and if her experiences had activated an innate ability to remain steady under pressure. Or if perhaps the suffering she lived through had given her that gift.

There were more than a few places in my mother's memoir in which she describes her levelheaded plans of action regarding my health as a young child. Looking back on these times, I can see how experiences that we don't even remember can still stay with us. These events can form our character without our knowing it. I think her resolute care of me, when my very survival was at stake, was especially impactful on some level below conscious memory. My mother's skills at coping with fate's surprises were certainly instilled in me.

In the spring of 1948, Kashiyo started elementary school. I turned a silk serge kimono into a dress so that she would have new clothes.

About a month before school started, she came down with pneumonia and a high fever for a week. A doctor came by every day, but her condition did not improve. The doctor said the only hope was a new medication called penicillin, but this medicine was not easy to get. Even if we could get some, it was extremely expensive. One dose cost about 5,000 yen, or as much as about two months of my husband's salary. There was no way we could afford that.

My husband said he would go to Ibaraki and ask for a loan from his parents. I hated to have him do this, but our child's life was at stake, so I agreed. He set out on a day trip and came back with 5,000 yen but told me that he had borrowed the money from his sister instead. That was better than a loan from his parents. Of all the Enokido clan, his sister was the kindest to us. When we had returned from Shinkyo, she was the one who welcomed us. She was the one who gave us warm pumpkin soup and drew a hot bath for the children. I was determined that I would take care of her if she ever got sick or needed help in her old age.

I was relieved to have the 5,000 yen, but miraculously, Kashiyo's fever subsided all on its own. There was no need for an injection, after all. But this situation got me thinking. When one of our children was ill, or when our children had to study, we had no control over our living environment. Staying where we were was not ideal. We decided to move into one of the two units my second sister had bought, but she wanted to set the price at four times what she had paid. My oldest sister got very upset, because the second sister set the price so high, and she made no secret of it.

To make things worse, the available unit in the two-unit house was not empty. There were tenants in it, Mr. and Mrs. Yamada, who were good people. Mr. Yamada had the air of an educated person, and he worked for the city government. Mrs. Yamada, who was about my age, sometimes came to me to learn sewing, and I considered her a friend. Kashiyo would visit with them. They did not have children, so Mrs. Yamada treated Kashiyo like her own darling child.

Under these circumstances, it was difficult to ask them to leave the house.

I thought for several days about what to do. Finally, I went to visit them to discuss the situation. My second sister, who was the owner of the house, accompanied me. I was prepared for an unfavorable response, but their reaction was even worse than I expected. They flatly refused to move out because there was no other place for them to go. In addition to that, they were furious.

Several months went by, and we made no progress despite numerous discussions. It was a small house with just two bedrooms. Finally, we agreed that we would build an addition in an empty lot beside the house. Our family would live in one bedroom, and the Yamadas would live in the addition. The other small bedroom would be a common space. Happy that the disputes were finally settled, I quickly went to the Ward Office to obtain a building permit, but the permit was not issued. After a month had passed, I spoke with a carpenter who said the permit should ordinarily be granted within a week or ten days. I spent many days waiting, growing ever more anxious.

Mr. and Mrs. Yamada started getting even more impertinent, saying things like, "We won't let you build the addition. If you set one foot on our premises, we will sue you for trespassing."

I decided to visit Mr. Yamauchi, a member of the Diet (National Legislature). He was from the Socialist Party, and the father of a friend of my niece. After I told him the whole story, he said simply, "Leave it to me."

Two or three days later, the application was approved, and I obtained the building permit from the local government office. Mounted on a twelve-inch square piece of wood, the permit filled my heart with emotions. I called our carpenter immediately, and he nailed it to the Yamadas' front door.

I found out from Mr. Yamauchi that Mr. Yamada worked in the construction section of the Ward Office, and he had hidden my application. Mr. Yamauchi went to the Ward Office on my behalf, spoke to the head of the section, and ordered him to sign my application immediately. I was impressed by the great influence a legislator could exercise.

The carpenter started construction. While the addition was being built, Mr. Yamada offered to leave if we paid their moving expenses. He also demanded 3,000 yen. Two or three days later, he increased his demand to 3,500 yen. That was a lot of money. It was unreasonable, but I was exhausted from the prolonged battle and gave in. A few days later, they left.

We were finally able to move in, in July 1948. The foundation for the addition had been laid, but we no longer had any need to build it–and we had run out of money. My oldest sister gave me a kitchen cabinet, an old table, and some dishes. My second sister bought us a big, brand-new ceramic hibachi.

On the first day in our own house, after my husband had gone to work and the children to school, I sat alone in the six-mat tatami room. I just sat still there, savoring the pleasure of having a house of our own. But somehow, I felt I would not want to die in this little house as it was.

I was in the second or third grade when we moved into our own house, and I still remember it very clearly. I seemed to be fixated on us returning to a comfortable standard of living, similar to the condition of our Manchukuo days I had heard so much about. By winning the bitter legal fight with the tenant who had lived in the house we bought, my family had moved to a small house.

I came upon my mother sitting in the empty tatami room in the new place. The afternoon sun was pouring in gently. My mother smiled with great relief and said, "It is nice that we finally get our own house. But I don't want to die here. This should not be my final place."

She was still young, so speaking this way did not frighten me. Our own deaths were a very remote possibility then; we were just speaking in theory. I heard people say, "I want to die on my own *futon* in my own house, not in a hospital." This is an article of faith for a majority of Japanese people. It was natural that my mother would want her life to end that way, particularly after she had witnessed countless miserable deaths in Manchuria. I thought I should die on my own *futon*, on my own tatami floor too. That part was expected. What surprised me during that conversation was not what she had said, but what I understood of my mother's ambition to eventually move to a better house. There were tremendous housing shortages in Japan after the war, and we were lucky to have our own house. However, my mother was not satisfied. I felt very proud of my mother, whose dream was not limited to having a small house. I told myself, "Yes, we will do better!"

CHAPTER 25

THE LONGEST FORTY-EIGHT HOURS

The house was small for five of us, but it was ours. It had two bedrooms, one bathroom, and a tiny garden with a lot of sunshine. But fate did not allow my mother to remain worry-free.

Before I knew it, seven years had passed since our return to Japan from Manchuria. It took that long for us to feel somewhat settled. We did build the addition, and our two-bedroom house was enlarged to three bedrooms. We had furniture and desks for the children to study. It may not have been as perfect as a full sail on favorable winds, but we had created a comfortable little home.

When we left my sister's house in 1948, I did not have even one piece of fabric to repair torn clothing or to use as a dust cloth. Even if our life was plain, we had made great progress, and we were supporting ourselves. Our children were all good students and were growing nicely; this was my greatest joy and made life worth living. There was no question that all three children should go to college. I worked even harder, and our savings grew. My heart filled again with dreams and expectations.

Around this time, it became popular for groups of friends and neighbors to travel around the country together. My second sister took part in trips like that several times a year, but I was content to just look on, suppressing whatever desire I might have to join them. My pleasure at that time came when I accompanied my daughter, who was taking ballet lessons, to various places for her performances and to socialize with the mothers of other students. My two nieces were also part of this ballet school, but my sisters never accompanied them. I was the one who took care of all three. I even designed all their ballet costumes–great fun, as I had to create a design in accordance with the theme and music of their performances.

My mother would stay at the ballet school during my lessons, chatting with other mothers and watching their children dancing, all afternoon on every Saturday. Once a year, we had a performance day, similar to a recital for music students. We gave our performance on a big stage with our family members, friends, and general audience present; we also participated in dancing competitions.

As a participation fee, a student who wanted to be a solo dancer had to pay 3,000 yen; if she danced with another person, the fee was 2,000 yen. And it cost 1,000 yen if the student danced with three or more dancers. It did not matter how well the students danced; it was all about money. I never danced in a group of fewer than three girls. In addition to a participation fee, parents of students were expected to buy the bulk of the tickets for the performances. We usually gave away those tickets to our friends. We also had to pay our own traveling expenses and buy our own dance costumes. Needless to say, taking ballet lessons at that time belonged to a lucky group of children.

One year, I danced with my two cousins; the theme of the dance was "tambourine." Our teacher choreographed only four minutes from Johannes Brahms's "Hungarian Dance No. 5." My mother designed the costumes because she could, and because it was cheaper for her to make than to purchase. Three girls had to dance with tambourines on each hand, jumping up and down, swishing around the stage, and kicking the tambourines with our feet. Our dresses were bright red satin with wide green and yellow ribbons at the skirt. My mother painstakingly sewed small shining spangles all over the dresses, one by one. We also wore chokers around our necks made of the same red satin and glittering spangles. We won third place, and my mother was more excited than the three of us dancers.

She must have thought this was what she could accomplish while her sisters enjoyed group tours. I believe the conceited attitude my aunt noticed in me had been inherited from my mother. She looked down upon those neighborhood women who joined low-budget group tours. Her focus was her children and the family's well-being.

> Isao passed his entrance examinations and entered high school. I was thrilled. But one day, he came home from school before lunch. This was highly unusual; he was on the baseball team, and he usually practiced until late afternoon. Every day, he would come home late with a bright smile and a dirty uniform. That day, though, his eyes looked downcast; fear spread throughout my body.

"They say I have TB, and I have to go to a clinic."

Stunned, I could not believe my ears. It cannot be, I thought. I could not speak. At that time, tuberculosis was considered a death sentence. It was widely believed that few ever recovered from it. I was sure there had been some mistake. Perhaps someone had misinterpreted the X-ray? All the way to the clinic, I prayed. But the clinic confirmed the diagnosis.

That day was the beginning of the fight for our son's life. He followed his doctor's instructions faithfully. He only went out to visit the doctor's office. He was a good listener, and his disciplined attitude was remarkable. He had no symptoms; he seemed no different from a healthy person. It was heartbreaking to see this once active child confined to home at the age of fifteen. Two years passed this way.

Isao took his medication, got numerous X-rays, and visited a Red Cross Hospital where they took special images. The doctors told him he would be back in school by the next semester. We believed them, but still, we kept praying. Isao needed all the help he could get. Whenever we heard of a new treatment that was said to be effective, we did not hesitate to spend the money, no matter the cost. We even purchased powdered snake from a renowned Chinese herbal doctor; it was extremely expensive. But the two-and-a-half-inch shadow in his chest never disappeared.

It was decided that he should have an operation at a national hospital that specialized in TB in June of the following year. Neither my husband nor I knew how to manage our emotions. We felt more dead than alive. At the time, the surgery was considered extremely dangerous. The day before the operation, I took Isao's hands and told him, "Be courageous."

"I will be okay. Don't worry," Isao said calmly to comfort me.

The day arrived. We had to leave Isao at the hospital, but watching the clock, I pictured the scene in the operating room. Splattering blood, the sounds of forceps, camphor injections–I could visualize the scene based on my experience as a nurse. I was in agony worrying about my son. After several hours, assuming the operation was over, we went back to the hospital.

When I stepped into Isao's room with a trembling heart, I was shocked by how pale he was. Still under the influence of anesthesia, he slept on motionlessly, as if in a coma. Red fluid dripped from a thin tube in his arm into a glass bottle beside his bed. A nurse repeatedly took his blood pressure and pulse. Her serious and sincere attitude filled me with great appreciation.

The nurse said that if I called out to Isao, he would answer. She was patting his cheek lightly and calling his name, "Enokido-san, Enokido-san."

He responded with a faint grunt, "*Unn* (yes)."

I touched his cheek carefully and said, "Isao, this is your mother. Do you understand?"

Instantly and firmly, he responded, "Don't worry. Leave it to me!"

His eyes were closed. His voice came from beneath the oxygen mask. He was not fully conscious, but he didn't want me to worry. Tears rolled down my cheeks. I was worried to death about him, while he seemed to be worried about me. Hold on! I shouted to him in my heart, *Ganbatte!* (Don't give up!)

We met the doctor who performed the surgery. He gave us a detailed explanation of everything that had happened and Isao's current state. I asked him if my son would be okay. Would he survive? The doctor said the next forty-eight hours would be critical.

Forty-eight hours. Ahhh, forty-eight hours!

On the way home, we could think of nothing else. When we reached home, my legs were wobbly. My husband held me tight. With each passing hour, I counted how many more were left.

It was the longest forty-eight hours I had ever known.

Six months later, Isao was released in fine shape and seemed ready to return to a normal life. Ordinarily, he would have needed to recuperate for four or five more months, but he did not have that luxury. He had to prepare to reenter school. The public high school he had attended had given him permission to be absent for up to two years. It was now the start of the third year, so Isao would have to retake an entrance examination. He began to study while still convalescing but had less than a month before the examination. I agonized that, having been out of school and sick for three years, he might not be able to compete with the active, healthy students. School entrance exams in Japan were notorious for their severity. We encouraged him to apply to a private high school that was less competitive, as a safety net. We did not know how we would pay the much higher tuition for a private school, but his education was most important.

That same year his younger sister, Kashiyo, would graduate from junior high school. We were sure she would pass the entrance examination, as she was an excellent student. We did not like to think how Isao would feel if he were to fall a year behind his younger sister.

In February, Isao went to his junior high school to take the examination, surrounded by younger students. He passed! Kashiyo also passed. That same year our second son, Takashi, started junior high school. Having two children in high school and one in junior high gave me such a sense of fulfillment. I could not stop smiling. I felt great pride in knowing how bright our children were.

It was customary for parents to visit their children's teachers to show their respect and express appreciation. On the day the results of examinations were announced, I went to the teacher's room at the junior high school to report that Isao had passed, and that he would return to his high school. Many other mothers were there. Some had not received such happy news about their child's examination results and came away from the room in tears, and some mothers cried as they talked to each other. I hesitated to enter the room, as I felt guilty about being so happy myself. Only 40 percent of students passed the entrance examination.

With the joy of our children's success, however, came severe financial hardship for the next four years. After three years of dealing with Isao's health crisis without proper insurance, our savings were gone. To make matters worse, I also had TB. My case was light, and I did not need to be treated in the hospital, but I was not supposed to work.

After long discussions, my husband and I concluded it would be difficult for us to send two children to college at the same time, three years hence. It was painful, but we had to tell Kashiyo that we could not afford to send her to college. Kashiyo understood. She was a girl. There was no question but that boys should be given priority. She sobbed quietly, saying that it was the worst day in her life. Our pain was as acute as hers, possibly more intense. We had determined for a long time that we would send all three children to college, and that plan crumbled. But we harbored no sense of resentment toward Isao. He had done nothing wrong. On the contrary, he was the victim who suffered most.

PART TWO

PREVIOUS PAGE
Isao 27, Kashiyo 24, and Takashi 21, January, 1966.
At the Sankei-en Garden in Yokohama, Japan.

CHAPTER 26

•

MISO SOUP TOGETHER

Even many years later—after I was married, finished graduate school, had children, and realized a successful career—the memory of the day when I was told my family could not afford to send me to college still brought me to tears.

It had been in 1956, when I was fifteen. My mother asked me to come to the living room.

"I have to talk with you."

That was a very unusual request from her. She never tried to make an appointment to talk to us. She just talked. I went to the living room and sat down on our tatami room floor. It was dusk, perfect timing for a gloomy occasion. Following our usual family practice, important messages always came from my mother; my father was not there. I could feel her anguish, and that made me nervous.

"I am sorry, but I must tell you that we will not be able to send you and your brother to college at the same time."

Isao was three years older. According to the Japanese 6-3-3 education system, Isao, who had not attended school for three years due to his diagnosis of tuberculosis, would soon enter high school, and both of us would be eligible for college at the same time. My parents made a natural choice between their son and their daughter; he was also the oldest child.

I had no definite ambitions or ideas about what I would like to do when I grew up, except the firm determination that I should be successful. My school record was good—not because I was smart, but because I worked hard not to disappoint my parents—and to make my grandparents notice. My parents' decision did not necessarily crush my future career path, but it gave me acute pain that I would no longer belong to a perceived "elite class." Even though I was a repatriate from Manchuria—or perhaps because of that—I wanted to be a leader. I had been a good student, active, a ballet student (typically available to the privileged group), and always wore pretty dresses. I was elected to be class president each year. No college for an arrogant girl? The illusions I had nurtured that I would attain something significant with a college education were smashed. We did not know about scholarships or college loans in those days. Japan was still an unsophisticated cash-based society.

Even if she had had knowledge of scholarships or college loans, my mother resolutely refused to ask for any support from anyone. For her, borrowing was a sign of weakness and shame; it was not honorable. Even though we were relatively poor, both my parents clung to the fact that they were from families with good reputations and proud heritages. They did not want to be looked down upon as pitiful repatriates.

While my father had still been in Siberia, Japan began to be dramatically transformed. The American general Douglas MacArthur, who had been pushed out of the Philippines in 1942 by the Japanese forces, arrived at Atsugi airbase on the afternoon of August 30, 1945. Now the supreme commander for the Allied Powers and a five-star general, MacArthur stepped out from his silver plane—named *Bataan* after the

Filipino province from which he'd been forced to retreat—wearing sunglasses, a casual khaki shirt and pants, and a corncob pipe in his mouth. He had no imposing military uniform, no glorious decorations on his chest. Nor did he make a formal entrance in a grand victory parade. He proceeded to drive himself to Yokohama, nearly fourteen miles east of Atsugi. At the Hotel New Grand, where he had stayed five years earlier on his honeymoon, MacArthur was served a steak dinner. It could have contained poison, but he did not show any hesitation, and savored it. His disarming manner earned the respect of the Japanese people, who had been told by their government during the war that Americans were rapists and devils. It was the end of the war and the beginning of peace.

Yokohama, where MacArthur initially set up office before moving to Tokyo to establish his command center, became a "Little America." The Allied Forces seized prominent buildings and elegant houses that had survived American bombings. Soon, many new houses were built for American GIs on confiscated land. These houses, surrounded by wire fences, were simply made, but they looked luxurious in the eyes of impoverished Japanese. The fences clearly separated the occupiers inside the fence from the occupied outside the fence. The wide green lawns and tennis courts around the houses were the focus of envy and resentment by the Japanese. While growing up near "Little America," I watched young American GIs playing tennis in their compound, and I wondered if I would ever be able to play tennis like that. It appeared to be an untenable dream.

The American occupation began on August 28, 1945, and lasted nearly seven years. I was ten years old when the Americans withdrew in 1952. My father's first full-time job after he returned to Japan in 1946 was with the American Service Club, probably because he could speak English. We were still small children, and we did not bother to ask our parents' views toward Americans. There was a sense of uncertainty and trepidation among Japanese people concerning Americans. But because our father was employed by the Americans, we had occasion to go on picnics with his American friends from work. My mother made pretty dresses for me from drapery fabrics that my father brought home from the American Service Club, probably discarded due to renovations. Our lifestyle must have been more Westernized than that of most Japanese citizens. We ate Christmas cakes, and our parents placed presents from Santa Claus at the top of our futon on Christmas Eve night. They did anything to survive and everything to give us pleasure within their limited means, suppressing their personal grudges against the former enemy.

Eventually, Isao started his college education, and Takashi began his high school years. I became a working girl for a large trading company in Marunouchi, a sleek business district next to the lush green Imperial Palace East Garden. Our family's small two-bedroom house had expanded to three bedrooms, and all of us lived in this house until after Isao's graduation from college, when he got a job and moved away.

My father never gambled, and never drank too much. He was a hardworking and faithful husband, but he also had expensive tastes. His watch was high-quality Swiss, and his camera was a German Rolleiflex, which was rare at that time. He even built a tiny darkroom at the back of our house to develop and print his photographs. It seemed to us children that our mother worked harder than our father. She got up early to prepare breakfast, started a wood fire to cook rice, warmed rooms with charcoal, sewed all day long, and stayed up late at night to mend our clothes and socks under dim light after we had gone to bed. I don't know what she did for pleasure, but she was always vibrant, and we took her long hours of toil for granted.

I commuted from my parents' house in Yokohama to my job in Marunouchi. I took a bus to a local train station, changed at Yokohama Station to an express train to Tokyo Station, and then walked to the office. The commute took about two hours each way. But marching from Tokyo Station to my office with crowds of crisply dressed young businesspeople was uplifting.

My job was to clean desks, serve tea, and do chores for male employees. Female employees were expected to resign when they were ready to marry. Therefore, there were few women in their thirties. I was a cheerful, naive young woman without much concern about my future, easily forgetting my disappointment that I could not go to college. I adapted to my new life, joining a group of fun-loving young people. Soon, I fell in love with a handsome engineer from another department. He would take me out for dinner, an extravagance for me. Dining out at restaurants with my parents happened only rarely. During the weekend, the handsome engineer and I would go shopping and attend ballgames, outdoor concerts, and movies. I reported to my mother where we went and what we did. She was pleased to hear my stories.

One night at a chic nightclub after dancing, my date and I sat down at a small white table. I clearly remember that night. I was wearing a new green-and-white dress that my mother had made. The entire room was bathed in blue light. The engineer held my hand and gazed at me. I was embarrassed. Then he asked, "Wouldn't it be nice if we could share miso soup every morning?" Miso soup, for the Japanese, was like a cup of coffee for Americans; every morning, we started the day with miso soup.

"What do you mean?" I asked.

"Well, we could have a life together," he said gently, smiling.

I was not prepared for this. My words came out instantly without thinking, "Oh, no. I am still very young." I was nineteen, and he was twenty-three years old.

I was not ready to receive a marriage proposal from such a fine young man—smart, handsome, tall, tender, intelligent, rich, and popular. It had given me great pleasure to date him, a man who had been sought after by many young women like me. I probably felt that I was winning some kind of prize by monopolizing him; I had beaten out many competitors.

I had never really dated anyone until that time. In high school, dates had been done in groups of boys and girls together. I had gotten several letters from high school boys who wanted to date me, and I shared those letters with my mother. We enjoyed making cynical comments about the contents, their handwriting, and the styles of those letters. My mother and I always concluded that those boys were not qualified to date me. I had been blown away by Rhett Butler of *Gone with the Wind*. This young engineer was nothing like Rhett Butler, but he appeared to be a white knight to me. My mother liked him, too, but had expressed her concern that he might be too good to be true.

After the night that he proposed, the young man stopped calling me. I was devastated. My mother was sympathetic. She felt my pain but said it was okay; I was still too young. I had not seen the world yet. I only shared those happinesses and sorrows with my mother, not with my brothers or my father.

I could no longer stay at the same company where the young engineer worked, because everybody knew I had been dating him. How could I cope with the humiliation that he had dropped me? I consulted my mother and decided to quit the job. I enrolled at the Tokyo YMCA Secretarial School as a full-time student where some classes were taught in English. My classmates were all female. Some had already completed two-year junior college before they came to the secretarial school.

The school was in Kanda, beyond Marunouchi. Kanda was the train station after the Tokyo stop, where several universities were situated. I was happy to be surrounded by college students; I could pretend I was a college student, commuting two hours with a heavy load of books every morning.

A year later, I graduated first in the class of fifty students. I was offered a well-paid job, more than three times higher than I had previously earned. I was young, could speak conversational English, and could take some shorthand. There were not many women with such skills in the early 1960s.

My mother used to say that her life had been better than her mother's, whose entire mission had been to be patient and obey her husband. My mother, at least, had a chance to be educated in Tokyo, and had her own career and an independent life for a short time before she was married. My mother did not seem to think an arranged marriage was a necessity for me. I was considered a progressive and modern daughter. Still, we received several resumes from matchmakers who wished to arrange a marriage when I was in my twenties, a desirable marriageable age. My mother and I shared those proposals and photos, and we had a good laugh, just as when we had shared the "love letters" I received from hopeful high school boyfriends. Again, we did not think these suitors were qualified. What an arrogant pair we were!

I was not ready to be married and settled as a "good wife" yet. Nevertheless, I started following the path to be a desirable *hanayome* (flowery bride) by taking lessons in cooking, sewing, conducting the tea ceremony, making flower arrangements, and studying the etiquette for weddings and funerals. In the 1960s, jobs for most young women were as "office ladies"—typically referred to as "OLs"—who ran errands and served tea to the male employees, as I had done. Being an OL was typically considered a stopgap job until we young women found husbands-to-be. However, all my classmates at the YMCA secretarial school were there to look for better job opportunities. I forgot that I had come to the school to get away from my "miso soup" engineer who had dropped me; I wanted to work.

My first job in 1963 was arranged by the school. The position was at an American pharmaceutical company that was endeavoring to get into the Japanese market. It was similar to today's start-up companies, and I was one of six founding staff members. I found working for an American executive challenging and exciting, and was delighted to earn a good salary. However, my role became increasingly minimized as the company expanded with more capable staff.

I went back to the secretarial school and asked if they could find me another job. They advised me to stay where I was, stating that I would not find a better position. However, I did find another job at a European shipping company with a slightly higher salary through a help wanted ad in the English language newspaper, the *Japan Times*. The job turned out to be a real bore, and I had no respect for my young British boss. The only thing I learned from him was the word "bloody" that he used often.

One day, I saw an ad in a local newspaper that Yokohama City was looking for young women to act as official hostesses for the 1964 Tokyo Olympics. I sent in my application to see what might happen. A few weeks later, I received an invitation to audition for the position, stating "no bathing suit necessary" but recommending that I wear a kimono.

On the appointed day, I asked my mother to help me dress in a kimono, and took a bus to *Yokohama Boeki Kaikan* (Yokohama Export and Import Business Association building).

The place was packed with over a hundred colorful kimono-clad young women. We were instructed to walk from one corner to the other of the room in front of six judges. After returning to the waiting room, half of us were called back before the judges, and we were each engaged in a simple conversation. Finally, after returning to the waiting room again, only a few numbers were called, and about a dozen of us lined up. For this third round, we had a lengthy question-and-answer session in front of the judges.

We all retreated to the waiting room. That afternoon, they announced that I was a winner. I was astonished and could hardly believe it.

I walked back to the bus terminal. Saturday was a workday, with many businesspeople and young OLs arriving at the station plaza from their offices. I looked around the crowds and asked myself in disbelief whether I was really Miss Yokohama. I was filled with joy and pride. I could not call my parents, because we did not have a telephone at home, but smiled at the thought of how they would react when I told them the happy news.

The next day, a local newspaper reported the selection of Miss Yokohama with my photograph. I received telegrams and letters of congratulations. My official functions as Miss Yokohama included wearing a kimono to welcome guests from overseas and presenting them with flowers, attending opening parties for new businesses, and appearing in parades and city celebrations. I was disappointed to be treated like a "pretty doll" without a brain. Every time I attended official functions, my mother had to help me with my kimono. It was a complicated process, and few women could do it without professional help. Witnessing my parents' pleasure upon seeing me appear on the TV news for various occasions gave me some satisfaction, but it was not enough for me.

During my time as Miss Yokohama, I became acquainted with a young man who worked at a recruiting company. I was a bit suspicious of him because recruiting was a completely new profession in Japan in the mid-1960s, but he introduced me to a major Japanese-American joint venture company where I got my third job in two years. With this company, I was quickly promoted to executive secretary to a young American executive vice president. He doubled my salary, and with the increased income, I could move out of my parents' home in Yokohama. I rented a newly constructed two-bedroom apartment in Tokyo where I had one roommate. My commute time shrank from two hours to thirty minutes.

My parents did not express any opinions about my choices. They might have thought I was becoming independent and doing well, or they might have, by that time, given up telling me what I should or should not do. I had a great deal of freedom and became more obsessed with the grand illusion of being a "successful woman." I did not worry about catching a train to go home any longer—I could stay out as late as I pleased. I did not visit my parents regularly, as I likely thought I did not need to rely on them as much anymore.

My boss was demanding, and I made an effort to meet his expectations. Not only did he encourage me to be an efficient worker, but he also instructed me how to graciously accept compliments. I used to dismiss any flattering comment by responding, "Don't be silly. I am nothing." My mother had repeatedly taught me this attitude by saying, "An ear of rice bows its head as it bears more fruit."

I was fortunate to have a job in one of the first US–Japan joint venture companies. I could observe firsthand how top executives of reputable American and leading Japanese companies worked together despite their different corporate cultures. The lives of secretaries for American executives appeared glamorous compared to ordinary female office workers. We all spoke adequate English, wore high-fashion clothes, and enjoyed fine dining. But it did not take long before I once more felt something was missing.

CHAPTER 27

•

GOING TO AMERICA

I enrolled in night classes at the international division of Sophia University in Tokyo to study marketing, which was taught in English, and took classes in French. My purpose was to place myself in an English-speaking environment. Within a year of starting my latest job as executive secretary, my boss hired an assistant for me. My assistant was nearly forty, while I was twenty-three. She had worked on an American military base, was divorced from her American husband, and had a son. We had fun together, but I saw my possible future in her situation. I felt I should not settle for the status quo; I needed more education.

A Japanese man whom I met at Sophia University had just returned with an MBA from Indiana University in Bloomington, Indiana. He suggested that I apply to IU and offered to write a letter of introduction to the vice president, whom he knew well.

I asked my parents if I could go to America to study, but they did not respond immediately. In the 1960s, the United States had become a shining light, especially for young Japanese eyes. It was amazing how we Japanese had turned so quickly from despising our occupiers to becoming their zealous admirers. I suppose we realized we had been misled by our leaders about the nature of Americans. We were tired of fighting, losing lives, starving, and sacrificing, and were eager to have peace and prosperity. Contrary to what we had been told and feared, we saw that Americans were not bad. The transition from militarism to democratization under the American occupation was welcomed. Hollywood movies, television dramas, and Sears catalogs were translated into our language.

The Roppongi area near where I lived was called "*Gaijin* Village" (foreigners' heaven); it was a lively entertainment district buzzing with stylish restaurants and crowded with Americans enjoying a lifestyle that seemed glorious to me. For Americans, life in Japan must have been inexpensive, considering one US dollar was worth 360 yen. To the average Japanese, Americans seemed rich and friendly. We yearned for the American way of life—while still maintaining some grudges against them for having defeated our country.

Going to America posed enormous hurdles for ordinary citizens. It was very expensive. Under the strict foreign exchange restrictions, Japanese students heading to America were allowed to take only $500 after paying tuition and room and board. And Japanese students also had to pass an English examination conducted by the Ministry of Foreign Affairs. Today, anyone can travel and attend school in America, provided they have been accepted. But in the 1960s, studying in America was largely for people who were wealthy, well-connected, or extraordinarily talented—and I was none of those.

By this time, my older brother, Isao, had completed college and started working, moving out of our parents' home to Hiroshima prefecture. My younger brother, Takashi, had been accepted by a prestigious Japanese university. He was living with my parents while earning some spending money tutoring high school students who aspired to pass entrance examinations for prominent colleges. I had already worked for several years and had some savings, but hardly enough to live in America. If I continued working and contributing part of my relatively large income to my parents, they could enjoy a comfortable and relaxed life. But they did not stop me from dreaming of going to America, even though they understood what a financial burden they would have to bear.

Thinking back, I admire how courageous my parents were, both emotionally and financially, to let me take this big step. They were prepared to make extraordinary sacrifices for my selfish desire. My mother might have been thinking that her father had done the same thing for her years earlier when he encouraged her to move to Tokyo for higher education.

I was accepted at Indiana University to pursue a major in office management. After months of preparation, the day of my departure finally arrived. Just going to the airport was a big deal in the 1960s—it was considered a place for those with an elite status.

My parents, brothers, their girlfriends, my friends, and even some cousins came to see me off, some with farewell gifts. I wore a new two-piece suit that my mother had made for the occasion. The rose-colored fabric with black embroidered flowers was soft and wrinkle-free. I wore neither a hat nor gloves, unlike most Japanese women passengers at that time. I was anxious, and determined to bring joy and pride to my parents.

On the packed plane, I sat next to a young Japanese woman who was returning to the US after visiting her family in Japan. She told me about her student life in America. While we chatted cheerfully, the announcement came that we had just crossed the international date line of the Pacific Ocean. It was an exciting moment. I looked at a map, and I felt a strange sensation—I had just left Japan and was about to arrive in America! We landed in Hawaii for refueling;

after two days in Honolulu, I arrived at San Francisco, then headed to Bloomington, Indiana.

Dr. Samuel Braden, a vice president of Indiana University, and his wife, Mrs. Braden, were extremely thoughtful; I was met at the Bloomington Airport by their daughter, Mary Beth, who was two years younger than me. It was 1966, two years after the Tokyo Olympics, and a year after US involvement in South Vietnam escalated.

Because my dormitory was not yet open, Mary Beth took me to her family's home. The house was large, and the bathroom on the second floor had a drinking glass labeled with my name. After lunch, Mrs. Braden showed me a dishwasher—I had never seen or heard of such an appliance. "Now the question is, who should place the dishes into the dishwasher?" Mrs. Braden said. I took it as a joke—I could not believe that simply putting dishes into the dishwasher was a chore to be discussed and agreed upon. In our home in Yokohama, we did not even have a hot water heater in the kitchen. Washing up had to be done by hand using cold water.

The American way of life seemed extremely advanced and luxurious. So, I was startled to learn that Mary Beth's younger brother David, a high school student, was working on the university's campus as a construction worker during the summer, wearing a dirty and sweaty T-shirt. In Japan, it would be unthinkable that the son of the vice president of a large university would be working as a laborer, even temporarily! That week at the Bradens' house was an ideal introduction to the American way of life. I reported to my parents how lucky I was, and they sent a Japanese doll in a glass case to the Braden family to express their deep appreciation.

Mary Beth left for college soon after my arrival, and I did not see her until she came back to Bloomington the following year, when she married Rich West. Mary Beth later told me that after graduation from the University of Michigan, she and two girlfriends went to Boston with the intention of meeting Harvard boys—and Mary Beth met one. After they married, the newlyweds soon left for California to attend Stanford University's law school. I never expected to see her again.

At the end of summer, I moved to a dormitory. Mrs. Braden brought flowers to the door of my small private room. Thus, my exciting college life in America began. I was impressed by everything—big cars, spacious houses, wide-open fields, and friendly people. There were so many "first times"—going to a barbeque party wearing my girlfriend's colorful pants (as a working girl, I had always worn suits with skirts or dresses); shouting for our football team on autumn afternoons with crisp breezes; attending opera at an auditorium; spending hours studying in the library; and dating different boys.

My only communication with my parents was by mail; international phone calls were prohibitively expensive. I used aerograms that cost eleven cents, rather than an airmail letter that cost twenty-five cents. Fifty years later, I discovered that my father had kept all those aerograms from me. When I reread them in Yokohama after his death, those letters made me ashamed because I only wrote about what I did, and how happy I was. I never asked how they were— and yet my father kept my letters all those years. What had I done for him, for his happiness?

When I completed my two-year program, my academic advisor urged me to stay and finish a bachelor's degree, but I knew my family could not afford two more years. So, I left Bloomington in 1968 and went to England to take a summer course at King's College School in Cambridge. I had persuaded my parents—again, brazenly and cunningly—that I needed four more credits to graduate, and that the course in Cambridge would fulfill the graduation requirement. I also argued that this would be my only chance to see Europe.

I was honestly convinced that I would never have another opportunity to cross the great oceans again.

It turned out that King's College School was a coeducational independent preparatory school for children ages four to thirteen. But an entrepreneurial teacher from the school organized a summer school for adults every year, where I met students of various ages from many countries. I became particularly close to a middle-aged couple from Norway who suggested I visit them in Oslo, and a Danish single mother in her late twenties who invited me to stay at her home on my way back to Japan. A French college student asked me to a casual dinner at the Latin Quarter in Paris. We all studied English history and literature, and discussed the Soviet Union's invasion of Czechoslovakia under a tree in the school garden. We traveled and enjoyed a Shakespeare play at Stratford-upon-Avon, played tennis on a poorly maintained grass court, and experienced punting on the River Cam. I was a subject of curiosity for the Europeans, because few had met a young Japanese woman in those days.

My mother had firmly told me that this trip was my last chance to be carefree; once I returned to Japan, I would have to return to "normal mode" and endeavor to do whatever it took to become a good wife and wise mother. And at the time, that was exactly what I wanted to do. After my summer course was completed, I traveled with the guidebook *Europe on 5 Dollars a Day* through France, Italy, Holland, Switzerland, Norway, Denmark, Sweden, Finland, and then on to Russia to see Leningrad and Moscow.

Once in a shaved-ice shop in Yokohama, my mother and I watched a performance of Olga Lepeshinskaya's *Swan Lake* on the shop television. I was in elementary school at the time, but my mother's reaction made an impression on me. She seemed filled with emotion. I simply thought she loved the Bolshoi ballet. But in retrospect, I wonder if she might have been reliving her youthful days when she had attended a ballet performance with a medical student whom she had admired. So, when I arrived in Moscow, I wanted to visit the home of classic ballet for her. As I walked into the theater, I thought, *Mother, I made it! I am at the Bolshoi Theater!* But because the ballet season was over, I had to attend an opera instead; still, I was in the Bolshoi Theater.

I flew Aeroflot from Moscow to Vladivostok, and from there took a Trans-Siberian train to Nakhodka. The Trans-Siberian Railway runs a total 5,867 miles, the longest single rail line in the world. Its construction began in 1891. The forests and large rivers that run through Siberia were obstacles to laying down track, and both the cost and manpower to build the railway had been considerable. The Russians solved the problem of manpower by using prisoners, POWs, and soldiers. Reportedly, it had been built in part by Japanese detainees under excruciating conditions—each wooden cross tie under the steel nails was said to be equal to one Japanese victim that died during the railway's construction. I assumed that the Russians did not use Japanese detainees in the area so close to Japan Sea for fear of escapes; Japanese must have been assigned to the area west of the deepest lake in the world, Lake Baikal. That ancient and massive lake was north of the Mongolian border.

I took a Russian ship from Nakhodka to Yokohama. When I finally arrived at the Port of Yokohama in 1968, all my family members came to welcome me back. My father did not ask anything about my visit to Russia then, or at any time after that. All these years later, I imagine that he did not want to revisit the painful memories of his imprisonment in Siberia.

Looking back on that time of my life, I feel both gratitude and guilt, knowing how much my parents sacrificed to give me such exceptional opportunities. Studying abroad was for children of wealthy families; I cannot imagine how they were able to give me that college education when they had not been able to afford it when I was eighteen years old. I was not thoughtful enough to think about it at the time. I was completely and selfishly immersed in my own happiness.

CHAPTER 28

THE PROBLEM WITH AMERICANS

My mother had two major concerns in sending me to America. Her first concern was for my health. I had nearly died twice from illness—once as an infant in Manchuria with dysentery, and then with pneumonia soon after we arrived in Yokohama. I'd been sick often as a child. As an elementary school student, I was a fast runner, and I was given awards at school athletic events. But afterward, I always got sick. At middle school, I came in seventh of 150 students in a marathon. That weekend, I had a high fever. Years later when I started working at an office, I fainted on a train on my way to work. I remember being taken to the station master's office to lie down for a while. My mother was worried about what she could do if I got sick in America, a distant foreign country.

Mother's second concern was American boys. Many of her friends warned her to make sure I was not going to be caught up with Americans. We had all been conditioned by our leaders during the war, "*Kichiku BeiEi*," meaning that Americans and British were demons and animals. We were taught to despise them but learned during the occupation that they were surprisingly friendly.

A friend of mine said that when he was a child, he saw American GIs tossing chocolates and chewing gum from a slow-moving jeep. Hungry Japanese kids rushed to pick up those goodies, but my friend's pride did not allow him to chase jeeps. One day, however, a GI handed him a chocolate bar. My friend had not chased a jeep, and he had not picked up anything from the ground. It was hard to refuse something that he had been given personally, even though he wanted to. He took the chocolate bar and opened the package when he was alone. The indescribably sweet taste was so pleasurable that it did not leave his mind for a long time. Even if he had wanted to erase that memory, he could not.

The admonition that I should only marry a Japanese man intensified while I was in Bloomington. I was exposed to a group of elite Japanese male students there. Many of these male students were bureaucrats sent by the Japanese government. They were young people from prominent families and future ambassadors, professors, and artists. Typically, only select citizens went to America during the 1960s; I was an exception. I was happy to join that elite group abroad, but they did not always approve of me. They wanted to know why a nice girl like me was there, and told me that I should be in Japan, preparing to be a good wife. These elite young men spoke freely of their distaste for interracial marriages, and their opinions convinced me that I would never be treated with respect in Japanese society if I were married to an American (what was then called an "international marriage"). They even frowned on dating American classmates. Maybe they were jealous because most did not have American girlfriends; some popular Japanese male students were more broadminded and enjoyed dating American girls.

My mother was among those who had been taught to think of Americans and the British as ogres and beasts. She recalled that a cold chill ran down her spine whenever she encountered Russian soldiers on the street in Manchuria. But when

Americans in Japan turned out to be amicable, she felt free from that fear. Her complacency was a mistake; not every American soldier was harmless.

One day, she went to Tokyo and returned after dark. She had to walk down a short, unlit alley to reach her home. She sensed danger, but with no other route available, she hurried through the alley, where she was grabbed by her shoulders. She turned and saw a big American GI. She struggled to escape without making any noise. Her small body was no match, and she almost gave up when his hand appeared close to her face. She bit it, and as he flinched, she jumped and ran away at full speed.

Another time, a very young American GI stood in front of her unzipping his pants and exposing himself. She shed tears of chagrin to think such a youngster was making fun of her. There were multiple occasions when American GIs approached her, suggesting they could have a good time together. She took these experiences personally. Rather than being frightened, she felt humiliation and tasted the bitterness and sorrow of a defeated nation. She assumed those individuals were just bad apples; nevertheless, her distaste for Americans intensified.

She also told me that she was afraid to pass the train ticket barrier. American MPs stood there to check all Japanese passengers. She had a reason to be fearful, because sometimes she was hiding goods from the black market under her clothes.

Under the circumstances, it was ironic that our father's first full-time job after he returned to Japan was with the American occupation forces. Many detainees who returned from Soviet captivity were treated with suspicion by the Japanese on the grounds they might have been brainwashed as communists, and they therefore had more difficulty in finding employment.

Despite the general sense of uncertainty and trepidation toward Americans, my mother gradually accepted the new order, in which her husband's and daughter's employment with Americans benefited our lives. However, as a proud Japanese mother, she wanted her only daughter to marry a respectable Japanese man.

After my return to Japan from living and traveling overseas in 1969, I was hired by Citibank as an executive secretary to the head of Citibank, Japan, replacing his longtime sixty-five-year-old Japanese American secretary from Hawaii. At the time, I was the youngest employee, including among tellers and currency exchange staff. Within a year, an American officer named Tom was transferred to the bank's Tokyo branch from Hong Kong. He was young, attractive, charming, and clever. He had been written up by *Nihon Keizai Shimbun*, the equivalent to the *Wall Street Journal*, as the youngest branch manager of any bank in Japan at the age of thirty-one. The youngest branch manager of a Japanese bank was nearly fifty and worked in Hokkaido, a remote northern island of Japan.

To assign a young American man to a top position in the Tokyo Branch over all experienced senior Japanese officers reflected the American occupation mentality. Most American organizations in Japan were run by Americans—probably because they did not consider Japanese staff to be appropriate at the time. Americans had beaten Japan in the Pacific War with their enormous industrial and economic powers, and must have thought that an American head of organization could teach the Japanese a thing or two. Even a junior officer like Tom was seen as better qualified to represent their home country's benefits than much older and more experienced Japanese officers.

One day, Tom asked me to accompany him to a coffee shop to translate the Japanese menu. A few days later, he asked me out. This time, he handed me an English language newspaper, *The Japan Times*. He had circled an advertisement for a movie and added a note, "Would you like to share my popcorn?"

After I had safely returned home from the US and Europe without an attachment to an American, I had met an American in my own country who demonstrated the sincere wish to get to know me. I thought it was immaterial, because I had somebody in mind for myself—a man from a solid Japanese family whom I had met in America. I knew I had to be careful about Tom. I would be looked down upon if I dated an American in Japan.

Nevertheless, eventually we began dating. I was afraid he would be taken for a GI, so I asked him never to chew gum or express any affection in public. Japanese women who married American GIs, generally known as "war brides," or those who otherwise entertained or had relationships with occupation soldiers, were often subject to contempt by the Japanese. Again, the root of this bias must have been due to the damaged pride of a defeated nation, a tendency that was particularly noticeable throughout the 1950s and '60s while most Japanese were still suffering from the aftereffects of the war. Despite this, some Japanese women strode about town wearing bright red lipstick and high heels, holding the hands of tattooed American soldiers. At the time, the Japanese considered tattoos to be a symbol of the *yakuza*, or gangsters.

Of course, Tom was not a GI but a banker. However, he had three strikes against him. One, he was an American; two, he was married; and three, he had a young child. Nevertheless, our friendship continued to become more serious.

I decided to leave the bank before my relationship with Tom became a scandal. I found a job at Time-Life as a circulation manager in charge of Asia's education market. I thought this move would end our liaison, but it did not. Soon after, Tom told me that he was being transferred to Indonesia. We interpreted that as being his punishment for getting involved with a "native" woman. The FNCB's corporate culture was believed to be intolerant of divorce as well as "international marriages" in those days. I was convinced that his departure from Tokyo would end our relationship, but, again, it did not.

My salary at the time was more than double that of an average Japanese male college graduate. I had been able to give part of my salary to my parents—my contribution to my family's finances after my parents had sacrificed so much to support my student days in America. Still, I decided to become a freelance writer, giving up stability and salary so that I could travel freely. This decision was in large part precipitated by my relationship with Tom, who by then was living in Indonesia and had separated from his wife. Again, my parents did not object or try to stop me.

My debut piece as a freelance writer to one of the most prestigious women's magazines at that time was titled, "My Friends, President Sukarno's Children." The success of this work led to more international travel, including occasional trips to Indonesia where Tom was living.

When my first byline article of eight pages was published, I was happy and relieved that I could provide proof to my parents that my departure from a salaried position was successful. But my mother's concern for me did not stop. I was nearly twenty-eight years old and unmarried.

She told me that a friend of hers saw me while she was visiting, and she had asked my mother, "How old is your daughter?"

"Not young anymore," was her response.

"How old? Twenty-three?"

"No."

"Twenty-five?"

"No."

My mother told me with a bitter smile that her friend then stopped asking. Obviously, her friend must have been thinking of making a match for me, but in Japan, a single woman past the age of twenty-five was called "Christmas cake." Like Christmas cake after December 25, there was no use for a woman after the age of twenty-five! Most of my high school classmates were already married. I was happy with my job and financial independence, but sometimes I did feel uncomfortable to still be single.

Typically, a daughter marries first before her brothers. My older brother, Isao, did not wait for his sister to be married before he was. Then even my younger brother, Takashi, married before me. I wondered if my mother felt that she was losing face. Having a daughter who was not married after a certain age was a curiosity and source of gossip by neighbors and friends. My mother finally pleaded with me by saying, "Just marry once. You may divorce later, but marry once." We used to be an arrogant pair, but we became a desperate duo. Was she concerned about my happiness, or about our family's reputation by having an unmarried—old—daughter? It hurt me to give pain to my mother.

One day I invited Tom to my parents' home for a casual dinner while he was visiting Japan from Jakarta. I did not want it to be a big deal; we ate at the kitchen table. Tom was polite and cheerful. I translated two-way conversations among my parents and me. After dinner, Tom and my father went to the living room while I helped my mother with the dishes. The two men sat on the sofa, placing their hands on their knees. Silence. Then all of a sudden, my father apparently started speaking English. Tom shouted, "Kay, Kay!"

He had not known my father spoke English, and I had not bothered to tell him. My father's English was not fluent, but he knew it well enough to communicate.

After Tom left that night, I knew both my parents liked him. I had not tried to promote him, because I knew my mother's nature. If I spoke highly of him—or anyone— my mother would find a reason to dispute my assessment. Sometime after that dinner, my mother asked me, "Tom is a nice man. How about him?" I responded, "But he is an American!" "That's okay, if he is a good man," was my mother's response. She had fallen for my trick.

Of course, I did not disclose to them the three strikes against Tom either. If I had, I knew it would lead to a terrible clash with my parents, particularly my mother. I wanted to keep peace with her a little longer.

In response to Tom's persistence, I was ready to happily commit to a future with him. Our mutual passion made us feel that nothing could stop us. I felt I had fewer things to lose compared to Tom. His employer, Citibank, seemed to have an unspoken taboo; no American officers could marry local women. Tom's future could be doomed if we were married, but he said he did not care. He even surprised me by saying that he would not mind leaving the bank. That shocked and impressed me. In Japan, lifetime employment was the norm for most men. Here he was, with a potentially bright future at a prominent financial institution—but he would give that up? For me? A girl from Manchuria?

Tom might not have realized that he had also used a *koroshi monku* (literally "a killing expression"), meaning a clincher that ensured I would marry him: He told me that he was willing to be buried in Japan. I had always fixated on the idea that I would be buried in Japan, in a solemn moss-covered gravesite with a proper tombstone. I did not care for the wide-open American cemeteries where I had seen dogs chasing Frisbees.

In a Japanese cemetery, I knew that Buddhist monks and family members would visit my grave on commemorative days, sweeping the ground, polishing the granite tombstone engraved with my name, splashing it with clean water, placing freshly cut flowers, lighting new incense, and kneeling and praying. I was accustomed to the tradition-bound Enokido family gravesite, with its dignified tombstones. And perhaps, deep inside, I had been affected by the atrocious deaths I had heard of or seen in

Manchuria of those who died far from Japan and never had a proper burial.

What more could I expect from a man who wanted to marry me? I wanted to be with him every minute of my life and beyond.

CHAPTER 29

●

SHINTO CEREMONY

Tom and I were married in a Shinto ceremony in Yokohama in 1974, nearly thirty years after the end of the war. Shintoism is a way of life meant to promote harmony and purity. Humans are thought of as being fundamentally good, while evil is caused by evil spirits. Therefore, the purpose of the *shinto* is to keep evil spirits out by prayers and offerings to *kami* (the gods). The Shinto wedding ceremony is called *shinzen kekkon*, meaning "marriage before *kami*." It is a purification ritual, typically attended by immediate family members, *nakodo* (matchmakers), and close friends. Tom flew back to Japan from Indonesia, and he asked his colleague, Bruce Brenn, and Bruce's wife, Cindy, to stand in as his proxy parents because his parents in Maryland were unable to attend for medical reasons.

In Japan, there is no custom of the groom avoiding seeing the bride before the wedding. Therefore, Tom changed into his tuxedo in the same hotel room where two women in white uniforms who did professional fittings laboriously put makeup and several layers of kimono on me.

My face was painted with heavy white makeup, and I wore a traditionally styled wig, ornamented with a set of auspiciously and elaborately designed hair accessories made of tortoise shell, gold, and silver. On top of that, I wore a *tsunokakushi* (horn hiding) headdress, made from a rectangular piece of silk cloth. The purpose of the *tsunokakushi* is to veil the bride's metaphorical horns of jealousy, ego, and selfishness. It took over three hours for me to get ready. When I was dressed, coifed, and made up, we took a limousine to the shrine.

At the shrine, the *kannushi* (Shinto priest) sat to the right of the altar. He was wearing distinctive court-style vestments with a long black *kanmuri* (tall hat). The ceremony began with the sound of *taiko* (Japanese drums). The drums were meant to drive away evil spirits and evoke the *kami*, or the gods. The priest read an incantation to appeal to the gods, followed by an ancient *shinto* dance to sacred music dedicated to the god by *miko* (a shrine maiden). *Miko* was wearing a white kimono, a pair of red *hakama* (divided pleated trousers), and a gold crown.

Tom and I were then offered to drink sake from three wide-mouthed shallow lacquerware ceremonial cups called *sakazuki*, each one larger than the next, and each containing only a few sips. We held the *sakazuki* with two hands, beginning with the smallest, then the medium-sized, and finally to the largest *sakazuki*, taking three sips each time, for a total of nine sips, called *san-san-kudo* (three-three-nine). Then we said our marriage oaths, exchanged rings, and finally were toasted by family members with sake in *sakazuki*.

It was an elaborate ceremony, but it lasted less than an hour. When I look at the photographs of the ceremony today, I am struck that at no time was anyone smiling—not my parents, my brothers, or their wives. After the Shinto ceremony, we were taken by limousine to a reception at the

New Grand Hotel, where General Douglas MacArthur had spent his honeymoon.

Young couples often ask their superiors—officials, prominent businessmen, well-known artists, or politicians—to take on the role of *nakodo* at their wedding reception, and thus boost a young couple's social standing. The *nakodo* represents the bride and groom, and he introduces the newly married couples to families and friends from both sides at the reception. Our *nakodo-san* was Tom's classmate from Columbia University's Business School, Mr. Yuzaburo Mogi. He was a member of the founding family of Kikkoman Corporation, the world's largest soy sauce producer. The company's roots go back to the mid-seventeenth century.

The Enokido family had not been happy about having an American join the clan, but family members from Ibaraki nevertheless came reluctantly to show the family's solidarity. Their presence was more out of a sense of duty than for a celebration. Family members sat in a corner at the front row of the room with their mouths curled downward.

Mr. Mogi made a grand speech about Tom in which he said Tom might be a future Secretary of Treasury in America, in the custom of an effective *nakodo-san*, when some exaggeration is expected and accepted for the occasion. Listening to Mr. Mogi's speech, the lips of the Ibaraki family representatives gradually relaxed and turned to faint smiles. They thought it might not be such a bad idea to accept this *gaijin* (foreigner) as a family member, if the young man had such remarkable prospects. I believe they were also impressed by our perceived close connection with the prominent Mogi family as well as Mr. Mogi's grand speech.

Later, Tom and I went to register our marriage at the Tokyo ward office where a middle-aged Japanese officer met us with a grim expression. He only said one thing to me. "You are not going to change your nationality, are you?" Decades after the war had ended, this man was still motivated by a love of country that bordered on exclusivity. Today, this attitude might be called racism. When we went to the US Embassy to register our marriage afterward, we had a very different reception. Those American Embassy employees, although strangers to us, joyfully congratulated us. I felt that I was going to be welcomed into their society.

However, I had promised the Japanese ward officer that I did not intend to change my nationality. I honestly thought I would forever remain a Japanese citizen. The permanent resident status in the United States that had been granted to me by virtue of our marriage meant I could do nearly anything I wanted, anyway. I could study, work, pay taxes, and even join political campaigns. I just could not vote.

CHAPTER 30

•

A HAPLESS HONEYMOON

When we arrived at the airport in Jakarta, Tom's driver picked us up. As we approached the iron gate of his home, next to the Canadian Ambassador's residence, it was opened by a gatekeeper. Then the glass doors of the marble entrance were opened by the smiling head housekeeper. Inside the huge living room, I was overwhelmed by masses of gorgeous orchids in vases with pink ribbons from his staff and clients, congratulating us on our marriage and welcoming us home.

Upon our arrival, I went to the upstairs bedroom. A caretaker brought me a pot of hot tea, and I sat down at the rattan chair on the balcony, overlooking pink bougainvillea bushes spilling over the fence. I was happily married to the one I loved and had moved into his dazzling residence in Jakarta. There remained one thing I had to do—call my parents and tell them the truth.

My mother quickly picked up the phone. I reported that we arrived at Jakarta, and we had been warmly welcomed by Tom's staff, clients, and friends. Then, breathing deeply, I confessed with great determination that Tom had been divorced and had a small child. My parents had known Tom was an American, of course, but did not know about these two additional strikes against him. There was a silence, then my mother said I had deceived her. I did not know how to respond to her disappointment. We hung up, and I was determined to prove to my parents that my choice was the right one.

Busy social activities as a wife of the head of the bank followed. It was a blessing to have six live-in caretakers, but I was not completely comfortable being surrounded by people, even if they were wonderful. I did not want the life of a colonist.

Three months after I arrived in Jakarta, Tom's four-year assignment in Indonesia ended. He received the notice of transfer to the New York head office of Citibank, and our earlier welcoming parties soon switched to frequent farewell parties.

Indonesia was still a developing country in the 1970s, and Citibank was the major foreign financial institution in the country's economy. As the head of Citibank in Indonesia, Tom's team had been able to make significant contributions to the country's development. He was busy, lively, and appeared to be highly effective. I was proud to be his wife, and we developed genuine friendships with the Indonesian people around us. He also built an interesting relationship with a Russian diplomat and his wife. When they learned that Tom would be leaving for New York, they and the Bulgarian Embassy offered to make arrangements for us to visit several Eastern European countries as our honeymoon. At the time, it was not possible to visit those countries without special permission.

We left Indonesia in July 1974 with plans to stop in Singapore, Thailand, Taiwan, Hong Kong, and Japan before eventually heading to the Eastern European countries on our itinerary. However, I soon became ill with high fevers, chronic headaches, and a loss of appetite. As we traveled, I visited several doctors in different countries, and it seemed that every doctor gave me a different diagnosis and prescribed different medications. I would be fine for a short time, but my fever and headaches always returned. It became clear that no one knew what was wrong with me. When we arrived at the Japan leg of our trip, we stayed at my parents' home in Yokohama.

Tom called an Indonesian friend who was a medical doctor. He immediately diagnosed me as having paratyphoid, designated as a contagious disease in Japan. An ambulance arrived at my parents' home with its red blinking light and sirens, taking me to a quarantine hospital on the outskirts of Tokyo. Soon after I left for the hospital, Yokohama City's sanitation department was sent to fumigate my parents' house. While I was lying on a hospital bed, Tom jokingly told me that the house was being fumigated because a *gaijin* (foreigner) was staying there.

I was detained at the hospital for nearly two months. I was ordered to have complete bedrest, and the only things I could move were my eyeballs. Paratyphoid was rare in Japan, so I endured a parade of young medical interns wanting to see the telltale pink spots on my chest. Once symptoms of the illness disappeared, I had to swallow a long tube that sucked up liquids from my stomach. Doctors said it was necessary to examine my stomach contents thoroughly to determine that no more bacteria were hiding in my intestines. The procedure was painful, and I had to endure it three times, every ten days. Tom could visit me only twice a week. He had to travel nearly three hours by train to see me for fifteen minutes in the morning and another fifteen minutes in the afternoon, while wearing protective gear.

We had to cancel our Eastern European trip, as I would be spending our entire honeymoon in bed at the hospital. Tom stayed at my parents' home. I worried whether he would get along with my mother, who was not yet totally happy about our marriage. My mother did not speak English, and Tom's Japanese was rudimentary. My father, who did speak English, would not be at home because he went to work every day. But all those obstacles became unimportant because my life was in peril; all three of them focused and were united on that one cause—my life.

When I finally was discharged and returned to my parents' home, I discovered that Tom and my mother had invented a third language, and while they could understand each other, I could not follow their conversations! My illness had managed to melt the hard rock in my mother's heart. She saw Tom's devotion to me and realized what a wonderful husband he would be for me.

CHAPTER 31

LIFE IN NEW YORK, CALIFORNIA, AND WASHINGTON, DC

When I was finally released from the hospital after my bout with paratyphoid, I could not stand. My leg muscles had atrophied after nearly two months of complete bedrest. Doctors assured me that I would be healthy for the rest of my life, that I had been given a rare opportunity to have my body totally rested and cleansed.

Tom and I moved to Manhattan in 1974 from Indonesia and found a newly built apartment building five blocks from his bank office. As soon as we had settled, I decided to go back to school to complete the bachelor's degree my family could not afford in 1968, and I was accepted by New York University. I was thirty-three years old and felt closer in age to the young professors than my fellow classmates.

In April 1975, Saigon, the capital of South Vietnam, was teetering on total collapse. Mr. Walter Wriston, chairman of Citibank, instructed the Asia Pacific Group to order all American expatriates to evacuate to Hong Kong after first burning the bank's important files. Tom, as part of the Asia Pacific Group, was involved in this operation from the New York head office. The bank chartered a Pan Am jet and flew the American staff out of Saigon to Hong Kong, leaving the bank's thirty-four Vietnamese employees in a dangerous situation during the communist takeover. Tom's group chartered a ship from the Philippines, as well as another flight, to remove Vietnamese staff from the country—but those efforts were unsuccessful. John Riordan, an assistant manager of Citibank's Saigon branch, flew back to Saigon from Hong Kong, defying the objections of his superiors and against the official policy of the United States. He was prepared to risk being fired from the bank.

Amid the extreme chaos in Saigon, John met a CIA officer who told him that the only way that John could remove any Vietnamese from Saigon was to adopt them. So he proceeded to do the paperwork individually to adopt employees, their spouses, parents, siblings, and relatives. He made fifteen harrowing trips to Saigon's airport, maneuvering through the bureaucratic shambles, claiming that the Vietnamese were his wife and scores of children. John was single, and some of those purported children were much older than him. Nevertheless, he succeeded in removing 106 Vietnamese from Saigon, via Guam, to the Philippines, and then to Camp Pendleton in California.

Citibank resettled all the Vietnamese employees at great expense, giving them and many of their spouses jobs. Later, when I visited Citibank's head office at Park Avenue, I was greeted by a security guard who had been a high-ranking Vietnamese military officer. John was not fired; instead, he was awarded the highest honor by Citibank for his heroic conduct. He still hears from many of his adopted "family" members who call him "Papa," and our friendship with John continues today.

I finished my studies at NYU after two years and received a BA in journalism and East Asian studies. Reading my mother's writings about our life in Manchuria had stimulated my curiosity about Asia, and I wished I could continue my studies. Contrary to our expectations, Tom had not been transferred back overseas, so we bought an apartment on the Upper East Side, and I took the opportunity to further my education. My NYU professor recommended that I apply to the School of International Affairs Program at Columbia University (now School of International and Public Affairs). I was pregnant when I started, and my advisor encouraged me to continue, because she had attended university while pregnant.

I had a baby girl and was fortunate to know our apartment building superintendent's wife. He was a no-nonsense Hungarian, and she a sweet Paraguayan woman with a bright smile. They had a one-year-old daughter and agreed to take care of our newborn baby. They lived on the ground floor of our building. On days I had to go to classes, I dropped my daughter at the super's apartment, and I picked her up when I returned.

Life in New York was good for me. We had complete privacy, unlike in Jakarta with our six live-in caretakers. They had all been good people, but managing them was work—their relatives got sick, they sometimes had emergencies, and they complained about their working relationships with each other. By contrast, our New York apartment had a washing machine that worked with just the push of a button, a vacuum cleaner that was easy to operate, and the absence of a staff I had to keep happy. I was not a good cook, but I could manage most of our daily meals. I even prepared a dinner party for thirty. However, I had to call my mother to ask how to make *osechi ryori*, a traditional Japanese New Year's meal packed in multitiered red-and-black lacquer boxes. Eventually I learned that anyone could cook if one could read cookbooks.

In 1978, a little over one year after we had our daughter, Tom was recruited to Crocker National Bank in San Francisco. I still had one more semester to finish my graduate work, so I stayed in New York with our baby while Tom left for San Francisco. We agreed that Tom would return to Manhattan every two weeks to spend time with us, but while he was skiing at Lake Tahoe, he badly injured his knee and could not easily travel. I struggled to complete my classwork while caring for our baby and trying to sell our apartment. I was pregnant again by graduation. Tom returned to attend the graduation ceremony and helped pack up for our move to San Francisco where he was renting an apartment.

While Tom went to the office, a real estate broker showed me houses in San Francisco, Sausalito, Tiburon, and Mill Valley. Eventually we saw a contemporary-looking house with wide windows and gray and black stones in Mill Valley. The garage was draped with wisteria vines covered with purple flowers. A gracefully twisted pine stood in front of the house, an image that figures into Japanese kabuki stage sets. I fell instantly in love with the house.

I knew nothing about Mill Valley. Soon after we moved there in 1978, NBC television aired a documentary special, *I Want It All Now!* The program portrayed the hedonistic and narcissistic lifestyle of Marin County's affluent population, with more hot tubs, more therapists, more divorces, more foreign cars, and more alcoholism than in other California communities. We had entered a world that was on the forefront of what became a trend in much of the larger American society in the late 1970s.

I had decided to relax and enjoy life in California, as I was expecting our second child. I felt I should have that special privilege but had been too busy as a full-time student and a corporate wife. So, I did take advantage once we moved to Mill Valley. Our new house was just behind the local country club equipped with a swimming pool and tennis courts. Tom brought members of his staff to our house for tennis and dinner. Our guests from chilly San Francisco enjoyed the warm, beautiful weather in Marin County as soon as they crossed the Golden Gate Bridge.

Our second child, a son, was born in December. Soon after his birth, while watching a television news documentary, I learned about the hospice movement. In the film, a young woman in her mid-thirties—about my age—said, "Yes, I have cancer, and I know I am going to die soon." It was a shocking statement to my ears. In Japan, people never spoke openly about having cancer. She continued calmly, "I don't want our young children to think that their mommy had gone out to milk the cow and did not come back." I was breathless. Her children were just a little older than ours.

"Hospice is helping us cope with this situation," the woman went on. I was stunned. Then I was annoyed. In America, it seemed, even a misfortune such as terminal illness could be presented as a new venture. Did some enterprising people hope to make money from tragedy? Later I discovered that the Hospice of Marin was the second-oldest hospice opened in 1974 in America, the first being the Connecticut Hospice in Bradford, Connecticut. The Hospice of Marin was less than five miles away from our home, and they were holding meetings to explain the hospice movement a week later.

I drove to the meeting with uncomfortable expectations, but I quickly learned the value of this new concept and signed up to be trained as a volunteer. I was eager to learn more about this new movement, but I also confess that I thought it would be something I could report on; I was still a freelance journalist for Japanese magazines and newspapers that were interested in anything new, surprising, and exciting in the American way of life. The Japanese believed that whatever was happening in America would eventually be copied in Japan. So, I became active in the hospice movement and was the first Japanese person to take intensive training as a hospice volunteer. I was amazed to be treated like anybody else and pleased that I, a foreigner, could assist Americans who needed help.

I relished being more or less a full-time mother of two young children. I followed Dr. Benjamin Spock's book *The Common Sense Book of Baby and Child Care* and enjoyed tracking our children's development. I organized a playgroup with new neighbors and got to know other young mothers.

At the same time, I tried to maintain my working relationship with Japanese editors and a movie producer. I took whatever tasks came my way, whether as a contributing writer, a television reporter, or an assistant to documentary film production. It did not take me many months to recognize that my time was not my time alone any longer. The care of our children took that freedom from me and dominated my life.

Through a friend of Tom's in Germany, we were introduced to a German teenager as a possible au pair. Her English was fluent, and she wanted to experience life in America before going on to college to study psychology. I seized the opportunity, and proceeded to seriously explore how to pursue my goal to be an independent working woman; I did not have a clearly defined goal other than achieving success.

I still wanted to prove to my parents that my marriage to Tom had been the right decision. Further, I was motivated to repudiate my grandparents, who had treated us so shabbily after our arrival to Japan, by demonstrating how well my mother had raised her children. In my mind, being successful was a retaliatory measure. But my grandparents likely did not care that their daughter-in-law had, despite everything, raised three well-educated and respectable citizens. Still, my success felt necessary to make clear to anybody who might question this Japanese secretary's marriage to the bank vice president. For me, achieving the Japanese paragon of *ryosai kenbo* (good wife and wise mother) was not enough.

Our German au pair was smart, active, and creative, and she took wonderful care of our healthy, cheerful, smart, and athletic children. We were all happy; I did not realize then that I would miss invaluable opportunities to understand our children's minds until years later during their teenage years when we encountered unexpected difficulties. I became aware that there was a high price for my hands-off approach.

In 1981, the Crocker National Bank was acquired by a British financial institution. By then, Tom had had enough of being a banker and wanted to do something new. In 1984 we moved to Washington, DC, where he eventually set up his own investment company, CIG International, with support from US and Asian partners.

Once we were settled in DC, our children attended Sidwell Friends, a Quaker school. It was through their school experience that I discovered many differences between Japan and America. When I attended a public school in Yokohama in the 1940s, a classroom typically had more than fifty students. But in American classrooms, parents felt that twenty students were too many for one teacher with an assistant. I also found it strange that in our children's school, young students often addressed their teachers by their first names, and that most elementary school teachers were female. In Japan, there had been more male teachers than female in all grades, from elementary through high school.

It was pleasant to discover that American parents were involved day-to-day in classrooms as volunteers, substitute teachers, traffic guards, or fundraisers. During my days in Yokohama, I had never seen our parents in my school except once a year for "observation day by parents." At Sidwell, I participated in annual fundraising events, volunteered to give Japanese flower arrangement lessons to our children's classes, and read popular Japanese children's books to the students. I even accompanied them to a local Japanese restaurant to demonstrate traditional etiquette while enjoying delicious Japanese food. In all these instances, I was impressed to see the young American children's positive responses and strong curiosity.

During their first year at the Quaker school, I sent my customary Christmas card to Mr. and Mrs. Braden, with whom I had stayed in Bloomington, Indiana, my first week at Indiana University. We had continued to exchange the traditional season's greetings every year since I left Bloomington. Soon after sending our Christmas card to them, I got a reply from Mrs. Braden. She told me that their daughter, Mary Beth, worked for the State Department and was living in Washington, DC. Her husband, Rick West, a Native American, was the founding director of the new Museum of the American Indian, and their son and daughter attended the same school as our children. Both our daughters were taking ballet lessons at the Washington School of Ballet. Our houses were a mere ten-minute drive apart. The hospitality originally extended to me by the Bradens was everlasting; I called Mary Beth my first American friend. It was an extraordinary coincidence that we ended up as neighbors, and our lifelong friendship was renewed.

Through a mother of our children's classmate, I was introduced to a Philippine woman who was looking for a housekeeping job. She eventually became our live-in housekeeper. Our children appeared to have adjusted to life at the Quaker school and enjoyed their school days.

Meanwhile, my experiences with our children's school provided interesting material for my writing. Occasionally, I received requests from Japanese editors to write on specific topics. All Nippon Airways' (ANA) in-flight magazine requested a brief story about the Hay-Adams Hotel. The legendary historic hotel was across from the White House, but few Japanese had ever heard of it; it was not well-known even among Americans. Many people thought that the Italian Renaissance-style building behind thick trees on a narrow driveway was a private club.

The late 1980s was the height of Japan's bubble economy. Japan's theoretical property value surpassed by four times that of all property in the United States, a country nearly twenty-five times larger than Japan, according to the May-June 1990 edition of the *Harvard Business Review*.[15] Golf club membership in Japan could cost in the millions, and memberships were traded as valuable assets. During this period, Japanese companies gobbled up prominent American properties. Those acquisitions sparked concerns among critics that Japanese interests were taking over the entire US economy.[16]

Mr. Satoshi Iue, a Japanese businessman and son of the founder of the Sanyo Electric Company, stayed at the Hay-Adams during his business trip to Washington, DC. In a fortunate coincidence, Mr. Iue had read my article about the hotel in the first-class passenger cabin flying from Japan to Washington, DC. During his short stay at the Hay-Adams, he fell in love with the hotel and decided to buy it instead of the golf club. He told me much later that he wanted to be close to the White House, because he was confident that his friend, Bill Clinton, a young governor then, would eventually be president of the United States of America.

The classic, elegant atmosphere and history of the hotel must have appealed to Mr. Iue. The hotel took its name from two earlier residents: John Hay, private secretary to President Abraham Lincoln, and later ambassador to the United Kingdom and Secretary of State under Presidents William McKinley and Theodore Roosevelt; and Henry Adams, an acclaimed author and descendant of US Presidents John Adams and John Quincy Adams. The Hay and Adams families bought lots at Sixteenth and H Streets in 1884. They hired renowned architect Henry Hobson Richardson, a friend of the Adamses from Harvard, who designed two elaborate Romanesque homes that became Washington's leading salons in the years that followed.

After both John Hay and Henry Adams died, Harry Wardman, a real estate developer, bought the two houses in 1927. He razed both but saved their classic wood paneling and intricate plaster ceilings, and constructed an Italian Renaissance—style apartment-hotel designed by architect Mihran Mesrobian, an Armenian who began his career in Constantinople and served as palace architect to the last Ottoman Sultan.

Mr. Iue's Japanese business associate and Tom's friend, Hidetaka Iijima, contacted Tom at his investment company, CIG International, to see if he could help with the acquisition. The owner of the hotel granted Tom two weeks to complete the transaction, allowing no negotiations on price, and a $2 million nonrefundable deposit. Remarkably, given the large amount of money at stake, the negotiations were quickly and successfully concluded in 1989. Mr. Iue's family became the new owner of this renowned but previously financially unsuccessful hotel.

During the negotiations, I was asked to help as an interpreter. After the sale, Mr. Iue said to Tom, almost nonchalantly, "Thank you very much. You did a great job. Now you take care of the hotel." My role as interpreter led me to join Tom's company as a low-paid, part-time employee. I did not want to give up my freelance writing, but soon I realized that to be effective, I had to work full-time. Tom made sure to convince his client and employees that I was working for his company, and not just because I was his wife. He was very cautious; my salary was lower than market standard despite my experience and education. I had to work harder to prove my worth. The plus side of working together was that we could completely trust each other's integrity, and my working hours could be flexible in case anything came up with our children.

In fact, I was able to take time off when my parents visited us in late autumn of 1989. They arrived with just one small suitcase between them for two weeks—my mother was an outstanding packer due to her experience during our several evacuations in Manchuria. During their visit, we celebrated Thanksgiving and prepared a turkey. Neither of them had ever seen a whole turkey served at a meal. In Japan most meat was cleaned, cut, and sold in small packages measured in grams (one gram is equivalent to 0.002204 pounds).

I was a happy tour guide for my parents. Tom and our children, then ten and twelve years old, accompanied us. We took them to a newly opened Japanese restaurant at Georgetown Harbor. We sat on a tatami floor expecting an authentic Japanese meal—although a *Washington Post* food critic commented that the only authentic thing in that restaurant were the high prices. I had also asked around and found a Spanish restaurant in Dupont Circle where my mother could enjoy a tango performance, her favorite dance.

We took them to Arlington Cemetery. They marveled at how vast and open the cemetery was, and stood in silence before John F. Kennedy's eternal flame. We then headed to the White House. It was a cheerful, sunny day. There was a long line, so we asked for a wheelchair for my mother. She was embarrassed, but we felt she was entitled at nearly eighty years old. A guard kindly let us cut into the line, and we wheeled her around the White House. At the exit, my mother bowed and said "thank you" in a strong Japanese accent and stood up, intentionally stumbling. She was not a bad actress.

Every morning during their visit, my parents would stand on the front porch of our home to bid our children farewell as they left for school. In the afternoon when they returned from school, my mother rushed to hug them while my father stood by smiling. Tom proudly reminded me that he was the one who had "taught" my mother to hug. She had never hugged me. It did not mean she was cold-hearted, but according to Japanese tradition in those days, most parents did not hug their children—or anyone.

During their visit, both my parents took brooms and rakes to clean our front yard. Their home in Yokohama had a very small garden, and my mother kept colorful flowers blooming year around. There were no tall trees, so it was easy to keep the garden immaculate. But in Washington, DC, they could not relax as our front yard became covered with layers of fallen dead leaves. The two of them swept our short, front walk in perfect unison. As soon as they thought they had thoroughly swept away all the leaves, they looked back to see more leaves and acorns as they continued to fall.

My father occasionally went to the bookstore at the nearby American University, where he bought a collection of postcards to send his friends. He was a good correspondent. My parents were with us for only a two-week stay, so we decided to celebrate my mother's December 27 birthday early, prior to their departure. Our children, who enjoyed birthday parties, decorated the family room with colorful streamers and balloons. After dinner, our daughter carried in a cake with candles. My mother's face brightened. It was a simple birthday party for the monumental age of eighty, but my mother said it was the best one she had ever experienced—indeed, she had never had a birthday party before in her life. It was unusual to throw parties in Japan, except for the New Year's Day celebration and *Obon*, when we show respect to the dead.

I vividly recall the day we took my parents to the airport for their return to Japan. Our daughter wore a white cotton sweater with pink flowers and green trim. The Dulles International Airport was not as large as it is today, so we were allowed to climb onto the rooftop to watch the planes take off; we waved as their plane started moving. Our daughter started to cry, and I felt touched to know that despite the infrequency of their visits and the distance between us, an emotional attachment between my parents and their grandchildren had been formed.

I have felt guilty that my parents did not have the pleasure of living closer to our children. When I married Tom, I was hopeful that we would end up living in a large, luxurious residence in Tokyo sometime in the future. Instead, I had to compromise with yearly visits to Japan with our children—but of course those brief visits were never as good as living nearby.

CHAPTER 32

CORNELL

After successful negotiations, Mr. Satoshi Iue became the owner of the Hay-Adams Hotel. Mr. Iue was content with Tom's team and asked them to "take care" of the hotel. During negotiations, I had proven valuable as an interpreter not only with the languages, but also because of my familiarity with both American and Japanese business practices. As an interpreter, I attended meetings, read the financial reports prepared by a CIG senior officer, Jim, and translated them into Japanese for Mr. Iue.

Once a month, Jim and I crossed through the dark, imposing lobby of the Hay-Adams to attend a meeting in a small room at the back of the hotel. It was all very formal; a table covered by a green felt tablecloth was arrayed with shining silver platters heaped with freshly baked pastries while a waiter in a black tuxedo reverentially poured coffee. Everyone on staff was very serious. I was uncomfortable.

Before each meeting, I reviewed the relevant materials and then translated Jim's meeting reports. While trying to absorb what had been discussed and written, I studied the numbers and spotted discrepancies. I asked Jim to explain those discrepancies; he said they were immaterial and told me not to worry. The next month, I would review new financial analyses, and the numbers still did not make sense. When I asked Jim about this again, he said, "Don't worry. They are not important."

Jim was younger than me, but he was more experienced in hotel business, having graduated from Cornell University's hotel school. Still, I could not accept his opinion. Rather than bothering Jim again, I decided to ask questions of the hotel's general manager directly. The Swiss general manager had been recruited from a major luxe international hotel chain. To my surprise, he could not answer my questions either. He suggested that I speak to the hotel's accountant. I was shocked to find out that the accountant was a part-time employee that worked for another hotel client as well. Finally, I consulted Jim's boss, CIG's vice president who held a PhD in economics. He suggested I discuss the situation with *his* boss—the president of CIG, my husband.

So, I went to Tom's office. As I sat facing him across his big desk, I felt as if I had returned to the days when I had been his secretary in Tokyo. I told him that I did not think Jim was doing his job, that he was not paying close enough attention to the details of the financial statements prepared by the hotel's accountant. Tom crossed his hands on the desk, looked straight at me, and said, "Then why don't you take over Jim's job and represent the owner?" Tom's tone was casual despite the fact that he was suggesting a major change by transferring tremendous responsibility to me. Surprised, I simply replied, "Okay." My sense of gratitude welled up. Tom trusted me, and I trusted his judgment. Jim was released from his responsibility for the hotel and returned to concentrate on other CIG investment projects.

I had not been trained in a hotel environment and had no experience as a hotelier. Despite this, I was convinced that I could do the job. After all, I had traveled around the world and experienced luxury hotels as a guest, so I believed I understood what guests wanted. The real advantage to this attitude was that I was ignorant. I did not know what I did not know. But I felt I had found my passion—a desire to achieve some measure of success.

At home in the evenings, I read several books about the hospitality business, hotel operations management, revenue management, and strategies for successful restaurants. I also studied Japanese books on these topics so that I would know the correct translation from English to Japanese for our Japanese owner.

I naively thought that I could capture the essence of an old Japanese *ryokan* (inn) in Kyoto. The famous Tawaraya inn had opened in 1705 and has since been run by the same family. It was described by *Condé Nast* magazine as "the finest in all Japan with excruciatingly understated splendor." It did not take much time before I realized that my life experience was not sufficient to make me an effective manager. I struggled; the proof of my failure was evident from the fact that we had hired multiple general managers, all of whom had fabulous resumes from their work at world-class large luxury chain hotels. I trusted their abilities based on their resumes, but because they were unfamiliar with the management of a small luxury hotel, they wanted to establish a hierarchical organization structure similar to that of a chain hotel. At a Japanese inn—the model I wished to emulate—the head is usually a woman from the ownership family who rolls up her sleeves and works among the employees.

My naive ideas conflicted with the experts' opinions. They told me, "You don't know anything about hotel management."

I could not be dissuaded from my vision for the Hay-Adams. I decided to enroll in an intensive two-week course called the Advanced Management Program at Cornell University's hotel school. I went to snow-covered Ithaca, New York, in 1995. Attendees came from all over the world, including hotel owners, presidents of hotel management companies, hotel investors, and general managers of prominent hotels. Most were older than their professors—I might have been one of the oldest students—but we studied and worked together with the same goals in mind. We became good friends and exchanged our hotel stories. I recounted the resistance I had encountered from our experienced managers at the Hay-Adams. Many of my fellow students encouraged me to pursue what I believed in, and they were willing to help me in any way I needed.

After two intense weeks, we had a graduation ceremony. It was held in one of the classrooms, and we were all wore casual business clothes while the dean was dressed in formal attire with cap and gown. His ceremonial appearance emphasized the fact that we had spent valuable time participating in the program. He made a speech, stating, "You, who have just finished our course, are the most dangerous people. With new knowledge, you will want to change everything immediately. But don't. Wait for two weeks while you digest what you have learned and assess your situation intelligently."

He was right; I wanted to implement changes quickly. Fortunately, I needed to go to Japan for a two-week-long business trip immediately upon my return to Washington, DC. The first thing I did after I returned from that two-week cooling-off period was to fire the general manager who had disagreed with my management philosophy. He had been my fifth general manager in the first five years of my involvement with the hotel. I knew my Cornell colleagues supported me.

CHAPTER 33

NEW BEGINNING

The succession of so many general managers during my first five years with the hotel had been discouraging, and I had started to doubt myself. My credibility was at stake. Then, Hans Bruland came to the Hay-Adams for an interview. Hans wore a perfectly fitted blue suit. My advisor was with me and asked him questions about his professional experience. He responded fluently and had an impressive resume, including working for Japan's ANA hotel in DC's Georgetown.

After the interview, I called a Japanese hotel employee who had worked with Hans and returned to Tokyo after the ANA hotel had been sold. Unlike Hans, who lost his job after the ANA hotel was sold, Japanese hotel employees did not; they were simply transferred to different locations. I asked him about Hans's practical skills and knowledge as a hotelier, his leadership qualities, and his character. He replied, "I can highly recommend." Despite many years of working in American society, I still had the tendency to place higher confidence in a Japanese person's perspective.

We hired Hans Bruland as our new general manager. His passion was infectious; the hotel became lively. Hans did not give orders from the top, but he was on the ground, joking with staff and working in the kitchen. I saw a bright new beginning. He got to know staff members individually, organized regular meetings with division chiefs, established employee incentive programs, and organized Christmas parties for staff with management serving them food and drinks.

Many of our hotel staff were from Latin America and Africa. They enjoyed soccer, and I learned that they participated in local competitions. Games usually were held at eleven o'clock at night at an indoor stadium in suburban Washington, DC. Tom and I decided to attend and cheer on our players. We were surprised that we were the only spectators other than several coworkers.

The next morning at the weekly breakfast meeting with Hans, I reported what we had seen and asked, "Why don't we spend a little money to buy the soccer team simple uniforms?" Eventually, the Hay-Adams team started wearing their uniform at the games. When they returned home, it was usually past two in the morning, and some of them had to be at the hotel by five that morning. Nevertheless, that year the Hay-Adams team won all its games.

One day several employee soccer players marched into my office. They proudly placed the championship trophy on my desk with big smiles and thanked me. I was delighted. At that moment, I felt the true intentions of the hotel ownership had been communicated to them. Since my retirement from the Hay-Adams in 2012, that trophy has been displayed prominently in a bookcase at our home in New Hampshire.

CHAPTER 34

•

GRACIOUSNESS

Under Hans's superb leadership, the hotel's performance was solid and the atmosphere harmonious. Guests returned again and again. Importantly for both guests and employees, the Hay-Adams staff was empowered to extend hospitality and assistance without restrictions. I once learned that a guest had arrived without his special dress shoes for an important meeting. A staff member quickly jumped on an Amtrak train, went to the guest's apartment in Manhattan, and returned with his shoes.

But not everything went smoothly. I might have had a sense of insecurity and even jealousy as Hans started exercising more initiatives without consulting me. We often had a conflict of opinions, which I concede were likely due to personality clashes. Hans was a German man who had years of experience and cultivated many professional friends in the field, while I was a Japanese woman who had studied business in university and did not have deep connections with others in the hotel business. The general manager of the hotel could concentrate on pleasing hotel guests, while I, as the owner's representative, had to focus on pleasing the ownership. Our goals were not necessarily the same. In addition to writing yearly evaluations on Hans's performance, I had to manage his expenditures. Hans did not like to be told to cut extravagant amenities to guests or to be criticized by me about customary practices in the hotel world.

I still do not remember exactly what I did that angered Hans. But one afternoon I got a message from him saying he had had enough and could not continue to work with me. He said he was leaving. I immediately wanted to say, "Oh, please. Go ahead."

When I told Tom about the conflict, he calmly said, "I understand your frustration. But you should know you can be gracious even while you are tough." On reflection, I had almost certainly taken a too firm and inflexible position. I often tried to force an issue if I had an opposing position, because I felt defensive and did not think I was sufficiently imposing. I was petite, and my voice was quiet. It was not easy for me to hotly argue with anybody in English, so I felt I had no choice but to push back hard. My expressions could be blunt. I was not good at the nuances of English despite having spoken it for more than forty years; it was still a foreign language to me.

From that day forward, I changed my business maxim to "deliver tough decisions graciously" as Tom had advised. I also reminded myself that any criticisms of me were not necessarily personal attacks; they were just different business opinions. If I let my insecurity show, I would lose; I had to be more self-assured than anybody. I made an effort to find something positive to say about anyone to whom I had to issue a correction or criticism. It was not as difficult as I had imagined, but there was no denying that I felt somewhat dishonest. However, this method proved to be quite effective, and giving compliments did not cost anything. As I became accustomed to this method, I found that it relieved some of the strains I had experienced with my staff. Needless to say, I mended fences with Hans.

As I grew older, I became aware of how much I have been influenced by my mother, her unique trait of the combination of optimism and stoicism.

I got bad news when I was still struggling to establish my credibility as an owner's representative for the Hay-Adams. I was told that I had breast cancer in May 2000.

Tom was more upset than I was. Our children, then in their early twenties, were distraught and crying. They thought I was going to die.

"Don't worry," I told them. "We should wait until we know more about the situation. Then we can think about how to cope."

I went to a local hospital to have the cancer cells removed, and the surgeon found that the cancerous cells from my left breast had already been removed during the biopsy. She then did a lumpectomy on my right breast. The cancer cells were small and at a very early stage, so I needed no further treatment—neither chemotherapy nor radiation. I was thankful for the radiologist who, during my mammogram, had insisted that I take the mammogram over and over again. I have become an ardent advocate of mammograms and early discovery.

CHAPTER 35

•

CRISIS WITH OUR CHILDREN

While I gained confidence in my work at the Hay-Adams, we encountered unexpected crises with both of our children. It was certainly not our intention to be inattentive parents. We went to parent-teacher meetings and paid attention to what was happening at the school. At one meeting, we heard several parents complaining how difficult their children's homework was and how the academic demands stressed their children. Our children never complained—because they were smarter, I believed. But I was foolishly overconfident and ignorant; I didn't know they did not complain because they were not doing their homework.

I thought I had managed to balance my personal ambitions as a successful businesswoman with being a good Japanese *kyoiku mama*—a Japanese mother passionate about ensuring the education and preparation of her children. I had been determined to send our children to Ivy League schools since they were born. Sending children to prestigious schools was proof of being a "wise mother." To fully achieve the elevated status of *ryosai kenbo* (good wife and wise mother), a woman also had to help her husband climb the corporate ladder, because social status counted too. It was common for Japanese businessmen to live separately from their families when their work took them to distant places to avoid disturbing their children's educations. My brother Takashi left his family in Tokyo when he was assigned to *Asahi Shimbun*'s Sendai bureau in the northern part of Japan.

Amy Chua published a sensational book in 2001 titled *Battle Hymn of the Tiger Mother*, in which she described spending enormous energy, money, and time closely supervising her two daughters' lessons and activities while teaching at Yale Law School. When I compared myself to her, I felt lazy. I asked my housekeeper to take our daughter to her piano lessons and a friend to drive our son to tennis tournaments. I did not take time off while I was working. But Amy Chua did everything herself—even driving nine hours for a half-hour music audition with a famous music teacher. The somewhat relaxed discipline I applied to our children was likely influenced by Tom's opinion that children should also have fun.

I was not a tiger mother, a traditional Japanese education mama, nor a lenient Western mother. Something in between, maybe the worst kind. I gave our children neither strict discipline nor generous compliments. I believed our children were exceptional, and I was not aware of their inner struggles in a changing world. I had been living according to the old world's standards, expecting our children would simply manage to achieve the goals we, their parents, thought desirable. We expected them to enter good colleges, get married, and have a happy family. These were the goals my mother had for me, although it did not work exactly the way she had wanted either.

Asian mothers did not send their children to psychiatrists. In my youth, psychiatrists only served severely ill people. We believed we could and should overcome any difficulties simply with hard work and tenacity. That was how my mother had conquered the unfathomable challenges she faced in Manchuria, and where we acquired our life's lessons.

So, when our daughter started refusing to attend classes in high school, we were baffled. We thought she was a healthy, artistic, athletic, strong-willed, smart girl with many friends; her elementary school teacher had said that she was bright, sensitive, and cheerful. We were puzzled—what had happened to this lovely child who now told us that she could not sleep, or eat, or study, and did not want to attend school?

Rather than trying to determine the root causes of her difficulties, I concentrated my attention on forcing her to go to school. Every morning was a struggle to make her get up, get dressed, get her into the car—without breakfast—and drop her off at the school on my way to the office. She fiercely resisted, but she was always willing to attend softball practices after classes. It was hard to believe she was suffering from major depression when she was written up in the *Sidwell Horizon* school newspaper as being the sparkplug for the team who demonstrated leadership and boosted team morale. Her photo in her softball uniform with a cap appeared under the caption, "Athlete of the Month."

Suppressing my sense of failure, tinged with shame, this Asian mother recognized it was time to become a Western mother, and we sought professional help. A friend whom I consulted told me that she had similar experiences with her daughter, and she introduced me to her daughter's psychiatrist. I learned that teen depression was not a weakness or something that could be overcome with willpower, but I could not help feeling defeated. I interviewed several psychiatrists to determine whether they would be compatible with our daughter. We arranged for her to drive herself to her appointments, and then on to her SAT prep classes—but we later learned she went somewhere else to be with her friends.

When she told me that she did not want to go to college, I was speechless. I remembered how terribly sad I had been when my mother told me that my family could not afford to send me to college. What had gone wrong? Our sweet daughter's transformation into a rebellious and stubborn teenager was intolerable. I could not understand, and I could not do anything. I just hoped that these agonies would go away. She decided to go to a West Coast college that she had never visited. It was her desire to get far away from me, and I was frankly relieved when she was gone.

While we had been fully occupied with our daughter's issues, Tom and I agreed how lucky we were that our son seemed fine. But again, we learned how willfully ignorant we were. During his senior year, I had a call from the tennis coach saying he was going to give our son an F in his physical education class. I was stunned. Our son was the captain of the varsity tennis team—how could he possibly get an F in phys ed? The coach told me our son had skipped practice more than once without any explanation. "He does not deserve to play on our varsity team." I rushed to meet the coach. I begged him not to give our son a failing grade, and said I would make sure he would not skip practices again. That seemed to work for a time.

Dating back to his elementary school years, our son was characterized by his teachers as being intellectually, athletically, and socially gifted. It seemed he could excel at almost anything to which he put his mind. Despite these sunny assurances, we received frequent notices and phone calls from the school concerning our son's problems with focus. In classes, he was distractible and disruptive, often talking and clowning with his friends. He always impressed his teachers at the beginning of the school year, but ended up disappointing them, because he did not live up to his potential. We all—parents, principal, the dean, and the academic counselor—tortured our son, all of us demanding to know *why* he couldn't sit still, stop bothering others, keep up with assignments, or quietly complete his tasks. He replied sadly, "Probably because I am a bad boy." It brings me to tears whenever I recall him saying that and hanging his head.

We eventually found the cause for our son's troubles after meeting in 1996 with Dr. Harold Eist, an expert on ADHD. He described our son as an appealing, intelligent, and alert eighteen-year-old with a good sense of humor. He also declared that our son suffered from classic, lifelong ADHD combined type with hyperarousal. Dr. Eist was startled that everyone had missed this. It was as if we adults had all ganged up on a nearsighted child and accused him of being unable to see without offering him eyeglasses.

I blamed myself for the difficulties my children faced. I could have paid closer attention to our children, rather than leaving them in the care of an au pair and a live-in housekeeper. I might have been too single-minded as I strove to be a successful businesswoman.

When I was young, my mother spent her waking hours sewing other people's clothes to support her three children. We did not have a hot water heater, an electric stove, refrigerator, washing machine, or even a telephone. Everything had to be done by hand to feed us, to keep a roof over our head, and to provide us with opportunities for good educations. She found a ballet school for me when I was a sickly child to increase my strength; she hired a tutor after I moved to a better school so I could catch up with my peers; she even put me in a playgroup when I was too shy. Despite her grueling schedule and long hours running the household, she was attuned to the needs of her children and managed to find solutions despite the lack of money. My mother's balancing act was superb. She probably did not consider that she was balancing her professional and personal lives; did she even have leisurely pleasure? She did what was needed.

Today both of our children are fine adults, happily married, and with healthy children of their own. I still cannot escape my feelings of guilt for not having been a more attentive mother. It is a big comfort that both of our adult children frequently visit us in New Hampshire, and demonstrate that they care about us. We speak intimately and affectionately with our children, far beyond the scope of what Tom and I ever discussed with our own parents.

CHAPTER 36

SEPTEMBER 11, 2001

September 11, 2001, was a lovely day after an uncomfortably hot and humid summer. I was having my weekly breakfast meeting in the Hay-Adams Hotel with Hans Bruland and Tom. The author David McCullough was sitting at a nearby table. He was a frequent hotel guest, and that day he was in the middle of busy book tours to promote *John Adams*, which had been released several months earlier. It was a little before nine in the morning.

Our catering director came to our table and whispered, "An airplane has crashed into the World Trade Center in Lower Manhattan." What a tragedy! We all thought it must have been a pilot error.

A short time later, the catering director returned and hurriedly said, "A second plane has struck the World Trade Center."

We were shocked and discussed what we should do. Then another staff member hastened to our table and said, "The Pentagon has been attacked, and it has gone up in flames." We threw down our napkins and ran up the stairs to the rooftop to see black plumes of smoke rising from the Pentagon and covering the blue sky. We were horrified.

Returning downstairs to the lobby, a crowd of people who had fled the White House had gathered. I saw several familiar faces. As we stepped out of the elevator, we were told that a fourth airplane was heading for Washington, DC, and the Capitol. Hans quickly arranged for a large-screen television in the lobby, and we watched the collapse of the World Trade Center towers.

When I learned that an airplane had deliberately crashed into the World Trade Center, I immediately thought of the WWII Japanese *kamikaze* pilots, and hoped no one would compare this attack with them. As news coverage unfolded, everyone thought that a war was imminent. And I found myself firmly standing on American soil, physically and emotionally. I was suffused with the powerful realization that I *loved* America. I had been advised to get US citizenship, but I kept hesitating. On September 11, I felt like I was an American, and was surprised to find that I was using "we Americans," instead of referring to Americans as "they" or "you." I was boiling with rage and was ready to fight for us, Americans. It was a breakthrough moment for me.

Tom went to the American Red Cross office to donate blood and met with David McCullough on his way there. When they arrived, the Red Cross workers told them that they had enough volunteers for the day. I was prepared to stay at the hotel to do anything helpful; I felt the responsibility of a ship's captain. However, everybody—including Hans, Tom, our daughter who was then working at a law office in Washington, DC, and our son who happened to be in town from New York—urged me to evacuate. They insisted that I go to a friend's home, a presumably safe place, perhaps because I was a woman. But there was no point arguing. It was an extreme emergency. I walked forty minutes to our friend's house, which was filled with many other people who had escaped from their workplaces.

It was a tragic day for America; it was a day our world was united. And it was the day that gave me a breakthrough moment.

CHAPTER 37

RENOVATION

Support and sympathy poured out for America from all over the world after September 11. Terrorists had aimed to stop three powerful institutions: the economic power of Wall Street, military power in the Pentagon, and political power at the Capitol.

After the explosive anger and uncertainty calmed down, I began to think about the future. We had been planning the hotel's total renovation for nearly a year. The scheduled demolition and construction start was set for November. But with this attack, I guessed that real estate development, construction, and banking businesses would all be slowed, if not frozen. We could not forecast the future; was it wise to start this expensive investment during such uncertainty? I was responsible for navigating our ship across the sea of the unknown. I made a phone call to Chairman Iue in Osaka and asked what we should do. I was prepared to hear him instruct us to cancel or postpone.

"Isn't it good timing?" was his surprising response. I understood his felicitous judgment. He had an ability to perceive business possibilities.

He did not ask further questions. I decided that we had no choice but to execute our original plan to gut most interior walls and some ceilings. Mr. Iue was right. In the aftermath of 9/11, little construction work was happening in the area, so it was easier to find construction workers. Materials were readily available, and our employees made no complaints when they were told to take unused leave. We promised that their jobs were secure, and they could all return after renovations were complete, in four months.

We posted a ten-foot-high poster at the driveway entrance to the hotel. It depicted three construction workers wearing helmets, with the inscription, "For the next four months, the Hay-Adams Hotel is fully booked with some very discriminating guests. Reopening in Spring, extensively refurbished, more elegant than ever."

The hotel was closed, but we set up a 24/7 command center. With key management staff in new office space, we reviewed sales and marketing strategies, hired a new executive chef, designed new menus and uniforms, tested new products, reviewed the progress of construction, and continued receiving future reservations while referring regular guests to competing hotels. Every day was a tug-of-war between time, budget, and changing designs; we faced unexpected developments because the original building was old. But I had no doubt that we would succeed, and we did.

In the wake of the terrorist attacks, I began thinking about pursuing American citizenship in earnest. I had never experienced any inconvenience as a permanent resident, but as Tom and I got older, our lives became more complex. Our wills were complicated. We were told that the tax laws could be unfavorable to a widow if she were not a citizen. Increasingly, I was being persuaded by lawyers and accountants to change my citizenship. I also wanted to be able to vote and serve on a jury.

I had participated in the presidential campaign for Bill Bradley in 2000. His daughter and ours had been close friends since elementary school, and we expected Bill to eventually run for the highest office in the land. When he finally declared his candidacy, I volunteered to be a fundraiser. I could give my money and unhesitatingly ask anyone I met to donate as well. I had a strong conviction that Bill would be an excellent leader. But because I was not a citizen, I could not vote for him.

I finally applied for US citizenship in 2005. I thought approval would take a long time, but it was given rather quickly for a variety of reasons: I had been married to an American citizen for more than thirty years, during which time I had been living, working, and paying taxes in the US; I was also a mother of two American-born children; I had kept meticulous records of all my travels outside the US; and we had an effective lawyer.

The naturalization ceremony in Fairfax, Virginia, was emotional. There were people from many different countries, many wearing their national costumes, and we were shown a videotaped message from President George W. Bush. His speech, combined with the national anthem, stirred my sense of patriotic sentiment.

Hans threw a surprise party at the Hay-Adams with staff members after the ceremony. I found he had decorated my office with red and blue balloons and streamers and had gotten a cake. A few days later, Mary Beth and Rick West gave me a painting of a Native American draping an American flag over his shoulder. Our children sent handmade cards of celebration. Our daughter's card had Japanese and American flags on the cover. Inside, she wrote: "*Omedetou, gaijin* (Congratulations, foreigner)! Congratulations, Mama. Now you can enjoy the right to vote, convene, demonstrate, carry a US passport, and bring your close family members over to this country, the Republic of the United States. But don't forget your roots! Love you!!" Our son's card was simpler, but he created an origami-like cover. Inside, he had written, "Happy birthday, Mom!!! You have done the Japanese people proud!!! I love you and will go to Japan with you as my gift to you. Love!" He added his name in Japanese *kanji* (Chinese characters).

    I had finally broken the promise I had made to the clerk at Tokyo's Ward Office when Tom and I had registered our marriage in 1974. The times had changed, and it was the right thing to do. Besides, he was probably retired by then.

CHAPTER 38

•

BEYOND MY WILDEST DREAMS

I n 1983, when we moved to Washington, DC, it was a small, sedate village with few commercial enterprises. People in neighboring Virginia and Maryland considered the city a dangerous place to visit; it was called the "murder capital" of the United States. But during our thirty years in DC, the city dramatically transformed into a vibrant place filled with fashionable shops and restaurants. When President Obama's family arrived in January 2009, they lifted the city's image from drab to swinging, young, dazzling, and cosmopolitan.

Prior to moving to the White House, the Obama family stayed at the Hay-Adams. Traditionally, every president-elect stayed at the Blair House, the nation's guest house, for a few days prior to the January 20 inauguration. The Obama family had to come to Washington, DC, earlier because their two daughters were going to attend the Sidwell Friends School, and the school term started January 2. But the Blair House could not accommodate them that early because the Australian Prime Minister, Mr. John Howard, had a conflicting booking. So instead, the Obamas chose to stay at the Hay-Adams for those weeks. President Clinton's family had also stayed at the Hay-Adams instead of Blair House before they moved to the White House.

The excitement and tight security surrounding President Obama's arrival was exceptional. When I came to my office, I had to stop at a security checkpoint to show my ID and open my purse. I got to know the officers, and we smiled and made small talk, but they still insisted that I go through the official procedure.

As I look back over my career at the Hay-Adams, I am grateful for my good fortune. I had the opportunity to work there because of Tom, but he eventually stepped aside and I had become independent. I managed two major renovations and established an unrivaled and uncommon brand. As our tag line promised, "Where Nothing Is Overlooked but the White House," every detail had to be perfect. Fodor's Expert Review claimed, "The Hay-Adams remains a timeless destination, full of history, of opulence, and gracious hospitality, yet completely modern, and exceedingly down-to-earth."

I was fortunate to be part of shaping the Hay-Adams into a sound and successful business, and it received many awards over the years. In 2006, the hotel was sold at a price higher than the Iue family had expected—though not to the highest bidder. They chose B. F. Saul Company, a respected American enterprise owned and guided by the Saul family. The decision reflected the Iue's conviction that a "family-to-family" transfer would best protect the hotel's essence and legacy. When the new owners asked me to stay on as "part of the package," I was flattered, and more than happy to remain. I loved my work and found joy in seeing the hotel grow in elegance and distinction. I also wanted to ensure minimal staff disruptions, as so often happened in hotel ownership changes. The Hay-Adams continued to flourish with grace, growing increasingly refined while remaining true to its spirit.

I thought I would stay on with the new owners for two or three years, but I ended up working for seven. During that time, we created a magnificent ninth-floor event space, dubbed *Top of the Hay*, with sweeping views of the White House and beyond. It was the second major renovation in which I was involved. I stayed to see the *Top of the Hay* thrive, but eventually I knew I had done my job. It was better to retire before people started to ask, *"Is that old lady still there?"*

Still, it was not easy to leave a place I had been passionate about for twenty-three years. As I looked around at that uniquely elegant hotel, I was filled with gratitude. My career there had surpassed anything I had ever imagined. Even my progressive, education-minded Japanese parents could hardly have envisioned their daughter finding such a path in Washington, DC. More than anything, I had wanted them to be proud of me.

PART THREE

PREVIOUS PAGE
Tom and Kay, August 23, 2023. Sunset above the Connecticut River under a venerable oak tree in their son's back yard, Westmoreland, New Hampshire.

CHAPTER 39

•

APOLOGY TO MY FATHER

When my father developed cancer in the late 1990s, my family did not inform him of his condition. In Japan at the time, cancer was considered a terminal illness, and telling a patient his diagnosis was like delivering a death sentence. One anecdote we often heard was of a certain Buddhist priest who had cancer. His disciples thought he should be informed. But when the priest learned his diagnosis, he lost the will to live and died prematurely. If even an enlightened person could be depressed by this knowledge, what would happen to ordinary people? It was judged cruel to tell the truth.

I felt differently, owing to my involvement with the hospice movement. I was an advocate of telling the truth; still, when it came to my own family members, I could not insist. I visited my father in Yokohama. I wanted to tell my mother and brother that they should tell my father about his prognosis so that they could communicate openly. But that would have been easy for me to say. I would return to America, while my family had to remain to care for my father. They had to cope with his condition, so they should choose the best way for them, not me. Even though my father had not specifically been informed, I believe he somehow knew, but acted as if he did not to avoid imposing an extra burden on his family. Open communication was not necessarily a priority. Living harmoniously and not giving trouble to others are considered essential for peaceful life in Japan.

After the cancer spread to his lung and prostate in 1999, my father spent more time in bed at home, using a wheelchair to go to the kitchen to eat. While I was still in Washington, DC, the rest of my family celebrated the New Year of the new millennium in Yokohama. Colorful and elaborate dishes for the Japanese New Year would have been spread on the dining room table at my parents' house, but when I spoke to my mother that evening, she said that my father did not have much appetite. On January 6, my father was sitting on a sofa and said quietly, "Well, it's not going to be much longer."

Three days later, Isao called Takashi and told him to return to Yokohama, but neither of my brothers called me in Washington, DC. Takashi and his wife, Taeko, arrived from Tokyo. When Takashi entered his bedroom, my father said in a weak voice, "*Akushi* (shake my hand)" and stretched his right hand from his bed. It was an unexpected request; the Enokido family had staunchly practiced no physical contact. The last time Takashi had touched his father's hand was when he was a very young child. Father's hand was big and strong then; and now, it was surprisingly small, boney, and had no elasticity. Takashi was afraid any grip would break his father's hand. A thousand feelings were exchanged between the two without saying a word. It was the first and only farewell ceremony, and lasted for several seconds.

On January 16, the family gathered at the kitchen table and had dinner together. My father did not eat; he stopped eating from that day forward and remained bedridden. My mother called to tell me it would be good if I could come home before he stopped breathing. I prepared to leave as soon as possible. On January 20, my brothers told me that my father started snoring loudly. The doctor told my family that he was not suffering. I rushed to the airport. He died the next day, at home, just before I arrived.

My father's body had been wrapped in burial clothes, and proper makeup had been applied to his face. He had been placed in a funeral home. But when I arrived at my parents' home, my mother was sitting alone in the living room of the empty house. She refused to go to the funeral home.

"I don't want to be with those people who are smiling," she said bitterly. "This is not a party."

It offended my mother that relatives who had not seen each other for a long time greeted one another with smiles at such a time, and she refused to join them. She would have preferred to grieve by herself at home, recalling her memories. It was my job to persuade her to attend the memorial service. I was not particularly progressive; I was simply concerned about our family's image as any traditional Japanese person would be. I chose the conventional path, taking my mother to a funeral home where her presence was expected. People coming to express their condolences would think it strange if the widow did not attend the service. Instead of letting my mother sit quietly alone where her husband's life had ended, I brought her to the funeral home to be beside my father's casket.

Later, she told me solemnly, "His last word was *arigato* (thank you)."

She choked as she digested what he had said. For a person who did not overtly demonstrate affection, his thanks to her was a profound expression of deep love. It was the ultimate conclusion of their marriage of sixty-three years.

I wish I could have had a chance to say *arigato* to my father.

It was ironic. I had been such an obedient daughter whose focus had been to please my parents, particularly my mother.

They had sent me to America, making great sacrifices, and I became a woman they had not anticipated.

In 2020, I posted a message on Facebook about my father, having been influenced by an article Maureen Dowd wrote in *The New York Times*. She wrote, "I never told my father I was proud of him." It prompted me to write, "It pierced my heart, as I never told my father the same. He was a good-looking, adventurous, romantic, and intelligent young man. But when he returned to Japan from Siberia in 1947, skin and bones wearing tattered clothes, he was a changed person. I did not ask him any questions, and he did not tell me anything. As I learned more about the history and tortuous conditions of hard labor camps in Siberia, I could not but regret deeply, really deeply, that I was not a more loving daughter." Completely agreeing with Maureen, I said, "So, on this Father's Day, I will say what I should have said a long time ago; I am proud of you."

I got many reactions to my post, most people saying they felt the same, and that I was far from alone. But what could I do now after he was long gone? I resolved I would try to do my part to figure out who my father was.

My sister-in-law, Taeko, offered me some reassurances. I first met her when she was an infant on Huludao Island, and her future husband, my brother Takashi, was two years old. She told me that at a dinner in Tokyo, my father said that he wanted his daughter to play an active role in the international world. Further, Taeko's father, Fujiwara-san, who had been my father's classmate in Ibaraki and was one of my father's few close friends, told Taeko that my father said he was proud of me. For a reserved man to praise his daughter's achievement was uncommon. Imagining how my father felt about my work for the Hay-Adams and in the surrounding area of the nation's capital gave me some comfort. I had given him an opportunity to happily, and uncharacteristically, brag about his daughter. Of course, I could have done much, much more. One thing I could do was to retrace his footprints.

I later made a remarkable discovery about my father's experiences as a soldier during the waning period of World War II. In September 2023, I was visiting my parents' home in Yokohama. By that time, both my parents and my older brother, Isao, were gone. The house was occupied only by Isao's wife, Itsuko. I was looking for old stock certificates that I knew my father had had, and Itsuko was not interested in getting those old certificates converted into cash. She did not need the cash and thought the value of old stocks would not be significant, but I was determined to find out. While searching for those certificates in an old cardboard box of my father's, I found his handwritten notes. They were drafts of letters he had been writing to his friends. My brothers and I had always believed that the only thing our father did during his military service in Manchuria was to dig trenches and cut giant trees in a snow-covered Siberian hard labor camp after Japan's surrender. But the drafts of his letters mentioned that he had held a heavy machine gun in a battlefield near the Russian border.

I translated his drafts and sent them to my brother Takashi in Tokyo. After reading them, he said, "This is our family's treasure." It seemed that my father, whom I had looked down upon, had not been an easygoing person. He was a fighter! I wanted to scream, "I am very sorry!" I felt like a terrible daughter. My remorse at not having shown proper respect and affection to my father swelled.

CHAPTER 40

•

SUICIDE MISSION

My father's handwriting was like stylish calligraphy, and it was not easy to read. I had to use my imagination while translating it into English. Takashi was a former newspaper reporter, so his urge to verify the newly acquired information took him to the National Diet Library in Tokyo. He discovered a book published in 1982, *Dedication to the Spirit of the Departed at the Bank of Amur River*. It included accounts by survivors who were at the battle in Sunwu, where my father had been stationed. The book stated that the 270th regiment had only six hundred soldiers and that they were engaged in digging trenches. But by the time the Soviets began attacking the Japanese on August 9, 1945, the number of soldiers gathered in Manchuria had grown to 3,860. My father's account describes their encounter with the Russians.

> Our base bunker was in a hilly region east of Sunwu where the Amur River is the natural border between the Soviet Union and Manchuria. The area was filled

with a few scrubby high weeds as tall as a man; there were not even distressed shrubs among the weeds. Our duty was to protect the trenches we had dug. The sweat we poured into digging trenches and *takotubo* (octopus pot, or foxholes) would save us from bloodshed when the time comes for fierce battles, we had been told. Then came August 9 and the Soviet invasion.

Their aircraft attacked our camp. Initially we thought those planes were there to help us, but soon they started dropping bombs. The only means we had to defend ourselves were machine guns and type-39 rifles. It was clear that we were doomed to defeat. We nearly crossed the threshold of death countless times.

[Our unit's commanding officers decided that] the mission of our unit was for selected soldiers to carry 3-kilogram bombs into the paths of Soviet tanks, thereby blowing ourselves up. The captain told me, "You are a bright cadet, and your training records were excellent. I therefore select you as one of three honorable soldiers with the special mission to attack the Soviet tanks."

As a reward for my self-sacrifice, I was given Imperial tobacco and a cup of sake. I bid my fellow soldiers farewell and prepared to throw myself at the enemy's tank. I was thirty-two years old. I rushed headlong at the tank that was speeding toward me. I was about to be crushed by the tank when it changed direction and ran toward a different bunker. It had been only ten meters away. Did I regret missing an opportunity to be a hero, or was I relieved? I don't think I had much emotion one way or another.

I reported back to the battalion commander. My action was praised as courageous, but it did not impress me. Just one of those military days.

Two days later, I was ordered to be on sentry at the frontline, only about four meters away, to observe the movement of the enemy. Bombs dropped constantly. The superiority of the Soviet military had been proved at the time of Nomonhan.[17] The Soviet bombs dropped very close to my station. Splinters of shells and showers of sand created a huge hole of approximately three meters, so I had to back up. I had six hand grenades for the purposes of both attacking enemies and killing myself. To be able to use them instantly, the pins had been pulled in advance. It was extremely dangerous; those grenades could explode with the slightest impact. On my way to return to our rear position, I got rid of them. As I approached, my comrades mistook me as an enemy, and a concentration of bullets was aimed at me. I nearly had the opportunity for an honorable death.

The next day, I was assigned to be an ammunition carrier. I was paired with a senior officer who was a marksman. While he was firing frantically, he was shot in the face. His blood spread and covered my body, but I was unharmed. The image of that senior officer shouting "Ah!" and falling dead remained vividly in my memory. He was less than two meters away from me. If the enemy's shot had deviated a bit, my body would have been blown up. I was amazed by my good fortune.

After the invasion by the Soviets, the fierce fighting continued. We were unaware of Japan's surrender on August 15. We were still pushing forward to destroy our enemy and carried on fighting on *Chusetsu* Hill until August 18. That morning, we received our commander's instruction that there was no other choice but to have our unit commit suicide together. We all put our personal matters in order. The last moment arrived–then, in the morning haze, we saw four or five soldiers coming up the hill, waving white flags. We thought our enemies had decided to surrender; instead, we were told that Japan was the one who had surrendered. The war had ended with unconditional surrender. We all cried bitterly. It was humiliating and mortifying; but at the same time, we felt relieved. Our emotions were complex. I could not afford to think about my future. We all heaved a sigh of relief that we were set free from the furious daily fighting.

All of our weapons were gathered together, and we were forced to commence a long and agonizing march under the supervision of the Soviet soldiers. Along the way, we saw Chinese flags with banners that read "Welcome Soviet Union" held by Manchurians. We were not told where we were heading, but we all thought we were going back home.

When my father's 270th regiment had surrendered and started its march toward the trains that would take them to Siberia, Takashi, my younger brother, had been at the brink of death in Andong. Our mother had just made the excruciating decision not to spend her limited funds on Takashi's doctor visits or medications, as he had failed to improve. She was sure she was about to lose her son. She grieved about whether she could ever explain his death to her husband, wondering if he would understand that she had done the best she could.

Yet she didn't even know where my father was, if he was alive, or whether she would ever see him again.

CHAPTER 41

RETURN TO PHANTOM PARADISE

In 2001, I made my first visit to Manchuria as an adult, a birthday gift for my sixtieth birthday from my husband. I had visited China, primarily Beijing and Shanghai, several times for business meetings in the 1980s and 1990s, but I'd never thought of returning to my birthplace. Had I been denying my past? More likely, perhaps, I regarded Manchuria as part of an unreal, imaginary world. When Tom said he would like to take me to Manchuria, I realized I had been foolish to think that the place called Manchuria had disappeared from this earth after 1945. The place certainly still existed; it had been reclaimed by the Chinese. It was a reminder of a terrible period for them; nothing good had been attached to the name "Manchuria" for the Chinese, just as there was nothing good about Hitler in Germany.

During our annual visit to my mother in Yokohama in 2001, after I had lost my father just a year earlier, we casually mentioned over dinner that we were planning to visit Manchuria.

"You are?" My older brother, Isao, reacted instantly. "I want to go with you."

I was surprised. He had had a stroke when he was in his early fifties but had recuperated with disciplined rehabilitation. Though his employer had continued to pay his salary for several months, he eventually retired. My parents had renovated their house to accommodate two families, so Isao and his wife moved into my parents' house in Yokohama. They had no children and led a simple life. Their favorite activity was to take slow local trains to visit remote Japanese villages and towns. Isao hated flying, and he never went anywhere without his wife. Still, he was enthusiastic about the idea of visiting Manchuria with us.

Isao was three years older than me. Might he have a sense of nostalgia for a land he remembered better than I did? And possibly fondly remembered? As a child of seven, he had been an effective right-hand man to my mother in place of our absent father. I wondered if he hadn't suffered enough. Didn't he want to push away memories of our difficult life in Manchuria? I did; I had distanced myself from that place.

I began to pay closer attention. In Isao's living room, I saw bookshelves filled with books about Manchuria. For the first time, I became aware of his intense interest in the place where our early years had unfolded.

"Look at this!" Isao pulled a thick photo album from his bookshelf. "I know exactly where we should go."

He flipped open the album and carefully picked up a piece of paper. The corners of the page were a bit worn. "This is a map of Shinkyo, hand drawn by our father."

The realization hit me. My father, too, must have had fond memories of Manchuria. I always assumed that everyone in my family hated Manchuria. But my father must have drawn his map many years after returning to Japan, dreaming that someday he would revisit this place. Considering the dreadful experiences that we endured there, that neither my father nor elder brother ever spoke about, it was both puzzling and comforting to imagine what had been in my father's mind. Had he longed for that shattered land? Had he wanted to return? My heart ached.

So, in the summer of 2001, Tom, Isao, and I traveled to northeast China. We took a China Southern Airline flight directly from Tokyo to Changchun, known as Shinkyo during the occupation. A direct flight—remarkable. The world had changed dramatically while I had been ignoring the existence of the place where I had been born.

When we arrived at Changchun, we did not see the flocks of bicyclists on wide cosmopolitan streets that we had seen during earlier visits to Beijing. Instead, we saw small, beat-up, red-and-gray taxis everywhere. We easily summoned one, but it had no air-conditioning. Hot and humid wind blew through our hair. Unlike most people in Beijing, our driver spoke no English, and our Chinese was limited.

We eagerly tried to explain where we wanted to go by showing the driver my father's map, and he nodded as if he understood. So, whenever he stopped the cab, we thought we had arrived at our destination. We got out and looked around unfamiliar neighborhoods. The three of us stood on the street, studying our map. A few Chinese men wearing undershirts and black rubber slippers approached us to help. We were soon surrounded by curious crowds of Chinese locals. Somehow, they were all men. They tried to advise us simultaneously, shouting in Chinese. We did not understand their words, but we understood their intention.

One place we definitely wanted to visit was the house where we had lived. I had been told many times by my mother that our house had been situated behind the *Man Ei* (Manchukuo Film Association), a well-known landmark since 1937, and my father's map showed *Man Ei* prominently. As a young girl, I had somehow developed a starry-eyed connection to *Man Ei* and imagined it was a place where gorgeous movie stars worked. I had been told it was in our neighborhood, but I was surprised to see on the map how close it was to our home. "Neighborhood" did not necessarily mean something was within walking distance for a four-year-old child.

The sad-looking *Man Ei* was still there in 2001. It was dilapidated, but a faint remnant of its glory days remained; it looked like an old actress who had seen better days. When the Soviets invaded Manchuria in 1945, they looted the film studio, from the straw *tatami* (mats) and *shoji* (paper screens) to all of the equipment used in movie productions. After that, the Communist Party of China and the Kuomintang fought over the rights to the building. The Communist Party won the dispute and officially took control in 1949, later changing the name of the building to the Changchun Film Studio.

We entered the room where Masahiko Amakasu, the head of *Man Ei*, had committed suicide when the Japanese had surrendered. Amakasu was legendary. He had been known as a sadistic and powerful man who enjoyed torturing and killing people while he had been an active military officer before he was assigned to manage *Man Ei*. On August 15, 1945, after the emperor's radio broadcast stating that Japan would accept the Potsdam Declaration, ending the Pacific War, Amakasu's staff rushed to his office and advised him to leave Shinkyo at once. They were afraid that Amakasu would be arrested, because he had earlier been a general in the Imperial Japanese Army. But he had remained calm, paid out the remaining wages to his employees, written a suicide note in this office, and swallowed cyanide.

We walked into his office as tourists. It felt surreal to be in the room where Amakasu, once a powerful kingmaker and mighty shadow trader of opium, had worked with famous movie actors and actresses. I touched his gray leather sofa. The studio was still used by the Communist Chinese, but the building was in disrepair. Toilets on the premises were of the primitive squat style, smelly and distasteful. My romantic notions of *Man Ei* completely vanished.

We left the site and returned to the busy street in search of our old house. It must have been obvious we were tourists in an unfamiliar place. One middle-aged Chinese man approached us, and we showed him our map. He nodded knowingly and started walking, crossing a wide, busy street. We followed him until he stopped in a residential area. We all paused and waited. He pointed to a five-story brick building, where two bicycles leaned against a faded red wall. A patch of gray stone tiles on the street were being broken up. We thought he said that the building had been used as a hospital.

"This is where you were born," Isao shouted, nearly choking as tears rolled down his cheeks. "This is your hospital, and where our Uncle Kunimitsu died of pneumonia in the middle of the war."

Isao stood in front of the building, a map in his left hand, a black backpack on his back, his feet planted on the ground. He stretched his right arm toward the exposed iron staircases of the building. "I clearly remember our mother rushing down these staircases, telling us that Uncle Kunimitsu had just died. I stood here watching her come down the steps." He could not stop, exclaiming, "Yes, I remember that!" He continued as if the words were pushing their way up from somewhere very deep inside him. "I was watching from here. This is the hospital!"

Isao's emotional outburst was overwhelming. I did not even think to ask why our mother was running down steps to let us know of Kunimitsu's death. Had she wanted us, her children, to know? Where was Uncle Kunimitsu's wife, Mama? Where was my father, his younger brother? Was my mother the only one beside Kunimitsu when he had died?

Tom and I stood a few feet away from Isao. The neighborhood men who had surrounded us watched with interest. Even though we could not communicate with them, I felt they were quietly congratulating us as we identified the place. They bobbed their heads as if saying, "Thank goodness, they found it!"

We were not ourselves and stood there for a while. More than anything else, I was stunned to see my brother's outburst. Like most Japanese adult men, he seldom showed any emotion. I had seen him laugh or get angry, but never cry. I felt that I had been accidentally exposed to my brother's deep-seated sense of attachment to Manchuria. And somehow, I was ashamed of my own absence of emotion. I looked at the building with detachment. Why was I not moved by the sight of the hospital?

I felt dispirited at the sight of the old building. I had imagined that the place where I entered this world would be much nicer. Our life as colonists was supposed to have been luxurious, but that shabby brick building with peeling paint was my birthplace? Perhaps the years of Communist rule had contributed to this neglect. We saw large holes in the ground around the neighborhood, which was being excavated for new construction. Economic advancement was slowly creeping into this area. I figured that the old hospital would soon be replaced by new apartment buildings as China's economy rapidly grew.

We could not find the housing complex where we used to live. It had probably been destroyed to provide space for mid-rise apartment buildings. We gave up our search and took a taxi to another well-known property, Yamato Hotel. The hotel was still there in front of the Changchun train station. This was a luxurious hotel owned and managed by *Mantetsu* (South Manchurian Railway). Isao seemed to remember the hotel well, and he was all smiles as we entered the dark lobby. We visited the zoo where my mother took a photo of Isao and me when we were four and two years old. We stopped at South Changchun Train Station, which my mother had mentioned several times in her notebooks. At each location, Isao's round face brightened as he recollected old memories, but I couldn't recall anything.

Just recently, in 2023, I found a letter Isao had written in Japanese to Tom in 2001, thanking him for the trip to Manchuria. I was moved by his neat but strained handwriting. It had not been easy to write, as he had initially lost the use of his right hand after the stroke. He had passed away in 2019, so this letter was very dear to me and reminded me how emotional he had been at the site of the old Red Cross Hospital in Changchun twenty-one years earlier.

> To Tom
>
> I cannot thank you enough for a wonderful journey you offered me. I am at a loss where to start. Particularly that town of Changchun, that avenue, and that building. It was hot and humid, but that did not matter. The scenes were just spectacular beyond words. I was beside myself with excitement when I saw that hospital building and those outside staircases.
>
> More than fifty years, they had remained the same as I remembered that morning when our mother came out from the staircases right after our Uncle Kunimitsu died. I wish I could see more here and there. The deep emotion will never leave me for the rest of my life.
>
> Our journey was long but looks very short. While I am writing this letter, memories of that town are flooding me, and I will never forget. Of course, the river in Harbin, shopping in Darien, and tasty food

in town were slightly different. I enjoy recalling those memories.

Thank you for the great experience you gave me, and I must add that I am full of gratitude to my sister who accompanied me. With deepest appreciation.
From Isao

I tried hard to recall a few scattered memories and join my brother in his apparent fondness for the place where I was born. There must be something, somewhere that would help me fill in blanks.

CHAPTER 42

MOTHER'S REGRET

My mother had always been strong-willed, but toward the end of her life, she became depressed, particularly after she lost her husband. She missed him terribly, and was lonely. When she was in her nineties, after falling from her bed, she underwent surgeries to relieve pain due to a dislocated hip joint. During those surgeries and the recovery periods, I stayed in Yokohama for an extended period of time. It was my small opportunity to relieve my brother Isao and his wife Itsuko who had been taking care of my mother after they had moved into our parents' house in 1989. They had lived on the second floor with their own kitchen, and Itsuko was a competent caretaker when my parents were sick. In Japan, it has been a custom that an oldest son inherits everything from his parents, but he had to take care of his aging parents. Whenever I visited my parents, I naturally visited them upstairs.

On one of those occasions when Takashi happened to be in Yokohama, I told my brothers I was "losing face" because they had never come to visit me in America. I traveled to Japan frequently, and my parents had visited us in

Washington, DC, but my brothers had not. Because they had never visited me, my American friends assumed I must have had terrible relationships with my siblings. In fact, we had very good relationships, but I was expressing how their non-visits were perceived by my American friends. In America, people do not hesitate to criticize their family members. I was stunned when I first heard an American friend disparage her own mother. I did not remember the details, but in Japanese culture, we hide anything unfavorable about our own family or we keep silent. Our family members were not viewed as separate individuals, but the extension of ourselves. We did not disclose any weaknesses of our family relationships, but rather protected their images. The fact that my brothers had never visited me was easily interpreted by my American friends as my brothers not caring about me. I hesitated to say so to my brothers, because I did not want to hurt their feelings.

But when I finally told them how I felt, my brothers were shocked. Apparently, it never occurred to them that not visiting me in America for those long years could be mistaken as a sign of a bad relationship. I was surprised by their reaction, and it gave me hope.

"Face" is important in Japan; "losing face" and shame are worse than anything. My brothers may have thought that I didn't need their support because I was happily married and satisfied with my life in the US. They probably did not know that in America, overt actions and gestures are important. Japanese tend to be content with the idea that we were tightly connected in our blood, so there was no need to display our affections. Now they knew that Americans saw it differently. They would visit me someday, thereby saving my face, as well as my brothers' faces.

In her old age, my mother told me that it had been a mistake to let me go to America. She had always been logical and proudly progressive. She would say that her children's lives were theirs and that she had no intention to meddle. As long as they were happy, she was happy, even if she had to look on from a long distance. So, it was surprising to hear her say she regretted that she had sent her only daughter to America. In retrospect, what may have been more surprising was the fact that she had not said so much earlier, or more often.

My mother had difficulty admitting her mistakes and regrets. But she had openly admitted her deep regret that she could not be with either of her parents in their last moments, because she had been living outside Japan's mainland. I, too, was unable to be with either of my parents at the end of their lives. The morning of March 30, 2007, I got a call from Yokohama. I was always scared by long-distance phone calls from Japan in those days.

"You should come back," Isao told me.

Bright morning sun was streaming into my bedroom. It was the day of the opening ceremony of the "Japan Wow Program" at the Smithsonian Institution, a monthlong celebration of Japanese history and culture, for which I had been working as the chairperson for over a year. I had already dressed for the opening ceremony.

"How is she?" I asked.

"She has been snoring very loudly."

I could be ready to leave right away. A direct flight to Tokyo left every day around noon from Washington's Dulles Airport. The flight would take twelve hours to get to Tokyo's Narita Airport. Then, after an additional four hours in long lines for customs clearance, collecting luggage, taking a limousine bus, and a taxi, I would arrive at our home in Yokohama.

"You probably won't make it," Isao said plainly. He advised me to finish my work before I took a plane.

To go or not to go; I decided I would attend the opening ceremony. I made a speech thanking the sponsors and those who had worked so hard to make the event a success, and greeted guests before rushing to the airport. I can't say that this was what my mother would have wanted me to do. I believe she would have preferred me to be with her.

I ended up sharing my mother's lifelong regret that she had missed her parents' deaths because she had been outside of Japan.

My mother did not want to be buried in Ibaraki with the other Enokido family members. But she did not want to be separated from her husband either. She had reluctantly agreed to be interred in the graveyard with my father's family. Thus, like it or not, she will forever belong to the Enokido family.

CHAPTER 43

UNABLE TO SAY "ARIGATO"

One Sunday evening in 2016 around nine o'clock, there was a knock at our door in Walpole, New Hampshire. I opened the heavy wooden door—and there were my brothers Isao and Takashi with their wives, all standing smiling under the dim light of the front porch.

I burst out screaming and laughing, as did my brothers. There were neither hugs nor kisses, in keeping with the Enokido family tradition, but we continued laughing, our happiness bubbling over as we shouted for joy. My ordinarily restless and active two- and four-year-old grandchildren, who were visiting for my birthday, were stunned by our astonishingly loud and endless laughs, and they stood still and watched us quietly.

This had been a big surprise gift from Tom when I turned seventy-five. He had secretly invited my two brothers and their wives to my birthday party in New Hampshire, along with seventy-five guests and a classic guitarist. I had lived in America for forty-two years and this was my brothers' first visit to my adopted country.

That night after the party, my brothers and I gathered on the porch in our backyard. It was a quiet night; the cheerful crowds had long gone. The July air was crisp but pleasant as the sun set. We could hear the murmuring of a brook around our house. It had been a long time since I had been alone with my brothers. Both are men of few words, and we are not a family that reminisces with sentimentality. But during this visit, we sat on our porch and talked for hours about our family and our past.

"It would be wonderful if our mother were here with us tonight," I said.

"Yes," Takashi responded, his eyes moist. Isao just tightened his mouth. I could sense they were trying to suppress their emotions. It was remarkable that we could have ended up here together this way—after such a long journey with tremendous hardships.

"What about our father? Do you think he would have liked to live in the countryside like this too?" I asked.

"No!" my brothers declared in unison.

"He loved cities. He loved adventure. He loved activities," Takashi said. My ears perked up with surprise. What else didn't I know about my father? I offered my conflicting opinion.

"I did not think he loved activities," I said. "Any adventurous spirit was long gone after Siberia. He was passive and easygoing. I thought our family was controlled by our mother, and he agreed to almost everything she decided."

"No, he did what he wanted to do," Isao corrected me.

Trying to recall more memories of my father, I said to my brothers, "I don't remember that I was ever scolded by him. He was always such a mild-mannered person." I resisted saying that I thought he was timid.

"Are you kidding?" both of my brothers responded simultaneously.

"He threw a teacup at me when he was mad. I barely escaped by ducking," Takashi said, tilting his head sideways to demonstrate.

"I don't know what I said, but he got very upset with me once," Isao contributed, as if confessing some grave and hidden truth. "I could feel his anger flaring up. I dashed away from the kitchen barefooted, and he chased me outside. He did not even bother to put his *geta* (wooden sandals) on."

After Isao reminded me, I, too, remembered that incident. I had been stunned by witnessing my father's temper. We had been having lunch together, four of us sitting at the round wooden table. I was not paying attention to the conversation. Next thing I saw was that Isao stood up suddenly and dashed out from the *Genkan* (front entrance), and my father immediately ran after Isao. I could visualize the scene in my memory, like watching an old film rolling. All of us became eager to present our own tales and recollections. It was as if we were competing to see which one of us had the more interesting stories to tell. These conversations took place long before 2024, when I had discovered our father's handwritten notes about his military service.

My brothers also stirred my emotions by telling me that it was my father who pushed the idea of sending me to America to study in the 1960s, even if it meant the family had to be absolutely frugal to allow it. The value of the yen then was less than a quarter of its present value, and the family's living standard was very low. I had not known that my father was working behind the scenes for me in that manner. My brothers confessed that they had felt so bad that I, an excellent student, had been told to give up a college education.

Where had I gotten my beliefs about my father from, I wondered, and how could I get a clearer picture of who my father truly was?

When we were growing up, there was the world for adults and the world for children. Children were not involved with the adult world. Whenever our parents had visitors, we greeted them properly, and then we were told to stay away. It is a distinct contrast with our own children who were born and raised in America. They know many of our adult friends, who they are, what they do, and what they say. We also know a lot of our children's friends and their parents. The distinction of two worlds is not as stark as it was with our generation. My mother had not explained many things. If we had asked, she might have said, "Don't worry. We adults will take care of it. It's none of you children's concern." Nowadays I have many questions that I should have asked my parents and gotten answers to. All I can do now is make assumptions about what happened.

I assume my father's old friend from Ibaraki initially invited my father to join his insurance company to sell insurance with a flexible work schedule. It must have been in the mid-1950s. He may have noticed our family's financial difficulty during Isao's prolonged illness. My father could never be a good salesperson. He was rather introverted, and as a member of the proud Enokido family, he couldn't be expected to condescend to beg people. Hearing the exchange between the two men, my mother must have jumped in and said, "I will do it." She became a life insurance salesperson. She was outgoing, and she was prepared to do anything to help the family's financial state. She became a very good salesperson and enjoyed her success. In her notebooks, she wrote about her tuberculosis but made little mention about her work or about my father.

> I had to start recuperating at home with Isao. Fortunately, I had insurance coverage from my employer. However, the coverage would only be activated after I had been employed for six months. Since I appeared completely healthy, I kept working for another month, but not too strenuously, so I would qualify for the insurance. As soon as I had paid for my entire medical treatment, I quit working.

It took only two years for me to recover completely. Fortunately, I had never been seriously ill before, and nobody knew I was then. My thoughtful, supportive, and reliable husband was amazing throughout my recuperating period. We did not have a washing machine, so he did all the washing by hand. I hung the wet clothes to dry on the porch. For the head of the household to be doing domestic chores was not deemed dignified, and doing them where neighbors might see was even considered shameful. Money was tight, but we managed without having to borrow from anyone. My husband was absolutely wonderful. He was considerate, broad-minded, and had no bad habits. He never complained. He and I completely agreed, and we devoted everything we had to daily necessities and to our children's educations for several years.

It seemed that both our parents had been forged by the fire at this point, although their forges had been in different countries. While my mother had struggled to keep herself and three children alive in Manchuria, my father was in Siberia suffering from extreme hunger, cold, and mercilessly cruel treatment. Japanese detainees were whipped like cattle and discarded like dead animals. According to my mother, our father had pneumonia, and he was lucky to have been released from the prison camp instead of thrown into a ditch to die, as many detainees were.

When he was reunited with his family in our aunt's home, our father was utterly worn out. His physical and emotional exhaustion must have been beyond our understanding. He must have been relieved to see his wife and three children were in good health. He also saw how strong his wife had become. She fought to survive; she learned to rise to challenges rather than be defeated by bureaucratic orders or treated unfairly by men. Even after she had returned to Japan, she had to be resourceful and clever to survive.

I had learned a lot about my mother through her writing. My mother's notebooks said that she had no regrets. Meanwhile, I have many regrets—one of the biggest is that I did not try to get to know my father better. It never occurred to me to ask him about his life, his work, or his experience in Siberia. It is extremely painful to admit that I was not a good daughter. My mother said that my father enjoyed giving me a bath when I was a baby. I recall that my husband did that with our baby daughter over forty years ago. I still remember the scenes that I watched and photographed of my husband lifting our baby daughter up and down, splashing warm water as she shrieked with happy laughter. As for my own, I have no memory, and I have no photograph to remind me of my life with him in Manchuria.

CHAPTER 44

•

THE SEARCH FOR MISSING PIECES

I had few ways of knowing what my father endured before he showed up at my aunt's gate in mismatched shoes in 1947. I know he suffered, but he never told us his story. In fact, he did not talk very much at all. This was not unusual for a Japanese man, particularly for men who had gone through traumatic ordeals during the war. I did not know where he served during the war or if he saw action in those final months of the war after he was drafted, until I discovered drafts of his letters in Yokohama in 2023. He was a meticulous man, and he always made drafts before sending any messages to his friends.

Before my discovery of his drafts, I had very little knowledge of what my father had done as a soldier. My understanding was that the older servicemen like my father who were called up at the brink of the surrender were given no training and no weapons. Their draft notices told them to bring heavy kitchen knives and two beer bottles when reporting for duty. Kitchen knives would be used as spearheads by tying them to sticks, and beer bottles would be converted into handmade firebombs. My mother's notebooks did not mention this. Despite the discovery of my father's notes, I still have many questions. How was he released from the labor camp, and how did he manage to return to Japan?

It had not been my place to ask my father questions. I had been brought up to respond when spoken to by adults, but not to initiate a conversation. Besides, I felt that my life was well protected by my mother, and I did not need to bother with issues outside of my control. What I do remember is that he wore a well-tailored white suit that my mother had made for him shortly after his return, while Japan was in ruins, and everybody else was wearing shabby clothes in the late 1940s. I thought he was incredibly handsome.

I sent the translation of my father's notes to Takashi. He was delighted to learn about the missing piece of our father's life. As a former newspaperman, Takashi wanted the proof of authenticity of our father's writing. He had been incentivized to research materials related to World War II after I started writing this book. He had inquired of the Ministry of Health, Labor, and Welfare in Japan whether they had any records for people like our father. After several months, Takashi had received report from the Ministry in 2022. The report included materials provided by the Russian government and copies of information passed from Japan's former army. Russian reports had been translated by the Ministry. Both Takashi and I had been astonished to learn that the Russians had kept such detailed records for Japanese detainees. Our understanding had been that there were no records.

The report from the Ministry clearly stated that our father had enlisted on May 17, 1945, in Infantry 23 Division of Regiment 270 of the Kwantung Army. After Takashi received the translation of our father's draft letters, he went to the National Diet Library in 2024. He uncovered the information that Regiment 270 had been organized on

March 10, 1945, in Sunwu with a combination of Japanese soldiers from Japan, and Japanese men and policemen recruited from Manchuria. The regiment lasted fewer than six months; therefore, there was no mention in any publicly recorded war history. When my father joined the regiment, he was one of six hundred newly recruited soldiers. Later, it was expanded to contain 3,860 Japanese from Manchuria. They engaged in digging trenches near their barrack in Sunwu, and they were moved to *Katori-zan* (*Katori* Hill) on August 9, when the Russians attacked Manchuria. My father's company of 170 soldiers moved to *Nihou-zan* (*Nihou* Hill) down south. They were attacked by the Russian air force during August 12 through 14. Starting on August 16, Russian infantry corps with tanks started attacking, and the Japanese troops had received a deadly blow. The plan to attack Soviets with suicidal soldiers carrying explosives failed. The Soviets pulled out that night, and the surviving Japanese soldiers retreated to *Chusetsu-zan* farther south, prepared to encounter the enemy. However, a cease-fire order and disarmament were conveyed. The war had ended.

My father's notes mentioned that the Japanese soldiers' long, painful march started after they had been captured by the Russians. We knew he had been one of about seven hundred thousand Japanese internees in Russia. It is estimated that as many as half of these internees perished in the brutal conditions in Stalin's labor camps in the late 1940s and early 1950s.

The Japanese who were held in the Soviet Union did not consider themselves prisoners of war. They referred to themselves as internees or detainees, making the distinction because they had not been soldiering when they were captured. Besides, the Japanese military culture despised prisoners. Minister of War Hideki Tojo had instructed troops in 1941, "Do not live in shame as a prisoner." Anyone captured by an enemy was expected to kill themselves rather than stoop to the level of being a prisoner.

After the atomic bombs were dropped on Hiroshima and Nagasaki in 1945, Japan eventually accepted the unconditional surrender according to the Potsdam Declaration. This Declaration states, "Japanese military forces, after being completely disarmed, shall be permitted to return to their homes with the opportunity to lead peaceful and productive lives." But this did not happen to the Japanese in Manchuria. There was a persistent suspicion among Japanese scholars and former detainees in Russia that the Japanese military had secretly offered the captured Japanese in Manchuria to the Soviets during the armistice negotiations in 1945. Proof of this backroom deal was discovered at the Russian Archive in 1993 by Mr. Rokuro Saito, a returnee from Siberia and the chairman for the National Conference for Compensation to Detainees. It was a letter drafted by Colonel Teigo Kusachi, approved by the commander-in-chief of the Kwantung Army, Otozo Yamada, and addressed to Aleksandr Vasilevsky, commander-in-chief of Soviet forces in the Far East.

A summary of Colonel Kusachi's instructions follows:

- Let the injured Japanese (about 30,000) return to Japan. If they are too ill to travel, keep them in Manchuria.
- Keep residents who had made lives in Manchuria (estimated to be 1,350,000) in Manchuria so they can be made to work for the Soviet Army.
- Japanese soldiers and civilians who had lived in Manchuria should cooperate and join Soviet military operations until they are to be sent back to Japan. Until the time of their return to Japan, we ask the Soviets to utilize them.

- Japanese can alternatively work at coal mining, on the Manchurian Railway, or in steel mills.
- Please pay special attention to those Japanese because they are not used to cold weather.[18]

Mr. Saito also discovered another crucial document entitled, "Report on Conditions for Truce by the Kwantung (Japanese) Army." It indicated that defeated Japan could not afford to accept the repatriation of enormous numbers of soldiers and civilians from Manchuria. Therefore, it suggested that those Japanese settle in Manchuria and in the Korean Peninsula under the protection of the Soviets. In essence, these documents show that neither the Japanese government nor military headquarters tried to protect the Japanese in Manchuria. Instead, they offered them as a labor force to the Soviets.

According to World Population Review, approximately twenty-seven million Russian members of the military and civilians died during World War II, the highest estimated casualties of any country in WWII. The country was in ruins. They needed a massive new labor force. Many former Japanese detainees published their memoirs in Japanese. They related that Russian soldiers had told them that Japanese would be sent home, repeating *"domoi, domoi"* in Russian (home, home). Japanese wearing summer clothes were crammed into cargo trains without windows and toilets in September 1945. When the trains paused, the detainees got out to relieve themselves under the watchful eyes of the Soviet soldiers, who did not hesitate to shoot anybody who left the railway track area, on the suspicion that they were trying to escape. Countless numbers of cargo trains transported the enormous numbers of Japanese detainees from Manchuria to the Russian labor camps, and those trains usually paused in the same areas. In order to avoid being shot, detainees had to use the same spots where previous detainees' feces had been dropped. It was difficult to picture my father as one of those soldiers, but I believe he was.

The long cargo trains kept running day and night, loaded with Japanese-made machineries, desks, chairs, clothes, buckets, window glasses, and even tin roofs—all looted in Manchuria. Japanese detainees forced themselves to believe that the trains were heading to the East. When they saw a large stretch of water after several days, they hoped it was the Sea of Japan, but they eventually understood it was Lake Baikal.

Due to the subsequent collapse of the USSR and inadequate recordkeeping, it was believed that there was no precise record regarding this period. It is known that there were more than two thousand concentration camps all over Siberia and Mongolia. Between sixty thousand and ninety thousand Japanese detainees died from various causes: starvation, with daily rations consisting of a piece of black bread and a half cup of porridge; exposure to subzero cold temperatures; grueling hard labor such as coal mining, woodcutting, constructing their own labor camps, and building bridges, ports, ships, and railroads; and illness. Some detainees tried to cover the dead bodies of their compatriots with blankets, but Russians removed them, saying "Dead bodies do not need blankets." The Russians even stripped shabby, dirty clothing from deceased detainees. Naked bodies reduced to mere skeletons were stacked up like logs.

Before I encountered my father's writing and Takashi's discovery at the National Diet Library in 2024, I searched for as many details as I could gather to understand what my father's life had been like in Siberia. On the porch of our house in New Hampshire after my seventy-fifth birthday party in 2016, I pressed my brothers, who had spoken to my father about his life in Siberia, for more information.

"Our father said that cutting giant trees in deep snow was the hardest thing he had to do," Takashi said. This was the first time I learned about anything my father had done in Siberia. Memoirs written by other Japanese detainees confirmed this type of labor. Incidents of detainees being killed by falling trees happened often. Although they knew which way the trees would fall, the starving men often did not have enough strength to move out of the way in deep snow.

In a book published in 1989, Jun Henmi sets the scene this way:

> Morning in Lager (a hard labor concentration camp in Siberia) began with the signal of a hammer hitting a piece of rail. That marked the beginning of the day for hard labor. During summer, the sun rose at three in the morning, and it stayed light until nine at night. During the winter, it was still dark even after nine in the morning, and dusk gathered at four in the afternoon. It was unusual to see blue sky and sunlight in the winter. Snow clouds hung low, and days with gloomy winter skies continued. But the hard labor had to be carried out unless the temperature went lower than forty degrees below zero.
>
> The food was horrible—only 350 grams of black bread a day, and in morning and evening, porridge called "*kasha*," or salty soup with two or three pieces of vegetables and a teaspoon of sugar, enough to only fill half a canteen. Every day was a struggle on an empty stomach.
>
> When the black bread was distributed to Japanese detainees, everybody's eyes were focused on the hand that cut the bread. One loaf of bread had to be divided among seven or eight people. All pieces had to be exactly the same size. No one ever overlooked the slightest difference in thickness of each piece.
>
> The black bread was intended as breakfast and lunch to take to the workplace, but at the beginning

of this ordeal, many people ate the bread in the morning, and they suffered from extreme hunger for the rest of the day. To endure long hours of hard labor on an empty stomach was unbearable. People eventually learned the technique of dividing the slice of bread into three pieces—one each for breakfast, lunch, and dinner; they tore them further into smaller pieces and soaked them in water to make them swell. Everyone taxed their ingenuity to divert their minds from their empty stomachs. Often even a tiny scrap of bread could cause a scuffle in which detainees beat each other up.

There were many wretched stories about black bread. One time there was a big commotion because someone had knocked out the person performing meal distribution and stole the bread. It turned out that the person on duty hit himself and pretended that the bread was stolen by someone else. There was also an incident where a detainee stole all of the bread in the middle of the night and frantically gorged himself. He drank water immediately after, and no sooner had he done so, than his stomach expanded quickly, and he died in agony. Fellow detainees who learned about this had no pity for him. Many simply said, "He realized his wishes."[19]

Henmi goes on to describe the cold in Siberia as "beyond any Japanese person's imagination."

When they stood in line for roll call at seven in the morning, everyone's mouth became white. Their exhaling breath instantly froze. Cotton padded jackets were provided, but cold pierced their bodies like needles. The nose was the first body part to become frostbitten. During their labor, Japanese checked each other's noses to see whether they turned white. There were some who lost noses to frostbite.

However, Russians seemed to have different body temperatures. When they said it was cold, the temperature was thirty degrees below zero. On a sunny day with twenty degrees below zero, they said, "It is warm today."[20]

The actual labor that was carried out by my father was illustrated in the writings of Shizuo Yamashita. Mr. Yamashita had been taken to Siberia when he was twenty-seven years old. In his book, *Detention in Siberia for 1450 Days*, published in 2007, he described his experience as a detainee in Siberia.

We had no idea why we had been taken to this hinterland. When we stood at a corner of the vast primeval forest, we recognized there was an enormous amount of work to be done. One Russian told us a story that gave us chills all over. According to him, we would not go home until we completed the construction of railways. He must be one of those Russian prisoners who was sent to Siberia's labor camp to work with us. We felt hopeless; we might [never] return to Japan...

Our work was to cut trees in forests, carry them out, plus loading up food, oil, various building materials, and clothes. We were rounded up for road construction, sewage works, construction of warehouses, establishing water supply facilities, farming, and more...

The first time we downed big trees, it felt exhilarating. But downing giant trees was a very difficult task, and unfortunately, it caused many accidents.

This is how it was done. Two people were paired. Each pair was given one saw and two axes. We were strictly ordered to keep a distance of 50 meters between the pairs. Depending on how the trees stood, we decided which direction the tree should fall. We stabilized our footing and used saws, followed by axes. Then we sawed from the other side of the tree and drove in wedges. After trees fell, we took off branches and cut the tree into round slices. We manually pulled them to the roadside and placed them on sleds. After that, we had to pull the sleds to the gathering place, sometimes assisted by horses.

Powdered snow was soft and the wind carried it everywhere. Valleys were often created by snowdrift with deep accumulation. This condition created many accidents. Trees sometimes fell in different directions than expected. People whose feet were buried deep in the snow were pinned under trees. Sometimes, people forgot that the distance between the next pair had been narrowed as they concentrated on their own trees, and they were knocked down by trees. There was a person who died instantly after being skewered by branches as he did not pay enough attention because the trees in question were small.

With so many sacrifices, we got used to the hard work. Our physical strength was depleted by carrying giant trees with little food in our stomach. In extreme cold, our slow movement invited frostbite. But we could not move any faster. The cold in Manchuria was nothing compared with that in Siberia.[21]

That winter of 2016 after my brothers returned to Japan, New England had the coldest weather in many years, along with heavy snow. The glittering icicles and white-clothed trees were breathtakingly gorgeous. But I had warm clothes and didn't feel cold inside the house no matter how cold it was outside. Hadn't Japanese detainees in Siberia been required to work in such weather? I saw in my mind the shadows of Japanese men with inadequate clothes and food, cutting trees ten times bigger and heavier than the ones in our backyard. When I looked at the well-fed birds and squirrels in our snow-covered garden, I thought about the detainees in Siberia who had killed snakes and insects to fill their empty stomachs. And then I thought of my father.

I would not be surprised if my father had suffered the equivalent of PTSD from his experiences in Siberia. He certainly had been exposed to extreme conditions and many catastrophic events, involving actual deaths and injuries and intense fear. Ken Burns, a documentarian who lives in our village of Walpole, believes that anyone who has been in a war situation has a damaged soul, one that tends to be difficult to heal. Many ex-soldiers and prisoners keep their heavy burdens inside. Some also feel guilty for surviving while many of their comrades died.

How could I have been so blind to my father's doubtless deeply rooted mental anguish? I had believed he had been fortunate to have lived a long life in comparison to so many of his fellow detainees, but perhaps he didn't think so, and suffered guilt instead. One thing is certain—his experiences in the war never left him. In the late 1980s, my father had an operation to remove a kidney. He stayed in a hospital for one week. The nurse who took care of him was impressed by my father's stoicism. He had tremendous discomfort, but he was always very polite, and he never complained. He must have developed great tolerance for every conceivable pain from his years in Siberia.

CHAPTER 45

NOT A HELPLESS LEAF

My parents were survivors. My mother's demonstration of strength was clearly chronicled by her three notebooks. But my father? I hated myself for having given up trying to know and understand him for such a long time. This passage written by Shizuo Yamashita, mentioned in the previous chapter, gave me a faint hope that my father might have been able to reflect philosophically on his time in Siberia.

> Beginning in March, a temperature of minus 40 degrees Fahrenheit became the exception. We felt the days were a bit longer and the light from the sky stayed brighter. There were days of minus 15 and 17 degrees Fahrenheit when we felt warm as we went out to work and took off our thick overcoats.
>
> Every morning, we left the camp and went to the mountain, cut giant trees, and carried them out. We repeated this back and forth several times, and then the day drew to a close. We returned to our camp in the evening, carrying firewood. We began to feel as

if the camp was our home and a place we could relax. I believe this was because we had become accustomed to our condition, but it was also due to the relaxing of the Russian guards.

One of the most painful things we experienced during our detention was when we woke up in the middle of the night. We all wished that we would not need to get up as we were totally exhausted from the hard labor during the days. Getting up during the night was sometimes necessary to do extra work, but mostly it was because we needed to urinate. We endured until the last minute. When we decided to get up because we could not contain ourselves any longer, we had to wear several layers of warm clothes and walk more than 100 meters away, paying attention that our feet did not slip on the frozen path. We must have looked frantic.

On some occasions, there could be a crowd ... but those busy nights were unusual. There were nights I was alone. On such dark nights, I was dying to be home. I keenly missed my family, and I could not help feeling sentimental.

The Great Bear constellation lined up neatly in the shape of a ladle. Innumerable stars were packed and shining as if they were about to pour down. There was nothing to disturb this gorgeous night banquet in the Siberian sky.

I was watching the infinite sky in the middle of the land of banishment in Siberia. I felt my existence dwarfed by looking up at the sky; it aroused awe in me about the mystery of the universe. I was standing here on the mother earth in Siberia where I was forcefully detained. Was this the rare opportunity to live and to observe this country? If I would be lucky enough to be able to return to Japan alive, this could be considered a great journey that would not be possible under normal circumstances. By thinking that way, everything I saw and encountered every day could be a valuable experience. I smiled bitterly and kept watching the night sky tirelessly, my body shaking from the cold.[22]

My parents had been presented with a "rare opportunity to live," just as Yamashita wrote. It became my deep-felt desire to explore their lives by doing research, reading books, learning history, and translating my mother's memoir. My husband, Tom, started doing the same with his family.

There is a sort of romance in mystery, as we don't know about our parents as much as we would like, and perhaps we never will. My children, by contrast, see Tom and me as two people, beyond simply being their parents. Our children are very close to us; they communicate with us constantly about their children, their jobs, their investments, their plans for the future. They are not embarrassed to pour their overflowing sense of love to their parents. Our daughter wrote on Mother's Day in 2022, "Happy Mother's Day, ageless, beautiful mama. I am so lucky to have a loving, spirited, bold and brave mother to show me how to be the same. I love being a mother with you—sharing this experience fills my heart. Thank you! Your daughter, Alissa."

Our son also sent me a card from Berlin, Germany. "Happy Birthday Mom! So happy to be able to spend so much time with you. And we look forward to many days bothering you in the coming year. Love, Kai."

I had seldom received any card from my parents, but they did send me one on my fiftieth birthday, written with black ink in Japanese calligraphy:

"You have a memorable life, celebrating your best 50th birthday. Happy Birthday! From Father."

"Happy Birthday! *Omedetou Gozaimasu* (Many happy returns). I send my sincere wishes for your good health! From Mother."

We never said to our parents that we loved them, and we never disagreed or argued with them. We trusted them, we respected them, we adored them, but we never expressed our raw emotions to them.

Neither Tom nor I ever consulted with our parents about our life choices. We chose our own courses of action—to get married, change jobs, move to different countries and cities, to buy and sell houses, or to build our house in Walpole. We kept our parents informed but did not solicit their opinions. Perhaps it was because our lives in a radically changing world were so different from theirs. The emotional and physical distance between ourselves and our children is much less. Our children and even our grandchildren know more about us than we will ever be able to know about our own parents. Both Tom and I have deep regret about this, but there are also benefits in imagining their youthful lives, and, in my mother's case, reading her remarkable notebooks.

> Thirty years have passed since our escape from Manchuria. I started writing this in response to my daughter's request. I have never written this many words, but I am pleased to have done this. I feel I have gone through a wonderful adventure by writing this account. Various scenes and words came to my mind like watching a kaleidoscope. Numerous memories have flowed into my mind, including the joyful days of my youth. I had those sweet days, too!
> There was always the twilight time in April, the time of the year when ice cream became a bit tastier, and my heart leaped with fond memories. Evening in the Ginza section of Tokyo was illuminated by

colorful neon signs, and people on the busy streets were dressed in their fashionable spring clothes. This part of town always made us feel we were at the center of sophisticated society. I remember one day walking in that district with two of my girlfriends, young students from the countryside at a medical school. As we walked among the crowd, our feet felt light, bursting with youth and vigor.

We had ice cream on the second floor of a fruit parlor. We window-shopped and squealed with delight. Our feet were taking us in the direction of Hibiya Park. I was invited to a ballet performance by a man whom I secretly admired. He was a medical student from the same school I had attended. For a young woman to be with a young man alone was the source of scandal. So, I always asked my girlfriend to come with me, and he always brought his best friend. That night, we would see a ballet. I could not restrain the excitement with my heart pounding.

We arrived at the hall long before the doors were opened because I could not contain my enthusiasm. We did not know how to be "fashionably late." There was no pretense.

Reflecting on my life story now, on all that transpired since those very early days, I recognize that I took care of numerous people. Was it due to my kind heart, meddlesome nature, or curiosity? I was very much appreciated at times. I heard some saying that they were grateful, but their gratitude did not last. It is natural, I suppose. I believe it is much better to have taken care of others than for others to have taken care of me. People may forget what I have done for them, but I will never forget the kindness that other people extended to me. Even people who were supposed to be hostile to us Japanese, like the Chinese, Koreans, and Russians; I remember the kindnesses they offered me. Each of these people warmed my heart, even if I could not do anything for them in return.

It is particularly regrettable that my husband's older sister in *Iwase* died in a traffic accident in 1969. I had been determined to take care of her in her old age. She was the one who had given our children a bath when we first arrived from our exhausting trip from Manchuria. She also treated us with a hot meal and gave us a comfortable *futon* on which to sleep, before I had to head to her cold-hearted father's house the next morning. She is the one who loaned us 5,000 yen when we needed to buy penicillin for Kashiyo when she contracted pneumonia soon after we arrived at Yokohama, and we had no money. I was also very shocked to learn that my sister-in-law, Kunimitsu's wife, "Mama," had committed suicide in 1954 in Japan. There was a period when I had looked down upon her in Manchuria. I thought she was outrageous and shameful. Thirty years later while I am writing this, I recognize that I was naive and unforgiving. People who are in extreme situations do what they have to do to survive. It was especially painful to learn that she drowned herself after she returned to Japan. She must have fought to provide for her family with everything she had, in her way. She was a strong-willed woman. But trying to make a living with four children without a husband in postwar Japan had to be extremely difficult, even for her. Her exhaustion coupled with deep depression must have been beyond my imagination.

Now [as] I look back on my life, I feel fortunate to be able to say, "There is no regret." I had years of joy and sorrow, but I realized many dreams. My husband's contribution was enormous, and my children all cooperated with me. I used up most of my energy, but I never thought I did not want to work or that working was hard. Was it because I was simply young, or because I had dreams and passion?

With the decline of vitality and physical strength, I have become quite passive. Where have I gone? I feel restless. We only live once, and I should treasure my life. I sometimes believe I need to inject new energy into my life, but frankly, I am quite happy. These are peaceful days that I relish for the first time since my birth. I live in ease. I am free, and I can do anything I want. I don't want anybody to disturb me. It may be too mundane, but this is the best for me.

Our children who are grown and independent are always in my mind, but I can observe and enjoy them from a distance with a certain sense of detachment. I have no desire to meddle in their lives.

And I am sure they will cope with any challenges wisely.

Both of my parents are gone now. I think of my mother often. When I contemplate the sacrifices of my parents and how far we came, it boggles my mind. How is it possible to go from eating weeds in Manchuria to some of the luxurious corridors I have traveled in my lifetime?

One story from my years as president of the Hay-Adams stands out to me. Every week, I had the privilege of receiving the list of VIPs who would be staying at the hotel over the coming ten days. The list was full of prominent people. I paid particular attention to VIPs from Japan because I thought our Japanese owners would want to know. One day I was informed that His Imperial Highness Prince Hitachi was coming to stay at the Hay-Adams with Princess

Hitachi. He was a member of the Imperial House of Japan and the younger brother of Emperor Akihito (now Emperor Emeritus).

Each time we had a very special guest, we would try to provide a unique amenity tailored to the guests' lifestyle. Those amenities had to be tasteful and not extravagant. We might provide embroidered pillowcases with the guest's initials and their favorite flowers, for example. We had to know what these VIPs liked, their hobbies and personalities, but we couldn't ask anyone; it was part of our professional pride to know that we could offer personalized care for anyone on any occasion as the best small luxurious hotel in Washington, DC.

So, we could not inquire of the Imperial Household what would be a good gift for Prince and Princess Hitachi, but we knew Prince Hitachi was an ardent bird-watcher. There was no online shopping then, so I went to several bookstores in search of books about birds. I was not a bird-watcher, so I had to use my imagination. There were many beautiful coffee table–type bird books. They were big, colorful, and heavy. But I was sure that the prince must have many such books. I wondered what might be a bit unusual, and decided to buy a paperback book of American birds illustrated in black and white. It was the size of a small dictionary and thick but lightweight. I asked Hans Bruland to place this handbook on the night table. It was not extravagant—perhaps the prince might not even notice.

The next morning, I was told that the prince was very pleased with this little book, and he wanted to thank me personally. So, I stood in the lobby with Hans. The prince and princess exited the elevator and came over to me. I bowed. He spoke to me in a friendly manner, as if he knew me. Everybody was watching, and a photographer was moving around.

I had not been raised in the type of society in which people exchanged conversations in an exclusively unique royal vocabulary. Part of me was praying for the prince to move on quickly; the few minutes he stood in front of me seemed like a very long time. I did not have enough vocabulary to carry on a long conversation.

Later I received several snapshots that had been taken by the professional photographer. I sent some of those photographs to my parents in Yokohama. I wanted my parents to be proud of me. But my mother sent me a letter with scathing criticism. The series of photos showed that I had not lowered my head deeply enough when I bowed. She imagined that I raised my head quickly.

"Your bowing is not proper," she wrote. "Your head was too high. And before you raise your head up, make sure you slowly count at least on-e, tw-o, and thr-ee."

I looked at the snapshots again. She was right. My head was not low enough, and my bowing was not elegant. I knew it.

Thinking back now, it was an unimaginable event. Prince Hitachi's father was the one hundred and twenty-fourth emperor of Japan from 1926 to 1989. During his reign, Japan had gone through the entire arc of a nation, from aggressive expansion to extreme destruction. Prince Hitachi's father, the Shōwa Emperor, was a controversial figure. He is said to have been a reluctant supporter of the invasion of Manchuria, which led to the second Sino-Japanese War that precipitated World War II. Under the name of Emperor, better known in English by his personal name Hirohito, 2.3 million soldiers lost their lives, and approximately eight hundred thousand civilians died.

The person to whom I bowed at our hotel facing the White House was the second son of the Shōwa Emperor. So, I could even say that we were victimized by his father's decision to fight the war. Prince Hitachi's father was also the one who announced Japan's surrender on August 15, 1945, leading up to our miserable evacuation.

The contrast could not have been starker, and yet there we were—Prince Hitachi, accustomed to the halls of highest influence, and me, from a family that had once been like leaves in the ocean—small, forgotten pawns pushed around by great powers as they rearranged the world.

The more I learn history, the more I recognize how merciless the world around us can be. Who are we? After all, we are just leaves in the ocean.

How many wars and military conflicts have we had after the end of World War II? How many do we still have today? In 2022 and 2023, I watched millions of Ukrainian refugees flee their homes on packed trains and on foot, carrying frightened children and meager possessions. Millions of Russians have been pressed into a war their leaders have lied about from the start. Lives are cut short in the killing fields. We must find a way to learn from the past and stop war from repeating and repeating.

I look at the trees in my backyard. Now it is November. All the leaves are gone. Only evergreen trees are standing with healthy green branches. They will be covered by snow soon. Then they will be joined with sprouts on surrounding trees in spring.

One day, I will be gone, just as some of our dear friends and people whom I have admired are gone. The former chairman of Citibank, Mr. Walter Wriston, who cultivated the culture of mutual respect and cooperation among fellow Citibankers like a close-knit family, once said at the end of his career, "There is a very short distance between Who's Who to Who's That?" He was right. No one expects anything from me anymore, and I do not envy anyone anymore. Is this how my parents felt when we were inconsiderate youths and so full of ourselves?

After we are gone, our children and grandchildren will be running around here. Soon, grandchildren will become parents, and there will be new small ones. While they will be romping around the garden, catching tiny fish from the stream, our grown-up grandchildren will tell their children, "This is the place that our grandparents built."

Japanese people often say "I am sorry" instead of "thank you." When you say thank you to somebody, you are thinking about yourself. You appreciate what somebody has done *for you*. But when you think about the trouble this person has gone through to do some good for you, you apologize. "I am sorry to trouble you for me," instead of "thank you for doing this for me."

I cannot thank my parents enough, and I cannot apologize enough for what they had to sacrifice for us.

ACKNOWLEDGMENTS

I want to thank many people who helped make this book a reality. The original idea of publishing this book in English started nearly forty years ago when I read my mother's memoir in Japanese. Initially, all I wanted was for my American husband and children to be able to share my mother's writing about our experience escaping from Manchuria. While I was translating it into English, I began to think of offering her story to a wider audience beyond my immediate family, because I realized that people in the West knew very little about Manchuria. I also discovered how little I had known about the country where I was born. So, my research began. As a result, I enjoyed uncovering facts about the history of that "country" and my family.

When my book about children with life-threatening illnesses was published in Tokyo in 1985, the process was smooth and fast. I was much younger, full of energy, and I had known many people in Japan's publishing world. Furthermore, the book was written and published in Japanese, my first language.

The process this time was completely different. I encountered many unexpected difficulties. This book is in English, which is not my mother tongue; I am much older; and I did not have a substantial author platform. Nevertheless, I was determined to write and publish my book. I did not want to give up that goal.

I was fortunate to have been introduced to Ernie Hebert, author and retired professor from Dartmouth College, right after I moved to Walpole, New Hampshire, from Washington, DC, in 2012. He introduced me to Joni Cole, his former student and an author and writing instructor, who opened doors when I did not know how to start writing. Much editing assistance followed, including Terry Gallagher who edited my English translation of my mother's Japanese writing; and Lisa Tener, writing coach, who gave me frequent and timely advice whenever I was stuck. Author, editor, and teacher Rahna Reiko Rizzuto's sharp comments led me to rewrite large portions of my manuscript.

I am particularly grateful to Evelyn Duffy at Open Boat Editing who urged me to include the story of my career at the Hay-Adams hotel. Many sharp questions and astute comments made by Karen Gulliver's editing process at Bold Story Press encouraged me to do further research for clearer explanations that would make this book more meaningful to more people. Responding to Karen's various questions and comments taught me how to pull the proper words from my head.

I appreciate the friendly and thoughtful reviews by Susan Howell, Sheldon Boege, Suzanne Bennison, Janet Francis, and Simki Kuznick. I am sad that Jim Rousmaniere, journalist and historian who gave me adept advice, passed away before I could finish this book. Jennifer Howard, Stuart Horwitz, and Jacquelyn Mitchard's professional comments were very valuable. I also thank Emily Barrosse, CEO of Bold Story Press, for her enthusiastic support. I cannot thank Katy Ehrlich enough for her support based on her own experience of writing and publishing her memoir, *Irma's Passport: One Woman, Two Worlds, and a Legacy of Courage*. I am very fortunate to have had as my special friend Marie Arana, an award-winning author of fiction and nonfiction books whom we have known more than fifty years. Marie's constant and timely advice based on her wide and deep knowledge and experience in the writing and publishing world were truly invaluable.

Smart and effective librarians Sachie Noguchi, now retired from Japanese Studies Libraries of Columbia University, and Kuniko Yamada McVey, now retired from the Japanese Collections of Harvard-Yenching Library of Harvard University, have given me utmost comfort and assistance whenever it was needed.

I could explore Hakata Harbor where my family had arrived in 1946 only because Kazuko Aso kindly invited me to stay at her home in Kyushu. My family was part of the more than 1.3 million repatriates from Manchuria and the Korean Peninsula in 1940s. Through her, I met Hiroji Hotta, who had been active in collecting records and publishing books about the role of Hakata Harbor. He also introduced me to several Japanese women whom I interviewed concerning their repatriation from Manchuria.

Special thanks to the Cao family, who hosted my husband and me in Changchun for a week to show us around old historical sites, and provided us the opportunity to meet with many Chinese individuals who had lived under the Japanese occupation.

My younger brother, Takashi, a former newspaper reporter, who majored in political science in his undergraduate studies and international politics at graduate school in Tokyo, is proficient in Chinese history and language, both written and spoken. He has been a tremendous assistant and corroborator. I also thank Kazunari Enokido, the head of the Enokido family in Ibaraki, who provided me with precious historical materials and photographs of the Enokido family.

Our children, Alissa and Kai, were quick and efficient in solving numerous technical glitches. Without their help, I might still be in the darkness of this digital world. The most and greatest appreciation goes to my husband, Tom Crouse, who provided enthusiastic encouragement during my long and torturous journey of researching, writing, and the numerous stages of editing my manuscript. I could not have completed this book without his unfailing support and patience over many years.

ENDNOTES

CHAPTER 2

1. Stewart Brown, "Japan Stuns World, Withdraws from League," UPI, February 24, 1933, https://www.upi.com/Archives/1933/02/24/Japan-stuns-world-withdraws-from-league/2231840119817/
2. Louise Young, *Japan's Total Empire: Manchuria and the Culture of Wartime Imperialism* (University of California Press, 1999), 16.

CHAPTER 6

3. 岩見隆夫「敗戦満州追想」原書房, Takao Iwami, *Memories of Defeated Manchuria* (Hara Shobo, 2013), 81 (translated by Kay Enokido).
4. 半藤一利「ソ連が満州に侵攻した夏」文芸春秋、, Kazutoshi Hando, *The Summer When the Soviet Union Invaded Manchuria* (Bunshun Bunko, 2015), 248 (translated by Kay Enokido).

CHAPTER 8

5. Rei Nakanishi, "Endless Summer: 75th Anniversary of the End of the War; Heaven Turned to Hell in One Day," *Yomiuri Shimbun*, August 7, 2020 (translated by Kay Enokido).
6. Akira Takahashi "Mother Killed My Brother—Living Hell in Manchuria," *The Asahi Shimbun*, October 13, 2020 (translated by Kay Enokido).

CHAPTER 9

7. Akira Takahashi "Mother Killed My Brother—Living Hell in Manchuria," *The Asahi Shimbun*, October 13, 2020 (translated by Kay Enokido).

CHAPTER 12

8. The Eighth Route Army was part of the CPC Central Military Commission of Nationalist Government Affairs Commissions. It is known as the 18th Group Army of the Nationalist Revolutionary Army of Republic of China, headed by the Chinese National Party, the

revolutionary committee of KMT during the second Sino-Japanese War started in 1937. The KMT-CCP alliance collapsed during the Northern Expedition, and Nationalists controlled most of China. From 1937 to 1945, the second United Front was enlisted to fight against the Japanese invasion of China with eventual help from the Allied of WWII, but cooperation between KMT and CCP was minimal and armed clashes between KMT and CCP were common.

CHAPTER 15

9   Homare Endo, "Mao Zedong, Founding Father of the People's Republic of China, Conspired with the Japanese Army," Japan Foreign Policy Forum, Diplomacy No. 33 May 17, 2016, https://www.japanpolicyforum.jp/diplomacy/pt20160517095315632.html

CHAPTER 17

10   Paul K. Maruyama, *Escape from Manchuria* (IUniverse, 2010), 198.

CHAPTER 18

11   Natsuko Tamaki, "Handing Down War Memories—63 Years Since the End of War," Yomiuri Shimbum Western Version, August 10, 2008 (translated by Kay Enokido).

12   John W. Dower, *Embracing Defeat: Japan in the Wake of World War II* (W. W. Norton, 2000), 173.

13   Dower, *Embracing Defeat*, 46–48

CHAPTER 20

14   According to an old Japanese tale, an old man dug holes in the ground as his dog told him to "dig here and here" and he found treasures.

CHAPTER 31

15   Robert L. Cutts, "Power from the Ground Up: Japan's Land Bubble," *Harvard Business Review* (May–June 1990), https://hbr.org/1990/05/power-from-the-ground-up-japans-land-bubble

16   Ezra F. Vogel, *Japan as Number One: Lessons for America* (Harvard University Press, 1979).

CHAPTER 40

17   A dispute broke out between Manchukuo and Mongolia in Nomonhan in May 1939 near the border, and this led to a large-scale military conflict between Japan and the Soviet Union. The Japanese

army engaged in hand-to-hand combat while the Soviet army engaged in modern warfare with three-dimensional coordination between tank units and aircraft.

CHAPTER 44

18 臼井久也、「ドキュメント、シベリア抑留―斎藤六郎の軌跡」岩波書店, Hisaya Usui, *Siberia Detention, The Trail of Saito Rokuro* (Iwanami Shoten, 1995), 273-74 (translated by Kay Enokido)

19 辺見じゅん「収容所から来た遺書」文芸春秋, Jun Henmi, *Farewell Notes from a Prison Camp* (Bunshun Bunko, 2011), 22-24 (translated by Kay Enokido).

20 Henmi, 29-30.

21 山下静夫「シベリア抑留 1450日」デジプロ、, Shizuo Yamashita, *Detention in Siberia for 1450 Days* (DejiPro, 2008), 121 (translated by Kay Enokido).

CHAPTER 45

22 山下静夫「シベリア抑留 1450日」デジプロ、, Shizuo Yamashita, *Detention in Siberia for 1450 Days* (DejiPro, 2008), 148-150 (translated by Kay Enokido).

ABOUT THE AUTHOR

Kay Enokido was born in Manchuria. Her mother fought fiercely to keep her three small children alive during a harrowing escape from Manchuria after the collapse of the Empire of Japan in 1945. She inherited her mother's strong sense of determination and perseverance.

Kay was a contributing writer to major Japanese newspapers and magazines and traveled around the world. She eventually became a businesswoman in America. She holds a BA in Journalism from New York University, and a Master of International Affairs from Columbia University. She also attended Indiana University and Cornell Hotel School's Advanced Management Program.

After retiring from her position as President of the Hay-Adams Hotel Management Company, Kay and her husband built a house and settled in Walpole, New Hampshire. She enjoys life in the country; the life she had never experienced.

ABOUT BOLD STORY PRESS

Bold Story Press is a curated, woman-owned hybrid publishing company with a mission of publishing well-written stories by women. If your book is chosen for publication, our team of expert editors and designers will work with you to publish a professionally edited and designed book. Every woman has a story to tell. If you have written yours and want to explore publishing with Bold Story Press, contact us at https://boldstorypress.com.

The Bold Story Press logo, designed by Grace Arsenault, was inspired by the nom de plume, or pen name, a sad necessity at one time for female authors who wanted to publish. The woman's face hidden in the quill is the profile of Virginia Woolf, who, in addition to being an early feminist writer, founded and ran her own publishing company, Hogarth Press.

Thank you for reading my book!
If you enjoyed it, please tell a friend and
consider leaving a review on Amazon
or Goodreads—it really helps.

www.ingramcontent.com/pod-product-compliance
Lightning Source LLC
Chambersburg PA
CBHW020218170426
43201CB00007B/245